Up Close

Up Close

*A Lifetime Observing
and Photographing Desert Animals*

GEORGE OLIN

The University of Arizona Press ◈ Tucson

The University of Arizona Press
© 2000 The Arizona Board of Regents
First Printing
All rights reserved

05   04   03   02   01   00   6   5   4   3   2   1

Library of Congress Cataloging-in-Publication Data appear on the
last printed page of this book.

British Library Cataloguing-in-Publication Data
A catalogue record for this book is available from the British Library.

The Arizona people formerly known as Papago Indians have officially
changed their name to Tohono O'odham (Desert People). The change
was adopted as part of a new constitution approved by members of the
Tohono O'odham Nation (formerly the Papago Indian Tribe of Arizona)
in January 1986.

For Irene

Contents

Illustrations

Acknowledgments

When I began to write this book, I envisioned it as being a chronicle of the lives and surroundings of some of the small animals with which my wife, Irene, and I shared our lives for a good many years. However, as the effort progressed, I found that, no matter how much I tried to avoid it, our own activities became so involved with theirs that it drifted into an autobiography of sorts. I am not entirely pleased with this, for I write clumsily in the first person, but, for good or bad, I offer it for what it might be worth.

This account begins on the top of one of the highest mountains in southern Arizona and ends in the low desert along the Mexican border. Except for eight years spent in the eastern United States, we have spent most of our married life in this area known as the Sonoran Desert. Although it is an arid land, indeed, it boasts the richest number of plant and animal species of any of the world's deserts. The relationships of these varied kinds of plants and animals with each other and with their dry surroundings form an environment that is as delicate as it is ruthless. Any disturbance of the critical balance upon which it depends can be serious.

This being so, it seems that the more that is known about the participants of this interlocking society that we call "the environment," the more we should desire to learn about them. Science has recorded the animal species with the brevity common to scientific description, but comparatively little has been divulged about their everyday lives. This book represents an effort to add flesh and life to the dry bones of some of the descriptions given in the literature.

In the main, these tales are not about the spectacular species shown in some nature films. Rather, they are mostly of small creatures seldom encountered in our everyday lives. Some may be considered pests or perhaps vermin by unthinking members of our own species, but, insignificant as they may seem, they all play important roles in the harsh environment of the desert. Although separated from them generically, I have tried to enter into their activities as a participant to find out what they do and why they do it in their constant struggle for survival. This is not as simple as it might seem. My observations are full of gaps concerning the intricate activities of their lives.

During the years spent in pursuing this effort, I have been aided by so many individuals and organizations that it would be impossible to name them all. Foremost among them would be Irene, who has contributed so much to my efforts and endured so much in my behalf. We are indebted to Louis and Hazel Seeman, who opened their home and hearts to us while on the Reef; to Lee and Bonnie Price for giving us the run of their desert ranch at Ajo; to Dr. Stanley Alcorn, plant pathologist, who contributed so much to the saguaro story; and to E. Lendell Cockrum and fellow professors at the University of Arizona. My special thanks to John O. Cook, my superintendent at Saguaro National Monument, who has furthered my career at every opportunity. My appreciation goes to the various agencies of the U.S. Department of Interior and to the U.S. Department of Agriculture, which have not only furnished assistance in many ways but have given me employment as well. Finally, my grudging acknowledgment of the persistence of a gadfly named Burley Packwood, who has continually urged me to "get these stories down on paper; you won't be around forever, you know." Because of him, I have put my nose to this grindstone!

Part I

Two on a Mountain

Forest Service Lookouts

The year was 1951 A.D. It marked a time when the country was at an uneasy balance between the ending of World War II and the beginning of the space age. The war had necessitated a drastic change in national direction, and, as a consequence, new technologies were developed to satisfy its urgent demands.

Industry, ever alert to new opportunities, took advantage of these technologies at once, and most of them profited greatly by so doing. A few organizations found it difficult to forsake the old ways. One such was the U.S. Forest Service.

Since the Forest Service's inception, one of its prime objectives had been the suppression of forest fires, all forest fires. The Forest Service believed in this, the public demanded it, and Smokey the Bear emphasized it at every opportunity.

So it happened that, in the early spring of 1951, the Coronado District of the Forest Service, headquartered in Tucson, Arizona, let it be known that it would accept applications from married couples desiring work as fire lookouts.

This came as good news to Irene and me. We had come to Tucson several years before, and, while we had jobs, they were sadly lacking in possibilities of advancement. So it took little discussion for us to make the decision to at least take a shot at this chance of changing pace and, at the same time, escaping for a while from the extreme heat of the desert summer.

We Get the Job

Suiting action to the word, we arrived at the Coronado District offices in the federal building on the following morning. In response to our request for the application forms for married couples as fire lookouts, the secretary said: "I'm sure that Mr. Morris will wish to interview you first. Will you please wait here while I see if he is available?" Then she disappeared into his office. In a few seconds, the door opened and she beckoned to us. "Yes, he can see you now—please come in."

Roger Morris was a pleasant individual who looked more like a conservative businessman than our mental picture of a Forest Service official. After introductions, he waved us to seats and returned to his own, back of a large desk covered with maps and papers. Leaning back in his chair and clasping his hands behind his head, he regarded us steadily for a few moments. What he saw was a couple in their early forties: I, rather large and of lean build, and Irene, small and slim but obviously very fit. Seemingly satisfied with what he saw, he said: "Tell me about yourselves."

There was little enough to tell. Both of us were products of small towns, both had a high school and some college education. We both had worked in Los Angeles and had left because of the smog and crowded conditions there. For two years, we had trailered about the West looking for a place where we wanted to live and had finally settled on Tucson. We both had steady jobs from which we could get a leave of absence for the summer. Finally, since we had lived near Forest Service areas and camped in many of them as well, we hoped that we might be qualified to be lookouts, and we very much wanted the job.

Mr. Morris smiled at our enthusiasm. "I understand that," he said, "but there are conditions attached to these jobs which I want you to consider very carefully. First of all, the two locations which we are going to staff with married couples are very isolated. The people who are selected will be expected to remain on duty for the full time of ninety days or more depending on the fire danger. Then you must remember that living conditions will be very primitive. We will provide a schedule of packing up your supplies and mail, but, beyond that, you will have to do without. The duties will vary from very monotonous to very exciting, and even dangerous at times. We must rely upon your own good judgment to solve most of the problems which are bound to occur. These jobs are not vacations, the responsibilities are great, the hours are long, and the pay is small. Do you two think that you can do the work under these conditions?"

"I'm sure of it," I said. "We've been on some pretty rugged camping trips in times past. You mentioned that you were staffing two locations. Could you tell us where they are?"

"Certainly." He pointed to a map on the wall. "One is in the Chiricahuas, and the other in the Huachucas."

"And which one is the more isolated?" I asked.

"Oh, Miller Peak in the Huachucas, without any question. It's seven miles by trail from pack base."

"Then that's the one which we would prefer if we are selected," I said.

"In that case, make a note of it on your application forms; you can pick them up at my secretary's desk. I have been impressed by your attitudes. Now, if you will excuse me, I must get back to work. Good-bye and good luck!"

There followed a period of agonized waiting. Could we be lucky enough to be the ones selected? And, if so, would we get the post on Miller Peak? Our anxieties ended with the arrival of a fat envelope from the Coronado Forest headquarters. In it was notification that we each were now appointed as fire-control aides (lookout) at grade G.S. 3 at a salary of $2,650 per annum; and, the icing on the cake, we were assigned to Miller Peak! Shortly thereafter, we received further confirmation of our appointment from Bob Schmitt, district ranger for the Huachuca area. He suggested that we appear at the ranger station at Canelo two days before we started duty at Miller Peak on May 1. As it was already late in April, this occasioned a flurry of activity in order to get our gear together.

We assembled sleeping bags, work clothes, cooking utensils, and canned goods on the back porch. Not the least of our concerns were items for the other inhabitants of Miller Peak, which we hoped to meet. So, we added birdseed, suet, peanuts, and rolled oats to the pile. On the afternoon before our departure, we loaded everything into the Desert Tortoise.

This was an army ambulance, vintage World War II. Because it was big and slow and had four-wheel drive, we thought Desert Tortoise an appropriate name. We had converted it into a recreational vehicle of sorts by installing a folding bed and an icebox. It had quickly earned our respect, and even affection, for its four-legged ability to carry us into places inaccessible to conventional vehicles.

All things taken care of, we locked up the house and bade good-bye to

Tucson early on the morning of April 29. Arriving at the Canelo ranger station shortly before noon, we spent the afternoon with Bob Schmitt discussing our coming activities at the peak. His instructions were brief but to the point. During daylight hours, we were to make a thorough survey of the area with binoculars every fifteen minutes—more often if the fire danger was high or lightning storms were in progress. At night, if thunderstorms occurred, we were to watch those areas of heavy lightning activity and search those locations particularly well on the following day. We were to use the radio only for official business, not for social contact with other lookouts. The telephone, if it worked, was under the same restrictions. Both were to be disconnected and aerial and line grounded whenever thunderstorms were in close proximity. Maintenance and housekeeping chores were routine; it was expected that we would police the immediate area around the lookout as needed to maintain a good appearance.

When he had finished, I said: "It seems to me that you are more concerned with our personal safety than anything else."

"I am," he responded. "Unless you have experienced a heavy lightning storm on one of these peaks, you have no idea how violent they can be. You may think that you have been through such storms, but, when the thunder rolls continually and you have up to several [lightning] strikes a second, you know differently. They are awe inspiring, but, beyond that, they are extremely dangerous. The lookout is well grounded, and you should be safe as long as you are inside, but don't be caught outside as long as there is any possibility of a strike anywhere close."

Our talk drifted to more mundane matters until late in the afternoon. As it terminated, Bob suggested that we spend the next day (April 30) circling the Huachuca Range, eventually to wind up at pack base on the Reef.

On May 1, Alex Gonzales, boss of the fire crew, was scheduled to arrive at pack base also, and he and I were to hike up to the lookout and ready it for the summer's occupation. Alas, how plans can oft go awry!

April 30 dawned bright and clear but with a bitterly cold wind sweeping in from the west and a line of ominous-looking clouds looming on the western horizon. These were minor developments, however, and Irene and I set out in high spirits in the Desert Tortoise to circle the Huachucas.

We Survey Our Area

The Huachuca Range is a short one, only about twenty miles long, with four peaks rising at intervals along its length. It runs north and south, originating at the U.S.-Mexican border on the southern end and with about one-third of it lying within the Fort Huachuca Military Reservation on the northern terminus. Rugged canyons swoop down from the heights on either side and eventually lose themselves in the grassy plains of the San Raphael Valley to the west and the San Pedro River drainage on the east.

Our road on the west side meandered through foothills dotted with scrub oaks and juniper trees. At an altitude of approximately five thousand feet, we were traveling through an ecological belt known as the Upper Sonoran Zone. In places, the rocky knolls were sparsely covered with manzanita, century plants, and cacti of the cholla type.

The road was an unimproved county road, and, although the precipitous walls of the upper canyons had broadened to wide sandy washes at our level, large boulders in the streambeds caused us to navigate them with caution. Occasionally, even more primitive roads than ours would turn off toward the upper canyons. Some of them were used by ranchers who needed access to the cattle they grazed on leases from the Forest Service; others led to mining claims. Mining was at a low ebb, though, the better lodes having been worked out years before.

The whole region was rich in history, however, and we recalled some of this as we encountered weathered signs marking the crossings of the various canyons. Garden Canyon was one of the first of these. It bore easterly into the military reservation, and we knew that it emerged on the eastern side of the range. An excellent trail had once followed it over the mountain, as it was an important link between the early settlers and the outside world. For years before the turn of the twentieth century, pack trains loaded with concentrates from the Copper Glance Mine in Sunnyside Canyon traversed their slow way over the ridge and across the San Pedro Valley to the smelters at Charleston, Arizona, on the river.

On their return trip, they hauled supplies needed by the community at Sunnyside. The trail had fallen into disuse at the time of our visit, for the military frowned on unauthorized travel on the reservation, but in our imagination we could still hear the sound of plodding hooves and the creaking of leather as the patient burros carried their heavy loads up the stony trail.

Sunnyside Canyon was but a little way from Garden Canyon. Only a short way above the point where our road crossed Sunnyside Canyon, it widened out into a relatively level flat of perhaps fifteen acres. In the early 1880s, a religious colony was established farther up the canyon at the Copper Glance Mine. When the mine worked out, the people moved down to this lower location.

At the height of activity, the colony is said to have numbered seventy-five individuals. In about 1900, their leader died, and the colony went into a slow decline. In 1921 the post office closed, and in 1940 the last inhabitant departed. Ten dwellings, the schoolhouse, the blacksmith shop, and several outbuildings remained in good condition. The area has been fenced and is watched over by descendants of the original members, so, hopefully, the little town will remain a monument to the industry and skills of those pioneers who created it.

Pushing on, we came to Parker Canyon. This is considered to be the largest canyon along the western slope of the Huachucas. It strikes out in a southwestern direction and eventually loses itself in the grasslands of the San Raphael Valley. It has long been one of the major avenues of entry for animals (and illegal aliens, too) from below the border. Wolves had been considered extinct in Arizona for many years, but sightings of these creatures, which could have come only from Mexico, have been reported at intervals, and this concerned the ranchers who ran cattle in the valley. Bob had stressed that, if we saw either animals or humans that seemed "foreign" to the area, we were to alert him at once. He carried a .44 on the seat of his pickup, as he said, "just in case."

After taking time out for lunch under a tree at the mouth of one of the many small canyons, we arrived at Montezuma Pass by midafternoon and crossed over to the east side of the Huachucas. The weather, which had been lowering all day, now intensified. As we started north along the range, we could see that the mountains had held the front back for a time, but it was now a foregone conclusion that we were in for a major storm. We increased our pace, for we now realized that we had dallied too long and darkness was fast approaching.

We crossed the mouth of Ash Canyon, famous for the twenty-six-ounce gold nugget found in the creek bed in the early twentieth century. Several smaller canyons followed, and then came Miller Canyon. In its upper reaches, a group of springs had been consolidated and directed through a pipeline to the town of Tombstone, thirty miles away across the valley. It seemed ironic that such a difficult and expensive project had to be undertaken, because one of the major problems in Tombstone was the flooding of the silver mines. However, such water was not potable because of its high mineral content; hence, the need for the pipeline.

As we left the mouth of Miller Canyon, we could see the imposing bulk of the Reef ahead and to our left. Several thousand feet high, it was a great rock buttress against the flank of Carr Peak. By now, the light was almost gone, and rain had begun to fall, but we could still glimpse a narrow road ascending the east face by a series of steep switchbacks. Knowing that we would have to go up in the dark, we turned into the Carr Canyon road with some misgivings.

We Arrive at the Reef

Now the wind before the storm fell upon us with heavy gusts, and the rain began to fall in earnest. The windshield wipers began the monotonous cadence that would continue for the next hour. The headlights burned into the darkness, though at times their glare was reflected back at us as the wind whipped sheets of rain across the road. A half-mile or so into the canyon, the road made a sharp turn to the left, and an increasing grade forced us down to second gear at once. Slipping the transmission into four-wheel drive, we prepared for a rough ride as we started up the switchbacks that we had seen from below. Under other circumstances, the road would not have been difficult. However, the streams of water running down the ruts had already washed away all of the fine materials, leaving loose boulders and slippery bedrock in their wake.

The Tortoise responded as we knew it would; with wheels alternately spinning and grabbing, it scratched and clawed its way ever higher up the face of the Reef. Buffeted by the wind, pounded by the rain, it lurched over the water bars and gave us its best. Some of the switchbacks were so sharp that, even with our short wheelbase, we were forced to back and fill to round them. On we went, with our load making alarming noises as it was bounced from side to side. This went on and on until, at last, when it seemed that our ordeal would never end, there was an abrupt change in the character of the road. It suddenly narrowed to little more than the width of our vehicle and became a shelf clinging to a sheer cliff on the left side, while on the right side there was a void, which in the darkness was apparently bottomless. After a hundred feet of this hazardous progress, we rattled over a cattle guard, and, suddenly, the Tortoise was on level ground once more.

Proceeding cautiously toward a dim light in the near distance, we came to a fork in the road, the left one of which, from Bob's directions, we understood led to the storage building at pack base. In a matter of a hundred yards, the headlights picked up a weather-beaten cabin among the trees. We pulled up in front of the door and cut the ignition. We had arrived!

Our first concern was to get something to eat, for we had gone without food for about four hours. In the cramped quarters of the Tortoise, this was no easy feat, but Irene rummaged about through our scrambled belongings and came up with the leftovers from lunch, which, together with coffee brewed over our Coleman stove, quieted the rumblings of our empty stomachs. "Supper" over, we assessed our situation.

The wind had died down as soon as we had gained the shelter of the pines, but the rain still drummed loudly on the steel roof and effectively prevented us from getting out of the vehicle. With the stove turned off and the motor providing no heat, it did not take long for the cold to penetrate the steel walls of the Tortoise, and we were soon beginning to get chilled. Under those conditions, we quickly evaluated our options; actually, there was only one. Letting down the bed, we shrugged and squirmed into our sleeping bags and retired for the night. I remember hearing the patter of the rain slowly subside and finally stop. Then I fell asleep, leaving tomorrow to take care of itself.

I awoke slowly in the morning as is my custom and reviewed the events of the previous day. Then I rolled over on one elbow and looked through, or rather at, the windshield. It was white opaque, covered with a thick blanket of snow! This was, indeed, an unexpected development; wishing Irene to share my consternation, I said: "Irene, look at the windshield."

"Oh, no, how terrible," she cried.

We were no strangers to snow, but neither of us enjoyed it and, at this particular time and place, it presented problems. Reversing our antics of the previous night, we struggled out of our sleeping bags and into our clothes. Over breakfast, we discussed our course of action. Technically, we were on duty and, therefore, should not leave the Reef for warmer weather at a lower altitude. At the same time, the whole area was soaked from the storm so fire danger was zero. At that time, we had no means of communication with our ranger at Canelo. Our decision was that we had best sit tight where we were and wait for the snow to melt. That might take several days, for while there was possibly a foot of snow on the Reef, it was undoubtedly much deeper on Miller Peak.

With that much resolved, we sorted out some warm clothes and prepared to go out and investigate our surroundings. First, however, there was one troublesome problem. After several seasons of desert wear, the leather of our boots was dried out and would soak up the slush like a sponge. Resourceful Irene to the rescue. Drawing upon experience gained in her early childhood in northern Idaho, she fired up the Coleman, put some of our "bird" suet in a pie plate, and soaked the soles of our boots in the hot tallow. With more of the same daubed on the uppers, we were prepared for the slush.

We were fortunate in meeting Louis and Hazel Seeman on our first venture away from the Tortoise. Owners of the home whose lights we had spied on the previous night, they owned the Reef Mine and several mining claims associated with it. We were also fortunate in that they were enthusiastic wildlife fans who fed and protected the animals that came to partake of their largesse. They invited us to come down that afternoon to see what might come to feed in their backyard.

In the meantime, we slopped around the area where, for the moment, we were being held virtually under house arrest. The Reef was sparsely covered with Apache pines, a species closely related to the ponderosa, the yellow pine of the West. Any rocky places under the trees were covered with thick stands of manzanita bushes, their smooth, red-barked branches contrasting brilliantly against the fresh snow. A shallow ravine carved from the solid rock marked the north edge of the property. Its banks were lined with low alders together with a few young narrow-leafed cottonwood trees. Full to the brim with snow melt, it led to the edge of the cliff in the vicinity of the cattle guard we had crossed on the previous night. There its waters plunged over the brink to join the main stream of Carr Creek a thousand feet below.

Several buildings in various stages of disrepair stood behind the Seeman home. Near their house, an open tank five feet high and perhaps twenty feet across held a water supply sufficient for the mining operation and whatever domestic uses might require. A thin trickle of water fell into it from a pipe that apparently tapped a spring some distance farther up the mountain. Close to the entrance road stood a massive head frame, its heavy timbers black with age. The whole area spoke of years of struggle against an environment that refused to part easily with its bounty.

Behind the cabin where we had parked the night before was the trail that led to Miller Peak. Through the trees, we could glimpse snowy Carr Peak rising another two thousand feet against the blue. The weather had cleared, but, surprisingly, the sun made slow headway at melting the snow at our altitude. We returned to the Tortoise at intervals and, by lighting the Coleman and running the motor, managed to warm up to some extent. Our feet were the main problem. They remained dry, but we had thin socks, and the steel floor of the vehicle seemed, if anything, colder than the outside air. We were glad when, at four o'clock, it was time to go down to the Seeman house and see their wildlife.

The deer had arrived before us and were milling around impatiently anticipating the food they were accustomed to receiving. These were *Odocoileus virginianus couesi*, a variety of the eastern white-tailed deer, named after the great western naturalist Elliot Coues. These small deer, known commonly as the Sonoran white-tailed, live in the higher reaches of the desert country, as opposed to the black-tailed, called desert mule deer, which inhabit the hotter and drier environments below. Except for their small size, they have much in common with the white-taileds of the eastern states. The bucks have dainty antlers commensurate with their small size; however, the white "flag" from which they get their name is, if anything, larger than that of the eastern species and creates quite a spectacle as it wig-wags from side to side in their flight.

They run at a gallop as a horse runs, rather than take the bounding leaps that characterize the mule deer's progress.

The deer were all attention when Hazel went out with a pail full of rolled barley. As soon as she had filled their individual coffee cans, they crowded in, each to its own place. This lasted only until those that had finished their ration tried to impose on others, which had been more deliberate in their eating. It was evident that a pecking order had been established: in this case, the older individuals were dominant. This was natural, Hazel explained, as she pointed out mothers, and daughters, and even great-granddaughters, some of which were descended from a pet fawn she and Louis had raised many years before.

Noting the affection the Seemans displayed toward the deer, we inquired about danger from hunters and predators. Louis explained that the deer did not range very far from the Seeman property and that, when hunting season came up, the deer seemed to sense that they were safe within that area and stayed there. Mountain lions recognized no such safe areas, however, and did intrude at times. They were attracted to the vicinity of the house because of the strong scent of deer, but they prowled the area at night. Louis pointed to a rifle and a powerful electric torch in the corner of the living room, which were kept ready for just such a contingency. Later he showed us the pelts of two mature and one juvenile lion that had trespassed on the yard.

The deer, once satisfied that no more food was to be provided, began to move away. Once they were gone, Hazel went out again, this time with a pail of cracked corn. She scattered this upon the wet mixture of snow and pine needles, scuffing it up with her feet so the grains would not be too easily discovered.

As dusk began to deepen, the turkeys came in for their treat. Unlike the deer, they materialized from the shadows of the darkening woods like shadows themselves, clucking nervously and with many a retreat from imagined danger. We sat quietly, almost holding our breath, for it was obvious they sensed that strangers were watching.

These were magnificent birds, much slimmer in build than the domestic variety, with plumage that had a sheen and a color unmatched by the Thanksgiving fowl. Once native to the Huachucas, the species had become so decimated that it was considered extinct. The birds we were watching were of a group that the Arizona Game and Fish Department had reintroduced several years before. Under strict protection, their numbers had increased slightly, and it seemed possible that the familiar "gobble, gobble" might once more be heard ringing through the forest in the higher reaches of the Huachucas.

As the turkeys, too, drifted away to roost for the night, we turned our talk to the problems that face wildlife in general and birds in particular. Southeastern Arizona has a wide reputation for the number of rare birds to be found there. Because of this, the Huachuca, Chiricahua, Patagonia, and Santa Rita Mountains play hosts to increasing numbers of scientists and bird watchers every summer. Some regrettably take specimens and eggs, others harass nesting birds by taking photographs, and still others want only to add to their life lists, but collectively they exact a heavy toll on species that, under the best of circumstances, maintain a precarious existence. I realize that I am tarred with the same stick, but I try to balance my enthusiasm with concern for my subjects' welfare. I endeavor whenever possible (by using bait or other seductions) to have them come to me rather than inflict myself upon their privacy.

As we returned to the Tortoise, Irene and I could feel a definite change in the weather. It seemed that a warming trend was to follow on the heels of the cold front that had caused us such trouble. We spent the rest of the evening in comparative comfort and retired with optimism for the happenings of the next few days.

Two days later, at ten o'clock in the morning, a loud rattling of the cattle guard announced the arrival of Alex Gonzales, foreman of the fire crew. His mud-spattered pickup indicated the condition of the road up to the Reef. He pulled up to our vehicle and leaped out with enthusiasm. Alex was a man of about thirty years of age, of average height, and with a wiry physique that seemed to be all muscle and sinew.

"Bob told me that I'd probably find you here. I'm Alex, and you are George and Irene," he stated rather than questioned.

"We are sure glad to see you," I said. "It got a little tiresome staying around here and doing nothing."

"We'll try to fix that; I'm supposed to go up and check out the lookout. Would you like to go up with me and look it over?"

I felt the subtle challenge in his casual question. Let's see what this guy is made of, he was thinking. "Hey, I'd like that." I lied. Actually, I had no stomach to tackle fourteen miles round-trip of a snowy mountain trail with this dynamo who was ten years my junior. However, there was no graceful way to avoid it, so, after Irene had made us a couple of sandwiches, he and I set off—Alex breaking the trail and I following, literally, in his footsteps.

Our route led first to the juncture of another trail that traversed the top of the range from south to north, then led south on it to another turnoff that ascended Miller Peak to the lookout. The first leg, like the road up to the Reef, wasted no time in reaching Carr Peak. It zigged and zagged up a series of switchbacks, all the while maintaining a steady grade, which, together with the altitude, had me gasping for breath.

Up and up we went, gradually leaving the pines behind and entering a new plant association dominated by aspens and Douglas fir. These, too, thinned out near the summit, and then, having reached the ridge trail, we went south down the peak to the saddle at the head of Miller Canyon. We paused at a spot where, at some time, someone had somehow hauled up an old-fashioned cast-iron bathtub that now held icy water dripping from a spring. We ate our sandwiches there, then set off to find the Miller Peak turnoff. This trail was even more arduous than that on Carr Peak. We had to make frequent stops to catch our breath, and it was getting late when, at last, we reached the lookout.

Our first task was to raise the shutters that covered the windows. When these were locked firmly against the wind, we entered the single room and checked out the contents. There was not much. The Osborne fire finder was in good shape, and the stove was operable. That about completed the work inside. After a superficial inspection of the privy, and a check to ensure that the cistern was full of water, we were ready to return to pack base.

As we stood on the very tip of Miller Peak looking across to the Reef, Alex turned to me and suggested with studied casualness: "We could save a lot of time if we would cut across."

Again it was a veiled challenge, even more than the one of that morning, and again I rose to the bait. "Let's go!" Let's go, indeed, 3,500 vertical feet down to the floor of Miller Canyon, then 1,500 more up to the top of the Reef. All this in a distance of about 2.5 air miles. Alex needed no further encouragement.

We traveled the first thousand feet down a steep slope composed of slide rock, which made for treacherous and dangerous footing. Alex at-

Figure 1.1 Miller Peak is the highest point along the Mexican border between the Gulf of Mexico and the Pacific Ocean.

tacked it with vigor. Leaping lithely from rock to rock, he bounded down the side of the mountain like a ballet dancer, while I stumbled clumsily along in his wake. We made good time, considering the footing, but then we ran into a zone of chaparral that slowed our progress. When we reached the canyon floor, my shins were barked and I had various and sundry abrasions and scratches all over my anatomy. The climb up the far side of the canyon was even more arduous; by the time we reached pack base, I was completely "used up."

Nevertheless, as we waved Alex good-bye, I had the satisfaction of knowing that I had passed his test. I knew, too, that whenever one of the local people asked him, "How are that new lookout and his wife doing up on the peak?" he would give us his approval. "If Alex says he's O.K., that's good enough for me," I could hear them say. Acceptance must be earned; the loss of some skin that would soon grow back was a small price to pay for it.

Miller Peak Lookout

During our absence, Fred, our packer, had arrived at pack base; because the snow by now was almost gone, it was decided that we should go up to the peak on the following morning. It seemed that now, finally, we were beginning to get somewhere. Despite my aches and pains, I went to sleep that night with a certain satisfaction in the day's accomplishments.

After an early breakfast, we busied ourselves getting our gear together while Fred was saddling the horses. When he saw the accumulation, he exhibited remarkable self-control. Camera cases, tripods, sacks of bird food, and all of the assorted cartons and bundles that held our everyday needs, along with the radio, batteries, propane bottles, and other look-out necessities of the Forest Service, presented diverse difficulties when packed on the backs of animals. Nevertheless, he set to with a will, and I, with some experience in such matters, joined him.

In a couple of hours, we had loads on three horses and were ready to set out. Fred took the lead, with the three pack animals trailing, then came Irene astride a sturdy pinto furnished by the Seemans, and I brought up the rear on an old veteran of the trail with the government brand on his hip.

The sky was clear, the air cold and still, and we made steady progress, arriving at the lookout shortly after noon and unloaded hurriedly. After a sandwich and a cup of coffee, Fred took off on the homeward trail with the pack string, and we were left alone on what, at that moment, seemed the most isolated spot on Earth. "Well, here it is. Just what we wanted," I told Irene, and she replied: "This is unbelievable." Carrying our gear into the lookout took some time, but, with that accomplished, we took stock of our immediate surroundings.

Figure 1.2 At ten-day intervals, Fred, the packer, arrived with mail, groceries, including fresh meat and milk, and propane for the stove.

Our home to be for the next three months was fourteen feet square, of frame construction, with a four-sided roof rising to a peak. It was set on solid rock on the south side with a masonry-and-stone foundation rising to about three feet on the north side. Underneath the east wall was a cistern that had been blasted out of the native stone. Gutters channeled rain and snow water from the roof through a filter into the cistern. Windows filled all four sides with the exception of the door on the northeast corner. Three steps descended from the door to the rock doorstep. A short lightning rod rose from the peak of the roof, from which four heavy copper cables ran to the corners of the building and thence to anchors in the solid rock. These served the double purpose of grounding lightning strikes and holding the building firm against the fierce winds, which at times would have torn it from the peak. The outside had been painted so many times that the walls and the windows were sealed against the wind, although Irene swore later that sometimes the wind came right through the glass.

The furnishings were sparse: two iron cots with steel springs—grounded, of course—the propane stove, also grounded; and two chairs against a small table. A wide shelf above the windows circled the room. A wall telephone hung on the northeast wall, and the shortwave radio stood on a stand next to the Osborne fire finder, which faced north against the window on that side.

Outside facilities included a flagstaff to the southeast of the lookout, a sign welcoming possible visitors at the trailhead to the west of the building and, last but not the least, a privy 150 feet downhill to the southeast. This was not just any privy. It was almost brand new, having been built just the year before with materials all packed up from below. An ample pit had been blasted out of the stone, and, in spite of its simple architecture, the little building bore an air of, shall we say, structural integrity.

The door modestly faced away from the lookout; when open, it afforded the occupant a superlative view of the San Pedro Valley—a nice touch, I always thought. One feature puzzled me, though. It was a two-holer, and, considering the small staff at the peak, I could never figure out why it was necessary to provide more than one. More than that, the holes were of equal size, which afforded the customer no choice at all. But I carp. The fact is that it was known as the finest privy provided for any lookout in the region, and we have always been properly proud of it.

As the afternoon wore on, we accomplished some of the many tasks that settling in entailed. Irene stowed away much of our gear on the shelves over the windows, unrolled the sleeping bags, and put away groceries, while I busied myself putting batteries into the telephone and the radio and connecting those instruments to proper grounds. Switches had already been installed so that lead-ins to both could be diverted directly to the ground in the event of a lightning storm.

We kept so busy that we hardly noted the passage of time, when, all at once, a phenomenon occurred that then, and in later appearances, never failed to impress us. As the sun slowly slid beneath the horizon, all of the visible world fell into shadow except our peak and a few others. These remained brilliantly lit up for a few minutes until the sun was entirely gone from them as well. It was, in a visual way, the "knell of parting day" and invariably left me with a sadness and a strange feeling with a world that had lost a day that it would never again experience.

Darkness fell suddenly as it does in a desert country, and, as the stars came out, other lights began to appear in the valleys below. We ceased our labors and, leaving the lantern unlit, sat entranced with the view from our darkened cubicle. It seemed that we floated as in a balloon above a world peopled with tiny ants, all carrying lights. Arizona Highway 92, almost a vertical mile beneath us, was a string of pearl beads all slowly moving in unison. There were other lights from ranches within a twenty-mile radius, and then, as total darkness settled down, the glow from Tucson, Nogales, Douglas, and Benson shone above the horizon.

We sat there for a long time speaking in hushed tones. When at last we turned in, we agreed that, while our little home away from home lacked most of the modern amenities, it had the best view ever.

On the following morning, we took inventory, so to speak, of the area over which we were to watch. Situated only a little way from the U.S.-Mexico boundary, this consisted of a great half-circle to the north, bounded by as far as we could see. Owing to the fact that the recent storm had cleared the air, this was a very great distance, indeed. To the east, the forested summits of the Chiricahua Mountains formed a dark line against the horizon. Between the lower Mules, Bisbee lay hidden in a deep canyon. At the north end of the Mules, Tombstone sprawled across a hillside quiet now that mining had been discontinued. Twenty miles beyond Tombstone, the rocky defiles of the Little Dragoons held the final resting place of Cochise, the famous Chiricahua chieftain.

Looking north over our own Huachucas were the low hills of the Whetstones, and dim in the distance loomed the lofty summits of the Grahams. Near at hand to the northwest were the Santa Ritas with Wrightson Peak very nearly as high as ours. Behind the Santa Ritas were the Catalinas, where our central radio control was located on Mount Lemmon. To the west, along the border, were the Atascosas and, finally, at the limit of our view, the Coyotes with world-famous Kitt Peak at the north and Baboquivari, the sacred mountain of the Papagos, rising up like a great shark's tooth at the south.

We were one of the five lookout stations scattered around the perimeter of this vast semicircle: Buena Vista in the Chiricahuas, Rose Peak on the southern edge of the Mogollon Rim on the north, Mount Lemmon in the Catalinas, and Atascosa Peak in the Atascosas were the others.

Locating a smoke in this vast conglomeration of mountainous terrain is not as difficult as it might seem. In each lookout, mounted on a permanent pedestal, is an Osborne fire finder. This instrument consists of a metal ring about two feet in diameter with its edge marked off in 360 degrees. Each finder is installed in identical fashion, with the zero-degree mark at the magnetic north. A cross bar with an upright on each end rotates on the rail. Each upright has a slot with a vertical hair in the upper part. In practice, the lookout rotates the bar until he or she can line up the two hairs on the smoke, then relays the reading in degrees to headquarters. At the same time, another lookout, at a second location, provides a reading from there. Where the two lines cross on the master map at headquarters is the location of the fire.

While fire detection is the prime responsibility of the lookout, there are other official duties to perform. Temperature and humidity readings are reported to headquarters to aid in gauging the degree of fire danger, and a log of activities is kept to provide a record of any happenings that might affect the safety of the area and its forest. There will be days, when the Thunderbird shakes its wings and the dry lightning flashes, that the lookout is busy from dawn to midnight, and there are other periods when time hangs heavy on a lookout's hands. The latter was the condition during the month of May that year.

After the late spring storm that had battered us on the first two days of the month, the weather cleared, and the winds subsided. As the days lengthened, the meager amounts of ground cover that shared our stony mountaintop began to emerge from the dormancy imposed by a long winter and send out new growth. That, together with food that we supplied, was enough to encourage some birds to join us.

Our facilities were rudimentary: feeding stands were not easy to come by, but, with some ingenuity and much work, they can be fashioned. We had a few basic tools in the lookout, and there were numerous lightning-blasted snags only a short distance down the trail. With a saw and a hand ax and a lot of elbow grease, it is possible to hew out a very acceptable piece of lumber in a few minutes. A careful scrutiny of the ground around the lookout netted some bent nails and various pieces of rusty metal. A prize find was an old teakettle that, when cut down, converted into an excellent tray for small seeds. Though not aesthetic by any means, our creations were accepted in the same spirit in which they were offered.

Birds on Our Sky Island

Our first guests were some of the small species that frequented the low, understory growth. Here, for the first time, we had the opportunity to meet with the Arizona junco. It also goes by the names of Mexican junco and yellow-eyed junco. The latter name indicates what distinguishes it from the many other members of the junco group. Many of them are somewhat drab in color and rather secretive in habits. Not so this little sprite! Rather light blue-gray in overall color, this junco has a bright rufous (reddish) back and a startlingly brilliant yellow eye. It has the familiar white feathers in the tail that are displayed in flight.

Our pair became very tame but did not stay in the vicinity long after they had eaten. We suspected that they had a nest nearby but were never able to locate it. No young appeared, so, if there had been a nest, it might have been vandalized by some predator. I was successful in finding a nest later in the summer much farther down the mountain. Built under the curving side of a downed log, it was screened from prying eyes by a dense growth of grass, and it was purely by accident that I stumbled across it.

Another of our early acquaintances was a green-tailed towhee. It is quite different from the larger members of the family. Small, close to the size of the junco, with its rufous head and otherwise sober markings, it reminds one more of a sparrow, to whose family it does belong. Green-tailed is somewhat of a misnomer, in my opinion; it is not that conspicuous in the field. The species is remarkable in that it migrates vertically, if it can be so characterized, from the Lower and Upper Sonoran Zones of the desert, where it spends the winter, to the Transition Zone and higher in the summer. We saw only the one during our entire stay.

Not so with the spotted towhee, of which we had several pairs. These are striking birds, mostly black on the head and back with rufous sides and white spots on the wings and at the end of the tail. They have red

Figure 1.3
An Arizona junco shows the brilliant eye that is unique to it among the several junco species.

eyes that contrast sharply with their black heads. Noisy birds they were, continually scratching about in the dead leaves under the bushes and occasionally giving their mewing call.

The last to come to our feeding stands were the jays. We had seen them flying about in the forest far below and, of course, had heard them, for they are brash, noisy characters, but they are also suspicious creatures not about to be lured into danger by the prospect of food. Consequently, they watched and discussed at great length what went on with the other birds. We made every effort to entice them, but they remained hard to get for some time. Finally came the day when they cautiously deigned to partake of our offerings. From that time forward, we were sorry that they had.

These were Steller's jays, big, handsome, dark-blue birds with a blue-black crest and a throat that seemingly held more food than the traditional "pelican's beak." These birds went from being hard to get, to impossible to get rid of. It came to the point that, when we put the food out, we had to stand by until the smaller birds had enough, or the jays would move in and haul it down among the trees, where they would cache it, and then rush back for more.

We were spared these problems with the jay's big cousins, the ravens. There were a number of them in the area, but we saw them only when they were sailplaning the updrafts rising from the desert around us. Their expertise in riding the air lanes is exceeded only by the vultures, eagles, and hawks—in that order, it seems to me. One might hover over

the lookout for some time maintaining its position by the tiniest movements of pinions and tail feathers. At other times, a group would join in a boisterous game of follow the leader, swooping and racing in the wildest kind of aerial play, all the while uttering their guttural croaks.

We first saw the golden eagles about ten days after we arrived at the peak. This was a mature pair evidently bent on nesting in the Huachucas, for, after remaining in the vicinity for several days, they began the preliminaries toward that objective.

Catching an updraft, both would climb in lazy circles until they were but mere specks in the heavens. There they would put on a dazzling courtship display, at the conclusion of which the male would half-close his wings and fall into a vertical dive of several thousand feet. Down, down he would plummet until, just when it seemed that he could not escape dashing into the ground, he would spread his wings and let his momentum carry him into the heights to rejoin his mate. They might repeat this several times and then float away until lost in the distance.

It always mystified me how a bird's body could be so streamlined and the feathers so perfectly aligned as to make such maneuvers possible. At the very least, one could expect to hear a whistle as the speeding form split the air. We never did hear a sound at the distances that separated us, but some months later, as I was working a trail along a canyon wall, an eagle came hurtling down the canyon and passed within a hundred feet of my position. The sound of his passage was clearly audible at that distance.

Figure 1.5
Brash, noisy, and beautiful, Steller's jays are common in the pine forests of the West. They are greedy beyond belief.

Like the ravens, the eagles seemed to be curious about the lookout and its inhabitants. Occasionally, one or both would sail in and circle the building at close quarters. It was the thrill of a lifetime to see one of these magnificent birds bank over so that its back and golden cape and head were visible only fifty feet away. After all, how often can one see the back of an eagle in flight?

The birds that we did not often see were the ones for which the Huachucas were best known; in fact, in later years Ramsey Canyon bore the title of "Hummingbird Capital of the World." There were several reasons why the hummers seldom visited the peak. Our bare and windy mountaintop was hardly appropriate for such delicate creatures, and, by the same token, it had few of the flowering plants whose nectar they required. Occasionally, we glimpsed a transient, but they came and went so quickly that we could seldom identify them. Exceptions were the blue-throat and the Rivoli, which we recognized by their larger size rather than by their spectacular colors.

Only one of these tiny, feathered jewels decided to stay with us; for what reason, we could never define. This was a calliope, one of the tiniest of the tiny. It is listed in *Peterson's Field Guide to Western Birds* (Boston: Houghton-Mifflin, 1961, p. 166) as "the smallest hummer normally found in the United States." Measurements are given as 2.8 inches to 3.5 inches in length. This minuscule bit of pugnacity chose the grounding cable on the northwest corner of the lookout as the vantage point from which he could see everything that went on below—or above, for that matter. Woe be to any bird that triggered his displeasure. He would fly at it, squeaking furiously, and, although he seemed never to come to actual blows, he fought a spectacular fight, darting in and out and harassing his supposed adversary until he became tired of the battle and returned to his post on the cable, there to rearrange his feathers and cool off. He became particularly incensed when any bird would fly at, or above, his level, and it was amusing to see him take off after one of the eagles, which would calmly soar along, never paying him any more attention than if he were a house fly. He would disappear at intervals, at which times we supposed that he went down the mountainside to a level at which the nectar-bearing flowers that he required could be found.

By the time we had become familiar to our feathered friends, it was getting along in the month of May. Despite the late storm, spring had been hard on our heels as we climbed up to Miller Peak. The groves of leafless aspens through which we had ridden were now decked out in shining green. This greening of the peaks was made all the more striking when set off by a deep blue sky dappled with the billowy, cumulus clouds characteristic of late spring weather in Arizona.

The temperature had now moderated to the point that we spent more time outside the lookout. Up to this time, we had been enticing our animal neighbors to come to us. Now, in a strange reversal of roles, we discovered that we were being allowed to come to some of them. We discovered this in a strange way.

Tubby the Rock Squirrel

We had water, to a point; that is, we had enough of a supply for some uses but not for all. We were forced to establish priorities—enough for drinking but not for laundry, enough for cooking but careful with the dishwashing, enough for an occasional bath in our galvanized washtub but scrimping on all of these uses so that we could eke out just a little for the birds. Our plumbing system for waste water consisted of a five-gallon pail set by the steps outside the door. When the pail had accumulated a couple of gallons of spent dishwater, we would carry it along on a trip to the privy and toss it out along the trail.

It was almost empty on the day when I decided to sit on the steps while constructing a glass container in which to imprison some butterflies that I was hoping to photograph. It was a difficult task, but, in spite of my concentration, I gradually became aware of a scratching sound in the waste-water receptacle by my right knee. Slowly turning my head in that direction, I saw a gray rock squirrel hanging by his hind claws from the edge of the pail while he was getting a drink. Hardly daring to breathe, I watched until he had drunk his fill. Then he pulled himself up and, to my utter surprise, jumped over on the step next to my right leg and began to wash his face.

At this point, I began to talk to him. This did not seem to disturb him in the least, so, after he had finished his toilette, I called: "Hey, Irene, come see what we have here."

"How cute," she said. "He must be hungry."

To Irene, any creature, man or beast, must always be hungry and needs must be fed. Bringing out a piece of biscuit, she offered it to him. He graciously took it from her hand, giving us the impression somehow that this acceptance sealed a bond between us. Naming him was no problem. What do you name a rather obese squirrel whose pear shape reminds you of a door stop? Why, Tubby, of course, and so Tubby joined the roster of our lookout group.

We gave him the run of the house, and he repaid our trust by never a

Figure 1.6 Because of his girth, Tubby the rock squirrel had a hard time squeezing through this knothole in the porch foundation.

nibble at the goodies that his sensitive nose must have told him were in the various sacks and cartons stacked against the walls. He would greet me in the morning when I went out to hoist the flag, then come in with me when I returned. It did not disturb him if the door was closed; he seemed to have unlimited confidence that we would let him out at any time he so desired. Actually, he found some of our indoor facilities more to his liking than those he enjoyed outside.

For instance, it is usual for ground squirrels to select a vantage point from which to check on the surroundings for whatever of interest or danger might develop. Tubby chose his observation post on top of the shortwave radio, where, out of the windows, he had a better view of a greater area than from any vantage point he might have found outside. He would sit there for long periods, apparently enjoying the security as well as the view. On those occasions when a hawk or one of the eagles would come into view, his tail would twitch, and the hairs on it would stand on end until the intruder had soared away.

On occasion, he would go foraging outside. Mock orange, sometimes called *syringa*, a relative of the state flower of Idaho, was then coming into bloom. Dwarfed by the poor soils and the punishing winds on the peak, it still managed to produce the beautiful flowers for which the genus is noted. Tubby enjoyed eating the showy blooms, and it was most amusing to see him stand up on his hind legs and reach up with his fore-paws to pull the flowers down to his mouth. On these outings, he was always alert to any possible danger, however, and any fleeting shadow was enough to send him scampering back to the lookout with his tail fluffed out like a bottle brush. Tubby's wants were simple enough. Other than a few gourmet items such as flower petals and birdseed, he ate pretty much what we did and seemed to thrive on it.

Much as we enjoyed Tubby, we could not feel the same way about his relatives. The bird feeders soon attracted two of them. They were young and suspicious, lean and hungry, and, despite our best efforts, they were making serious inroads upon our bird food. Trapping seemed to be the only answer to our dilemma. Inventory of our junk pile yielded a small wooden box and a piece of ancient window screen. The resultant box trap was a frail thing, indeed, far more suited for holding butterflies than a young, husky rock squirrel. However, it had to suffice. So, with some misgivings, we baited it and set it out by the feeders. In a few minutes,

Figure 1.7
Mock orange grows
to be a large shrub
on the peak. Both
leaves and flowers
are relished by deer
and lesser animals.

we had our first squirrel. I knew that it would tear its way out of the trap in a minute or two, so I rushed out and wrapped a burlap sack around it. We set off down the mountain at once, I jolting the bundle about so that the irate inmate could not concentrate its efforts in any one place. About a half-mile down the trail, I released my prisoner. Its partner was captured and released in the same manner, and it solved the problem, for we never saw them again.

Tubby stayed with us until we left the peak. We missed him, and, in his way, I'm sure he missed us, too. However, we had no misgivings as to his ability to readjust to the wild. By resuming his normal activities for the rest of the summer and returning to a natural diet, who knows, he might even have lost a little weight!

As summer became a reality, a change swept over our surroundings. The storm that had greeted us on our arrival at the Reef at the beginning of May, was the last precipitation that we were to receive from the Pacific Coast for the month. Some high cirrus clouds still drifted our way from the west, but, though beautiful to the eye, they yielded no rain to a parched and thirsty land. While the desert plains below us heated up for the summer, the Huachucas greeted spring.

The forest of aspens on the flank of Carr Peak through which we had ridden on our way up to the lookout, gray then with bare branches, had now become a vibrant light green mantle on the mountain. Miller Peak wore a necklace of aspens at the point where the bare rocks joined the dark green mass of the conifers. Dwarfed in size and contorted by the winds, they still bravely displayed the dancing foliage for which their species is noted. Known by various names—popple, quaking aspens, aspen poplar—surely the scientific name, *Populus tremuloides*, describes them best. The leaf stems are flattened vertically while the leaf surfaces are horizontal to the ground. This arrangement ensures that the slightest breeze will set the leaves to fluttering, or "trembling."

This rustling of the leaves can be heard for some distance; in fact, with a slight breeze from the north, we could distinctly hear the forest on Carr Peak, an air mile or more from the lookout.

With the aspens leading the way, the understory shrubs and forbs also awakened from a winter of dormancy. All of this activity encouraged the return of animals that, during the previous fall, had descended from the heights to escape the cold. This vertical migration is a device employed by some mammals and several species of birds in the Southwest. By spending the winters in the lower elevations and climbing to the "Sky Islands" in the summers, they enjoy many of the benefits of conventional migration but with considerably less effort.

Buck Joins Our Group

We became aware that deer were in the vicinity some time before we saw them. At times, when we carried a lantern outside in the evening, we would hear the alarm snort of one or more bucks who were suspicious of this, to them, unwonted activity. This snort, actually more of a whistle, can be heard for a great distance, especially in the rarified air at high altitudes. Other bucks will take up the alarm, with the result that the entire deer population of a mountainside will remain on alert until such time that all are satisfied that everything is once again normal.

We were pleased when, at length, a small group of does accompanied by one buck ventured in to browse the leaves of the stunted aspens below the lookout. Shy at first, they would appear only early in the morning or at dusk, but when they became more accustomed to our activities, they might be seen at any time of day. Not wishing to frighten them, we never called to them and avoided staring in their direction while we were outside, but we watched them from inside with the binoculars.

Quite often, they would be about when we fed the birds, and at those times they could hear us, for we kept up a running conversation with our feathered friends. It has always been our habit to talk to our animal neighbors. as it seems to assure them that we mean no harm and also gives them a point of reference indicating just where we are and what we might be intending to do. On one such morning, we saw the buck watching us with special interest. He stood stock still for a long time, staring fixedly at what went on between us and the birds. When we had finished with them and gone inside, we saw him come confidently up the slope and go to the bird feeder. He inspected it thoroughly and sniffed at everything until he apparently decided that all was in order, and, from that time on, we were adopted by "Buck."

Buck was of the race of deer known as Sonoran white-taileds, or fan-taileds, which we had already seen at the Seeman place. Native only to the mountains of southwestern New Mexico and southern Arizona in the United States, and to the Sierra Madre and adjacent mountains for a considerable distance into northern Mexico, they range only at high elevations. We have mentioned that they are small animals; one might even class them as dainty. A mature buck will average no more than a hundred pounds, live weight. Their winter coat is a salt-and-pepper gray, while the summer pelage lightens to a fawn color with cinnamon shadings. The tail, which hangs almost to the knees, is dark on the upper side and pure white underneath. In flight it is held upright and wagged from side to side, giving rise to the term "fan-tailed." Altogether, it is a charming species admired by all who are fortunate enough to observe them.

We, of course, were of that hierarchy. Buck, we judged, was a three-year-old. We estimated his weight at approximately eighty pounds. His antlers were in the velvet, small but elegant, the beams curving forward in fine fashion, and the tines seeming to be taller than they actually were because of their furry covering. He had shed his dark winter coat and now was all fawn and cinnamon above and lighter below with a fully haired fan tail. He was a handsome animal, and that he knew it was evidenced by his proud, almost haughty, bearing. Our relations that summer might be described as those of friendly acquaintances. We grew to have a great affection for him and yet . . . our feelings were tempered by caution.

Several seasons previously, we had stayed in a campground frequented by a small, tame, white-tailed buck. He was a great pet, loved by all of the visitors, and had no fear of anyone. As fall approached, the velvet on his antlers began to hang in shreds. To hasten the shedding process, he would thrash his antlers in the surrounding bushes and rub them against any rough surfaces he could find. Another of his habits at that time was to point his antlers at a visitor's thigh and push, gently at first but then, if the person offered any resistance, with more force. As more and more visitors experienced this treatment, they began to carry switches, and, whenever the buck offered to use his antlers against them, they would dissuade him with a sharp tap on the nose.

A middle-aged couple had been camped next to us for several days in a travel trailer. On the day of this particular incident, a pleasant fall afternoon, he was in the trailer, while she was outside putting things in order around and under it. She was bending over with her back to the road when the buck came ambling down the path. Apparently, her posterior offered him an opportunity to try out his new antlers, so he walked over and gave it several sharp jabs with his tines. Her screams summoned her husband, who came rushing out of the trailer to her aid. The buck, now aroused by all of this turmoil, promptly attacked him. Only by grabbing the animal by the antlers and holding its head down was he able to avoid injury from the sharp tines and slashing hoofs. Even though the buck was but a small one, the man had all he could do to back up to the trailer door, throw the animal to the ground, and jump inside. We all learned something from their experience.

We could never understand why "our" Buck took such a fancy to us. We never fed him, mostly because we had nothing to give him. We never

Figure 1.8 Buck, a Sonoran white-tailed deer, was puzzled to find that his harem would not join him when he frequented the area around the lookout.

touched him, although we were often at arm's length and could have very easily. We talked to him a lot, for he seemed to understand, and agree, as he never ventured to contradict. At times, he would desert his does; at other times, they might come up to the lookout with him, and, although they were not too timid, they would be uncomfortable if we went outside and would drift away down the mountain to the cover of the forest. He would watch them go, puzzled no doubt at their unwillingness to stay.

It was not unusual for him to come up to the lookout after dark and stand on the south side, where the windows were closest to the ground. There he would watch what we were doing inside. We might have no hint that he was there unless we happened to see the reflection of the beam from our gasoline lantern in his eyes. The ultimate test of his trust came midway in July when Bob Schmitt came up to inspect the facility and evaluate our performance.

After a leisurely lunch and a tour of the premises, he was about to leave when he said: "Oh, before I go, let's go down and have a look at the privy." As we started down the path, I glimpsed a movement behind the structure and realized that Buck was there browsing on the shrubs. I said: "Bob, if you don't mind, walk quietly behind me. I want to show you something." With a questioning look, he gave me the lead, and, as we proceeded down the trail, I began to talk in a monotone: "It's all right, Buck. Bob won't hurt you. He's okay, don't be afraid," and so on, until we slowly stepped around the corner and there stood Buck with his mouth full of leaves and a placid look in his eyes. He was only a few feet away so I told Bob: "Don't touch him; we never do." Bob's reaction was predictable. "I'll be damned. I wouldn't believe this if I hadn't seen it." Mine would have been the same under similar circumstances.

The Lookout's Life

Now let us go back in time to late May and review our duties as lookouts. The mountains were bone dry, the humidity down to the teens, and, in consequence, the fire danger was extreme. The "dry lightning" storms had not yet begun, so the source of any fires could be considered human. Any smoke, no matter how small, was a matter of grave concern to us, inexperienced as we were. We were often torn between whether to report them or not.

Henry Van Horn over on Atascosa Peak was a great help in those situations. Henry was an elderly bachelor who worked some scheelite claims in a canyon on the west side of the Huachucas during most of the year and was employed as a lookout during the fire season. For years he had been stationed on Miller Peak, and he knew the surrounding territory intimately. He was reputed to have the keenest eyes in the business. He sometimes called us to report smokes that he had picked up in our area. We might see a suspicious haze arising from under the north end of the range and call him for a fix from his station only to be told: "Oh, that's only the smoke from the dump at the Fort; they're burning it today." From long familiarity with our fire finder, he could, from memory, give us readings of several other points where legitimate smokes might be expected to appear. We had occasion to draw upon his wealth of experience many times in the next few weeks.

While the desert continued to heat up, other developments that would have a direct effect on our environment were taking place thousands of miles away. Every summer as the Earth in its orbit tilts the North Pole toward the sun, a high-pressure area forms over the Atlantic Ocean north of the equator. This phenomenon has become known as the "Bermuda high." With it as a hub, a great whorl of high pressure rotates clockwise and gradually expands in diameter, spawning weather disturbances as it grows. Most destructive of these are hurricanes that develop over the water but tend to diminish the farther they penetrate over land. However, great masses of humid air reach out as far as the southwestern United States and rotate farther north and east as the jet stream retreats to the north. They bring on the so-called monsoons, summer rains that arrive in Arizona in late June or July. The moisture they provide is augmented by humidity drifting north from the tropical storms, called *chubascos*, that form over the Pacific Ocean along the west coast of Mexico.

A weather system so vast and so complex does not develop in a day or a week. Rather, it advances by irregular stages, depending on local conditions as well as the amount of moisture provided. The first indications that the monsoons are at hand are the cumulus clouds that form in the daytime during hot weather. As humidity advances from the south or southwest, it encounters the hot blasts of air rising from the superheated surface of the desert. Whirled aloft to dizzying heights by these updrafts, the humidity condenses in the cold of high altitude and forms clouds that then continue to enlarge and rise until the great billowing masses assume the anvil configuration. This is the point at which the bottom of the cloud is flat, and the upper parts are carunculated (swollen and irregular) in the fantastic forms so admired by photographers and those of us who create fanciful castles in the air.

As a practical matter, however, the condensation has reached the altitude at which it is cold enough for raindrops to form. If they do, and if a sufficient amount is released, a cloudburst may result; if, on the other hand, the output is scanty, streams of rain may be released only to evaporate in the dry air of the desert before they ever reach the ground. This phenomenon is known as "virga." In many instances, enough static electricity is created by all of the activity of this process to trigger lightning.

When lightning occurs without appreciable rain falling, it is known as "dry lightning."

It was fascinating at our altitude to watch the formation and disintegration of these early clouds. At more than nine thousand feet, the sky is definitely darker in hue than at lower levels, and, with no haze to soften their outlines, the fleecy white shapes stood out with startling contrast. The shadows of the cloud patterns upon the surrounding plains were interesting as well, while, from our angle of sight, a cloudburst had all the appearance of a black column of rain holding up a canopy of cloud.

Up to this point, our life at the lookout was easy—wash the windows, do a little maintenance work on the surrounding paths, call in to the district ranger on the telephone, radio in the weather stats to headquarters on Mount Lemmon in the Catalinas, and, of course, survey the surroundings for smokes. This bucolic existence was due to change, however.

Our first intimation of this was one evening in June. Far down in Mexico, west of the Sierra Madres, sheet lightning flickered momentarily above the horizon, and then all was dark again. On succeeding nights, more sheet lightning and then actual bolts were to be seen as the evening storms worked northward. Even though we had been forewarned, we were awed by the amount and the intensity of the lightning as the storms advanced upon us. Eventually, the foothills below the border were set ablaze, and, since the Mexicans made no efforts to extinguish the fires, we had the added interest of seeing them spread from foothill to foothill on succeeding nights. Then came the night when our first lightning storm surrounded us with tremendous winds, searing light, and deafening sound.

As outdoor-oriented people, Irene and I have never been *afraid* of lightning; however, we have seen many evidences of its awesome power, and we respect it thoroughly. Over the years, much has been researched about lightning. We are told that it is electricity, that it can leap from cloud to cloud or cloud to ground and return. We are told also that lightning rods and proper grounding can prevent buildings from receiving lightning strikes. It all sounds very factual and reasonable as you sit in an armchair and see it explained on television in the comfort and safety of your home. But when, on a pitch-black night, you are two people isolated in a tiny cabin on the very tip of a mountain, with a gale shaking the structure like a terrier with a rat in his teeth, with rain and hail battering the windows and an unremitting glare from lightning strikes all about, and with thunderclaps like dynamite explosions assaulting your ears, then a doubt arises as to whether that little lightning rod on the tip of the roof, and the network of copper cables grounding the building, is enough to protect you. Reason tells you that it is; the cabin has been there for twenty years and, no doubt, has seen many storms as severe as this.

Our closest call came one night around the middle of our tour of duty. We had had a very severe storm, but, about eleven o'clock in the evening, things had quieted down to the point that we had decided to retire. We had no more than lain down when a lightening strike and a terrific concussion from thunder shook the building. My eyes were closed at the time, but I could see the flash through the lids, and I told Irene: "That was close. I almost believe that I heard the thunder before I saw the light." We went to sleep without investigating, but, in the morning when we went out, we found the wooden lid on the cistern shattered and a rock in the foundation split. The bolt had struck no more than five feet from my head!

That morning when I called Bob, he said: "Boy, am I glad to hear you! You had some lightning last night up on the peak."

I told him: "I remember what you told me about lightning and that I hadn't seen real lightning yet. Well, now I have."

In contrast, on those evenings when thunderstorms occurred in other parts of our territory, they were a delight to observe. Perched in our lofty aerie, we watched as vivid streaks of lightning stabbed at mountain and plain and thunder rolled. Part of our duty was to spot those areas of greatest activity and check them on the following morning for possible smokes. On that next morning, our eyes would be red from the ultraviolet rays to which they had been subjected.

Every night, regardless of whether it looked stormy, we would disconnect the telephone and ground the line with a separate switch. The first pole of the line was only about two feet from the west wall of the lookout, and the line came in about a foot above the window. Since it was a ground circuit system, only one wire was involved. In the roughly twenty miles to the ranger station in Canelo, a powerful charge of static electricity would build up on a stormy night. At times it would exceed the capacity of the grounding switch and flow directly from the incoming line to the grounding cable in a pulsating ribbon of violet light. It was fascinating, but also a little frightening, to see so much uncontrolled energy streaming by only two feet outside the window.

Moisture continued to surge north from the tropics in increasing amounts in July. At the same time, we were experiencing afternoon thunderstorms because the desert, at its peak of heat, was lofting that moisture into the sky at an earlier time of day. Clouds formed, climbed to unbelievable heights, and produced downpours in only minutes. This called for some judgment on the part of whichever of us was not on duty and happened to be out on the trail photographing or observing. It was a case of either get back to the lookout before the onslaught or seek the shelter of some overhanging ledge. In the lookout, we waited until the lightning was striking about a mile and a half away before disconnecting the radio and the telephone. We soon learned that the radio would give us warning when lightning was too close. When an electrical charge was building up in a nearby cloud to the point that the lightning was about to flash, the radio would set up a shrill whistle of oscillation, gradually rising in scale and volume until it ended in a crash of static as the flash occurred. It was then high time to turn off the set and ground it!

At this time, we were introduced to a type of lightning bolt new to us, which Henry Van Horn called "reachers." This was a horizontal bolt of cloud-to-cloud type, but, instead, it issued from a low-hanging cloud some distance away and traveled on a level line to the peak. Henry warned us that they were "sneaky," and we found them to be dangerous and unpredictable. It was unnerving to be in bright sunlight with no clouds overhead and suddenly have a strike explode only fifty yards or so away.

Of Mice and Skunks

The evening temperatures moderated to the point that we sometimes left the door open until we retired. One moonlit night, as I stood in the doorway admiring the scene, I thought I saw something moving around on the ground beneath the bird feeder. Taking the lantern outside for a better look, I discovered that a number of mice were foraging for whatever bits of food the birds had scattered from the feeders. Irene decided at once that this situation called for action, so, on the following night, we provided a large jar lid with a small handful of birdseed. This worked admirably; a dozen or so mice gathered around this "round table" and got along in perfect agreement. This was too good to last, however.

Several nights later, a large wood rat charged out from under the steps and through the little group, hurling can lid, food, and mice in all directions. It then returned to its vantage point under the steps. In a little while, when the mice had regrouped amidst what was left of the food, it repeated the performance and continued to do this at irregular intervals. By nailing the lid down to a piece of board, we managed to limit the loss of the seed, and, since the mice did not seem to be injured by the rat's rough treatment, we not only allowed the show to go on, but, in some ways, we even enjoyed it.

As we sat watching one night, a stranger walked into the circle of light cast by the lantern. This one was black and white and sported a beautiful white tail tipped with black. We carefully, oh so carefully, brought out some bits of leftovers from supper and laid these offerings before him. They were devoured in a moment, and, without so much as a look of thanks, he was on his way with the peculiar loping kind of gait that skunks have. On the following night he was back, and, since we then assumed that he would be a "regular," our next grocery list called for several tins of sardines, the "smelliest and oiliest possible."

Skunks tame very quickly. They have an arrogance of manner that proclaims, in so many words, "molest me if you dare." They are not greatly concerned about what you do as long as you move slowly. This one was ready to eat out of our hands almost at once, but this was not for us. Very early in our association, we discovered that he did not readily distinguish between the food that we offered and the hands that offered it but snapped enthusiastically at both. Because of his predilection to grab fingers along with his food, we named him "Grabby" and fed him with a fork. It would have been nice if our relationship could have continued on that amicable basis, but it was not to be.

We suspected that Grabby maintained his base of operations under the lookout because there were several holes in the foundation large enough for him to squeeze through. It was all right with us if he lived in our

Figure 1.9
Grabby, a striped skunk, became a regular evening visitor but was interested only in the food we provided. We maintained an uneasy truce throughout our relationship.

basement as long as he kept the noise down after ten o'clock at night. All went well until one night, shortly after our bedtime, a sudden series of bumps and thumps under the floor indicated that some sort of violence was going on down there. This had no more registered upon us than the first wave of skunk odor welled up into the cabin, followed by more of increased potency. This left us on the horns of a dilemma. We could hardly remain in the odor-saturated lookout, but the night was too cold to spend outside. We compromised by leaving the door open and using towels to waft as much as possible of the odor outside. All in all, we spent a miserable night. Eventually, the odor faded away, but we found it hard to forgive Grabby. We supposed that another skunk had challenged him and that he, or perhaps both, had used their armament in the struggle for territory.

Along the Trail

We continued to have experiences, mostly of a less personal nature, with the surprisingly large number of animals that shared the mountaintop with us. As required by the terms of our employment, I was to be on duty five days a week, and Irene was to serve on the two days I was off. This left us both with plenty of time to hike down the trail to the forested

Figure 1.10 Apache-plume is a large shrub bearing distinctive flowers with long plumose styles protruding from the center of the white blooms.

area on the west face of the peak. There, in the Hudsonian Zone, and lower were to be found a wide variety of plants, each in its own preference of soil and exposure. In the shady ravines, Douglas-fir, spruce, and white fir found the coolness to their liking. Lower down on the warmer exposure, ponderosa pine, Apache pine, and live oak were dominant. Random open spaces, resulting from forest fires of years before, were covered with grasses and rimmed with aspens. There, the butterflies fluttered and danced among the daisies and sunflowers, which also love the open spaces. Lower still, box elders and maples made their appearances, and, at Miller Saddle, we could look down into canyons crowded with sycamore, ash, and walnut trees.

Many of the shrubs and forbs came into flower during the three-month period of our stay, and it was a delight to wander among them and revel in the rich perfumes and varied colors of their blooms. After a winter of plentiful snow and the late spring storm, the floral displays were spectacular. Among the most conspicuous, because of their size, were some of the flowering shrubs.

The New Mexico locust *(Robinia)* occurred in small groves along the trail, its branches bending under the weight of clusters of fragrant

Figure 1.11
The thimbleberry,
also known as the
New Mexican
raspberry, is
important not for
its fruit but as an
ornamental. It is
browsed by deer.

pink-purple flowers. *Rubus neomexicanus*, actually a raspberry but better known as the thimbleberry, presented itself as a dense shrub, its surface spangled with large, white, five-petaled stars. Apache-plume, so appropriately named, grew luxuriantly in the rocky places, its white flowers and purple plumes (actually, purple styles clinging to the developing fruits) contrasting strongly with the more conventional shrubs. *Syringa*s were there, too, more lush than those harried by the winds higher up on the peak.

Yellow columbines were to be found in the ravines under the shade of the firs, and the hummingbird trumpet *(Zauschneria)* clung to rocky ledges, its scarlet tubular blooms brilliant against the dark stone. Any small seep or spring was certain to be bordered by *Mimulus*, the monkeyflower, in shades of yellow and red. In the open, clumps of *Penstemon* of various species sent up flower stalks as much as four feet tall, while banks of *Gilias* flaunted their firecracker-red trumpets in many places along the way.

It was exciting to be surrounded by that wealth of beauty, and, best of all, it belonged to us, for there was seldom anyone else on the peak. The great advantage of "owning" this relatively undisturbed environment was the opportunity given us to observe what went on in some of the many microhabitats represented on the mountainside. It took time and patience to accomplish this.

Our entrance into some sunny glade was analogous to throwing a stone into a quiet pond. Silent ripples of alarm spread out in all directions as the inhabitants took cover. Comfortably seated and with binoculars at the ready, we would wait. From their hiding places, the denizens observed the intruders and checked us out for possible motives. If we remained seated and quiet, it would not be long until some of the braver creatures would resume their activities, and then, one by one, the whole group would gradually join the coordinated actions that we had interrupted.

In the study of wildlife, I might paraphrase an old adage: "They also serve who only sit and watch." In the early days of exploration of the western United States, most of the naturalists who discovered, classified, and named the animal species had no time to study the life habits of their subjects. Had they done so, and stressed the importance of each animal and plant to the ecosystem, we might have avoided the stupid and uncalled-for extinction of several of our native species.

It was on one of my forays down the mountain that I discovered the nest of the Arizona junco that had visited our lookout. This pair had chosen to build it under the overhanging side of a downed log. Tall grass growing along the trunk effectively concealed the nest, but, by parting the stems, I found the tiny bowl, well protected from sun and rain alike by the rounded bulk of the log. Four blue-white eggs were already being incubated, and I had the pleasure on successive weekends of seeing the young mature and fledge.

An unusual sight for us along the trail was that of the Clark's nutcrackers. This medium-size gray-and-black relative of the crow is a northern

Figure 1.12
The Clark's
nutcracker is a
member of the crow
family. It frequents
pine forests and
depends largely
upon pine nuts
for food.

species rarely met with in the mountains of the southwestern desert. Invasions do occur at irregular intervals, however, and one of these took place in the Huachucas in the winter of 1951. We observed a flock of from twenty to thirty, which congregated in the upper edge of the Canadian Zone, feeding on the abundant pine nuts to be found there. Irene and I found them to be fascinating creatures. We had seen them before in the mountains of Idaho and Montana, but there they were in their normal habitat and were accepted as such. Here they were exotics, and in that role, took on an added interest.

The nutcracker is a handsome bird with a light gray body and black wings and tail. A prominent white patch in the wings and white borders in the tail provide an interesting contrast to the rather dull body color. Their call is a soft "khaa" or "khraa," which, once heard, is forever associated with the occasion where first encountered. These are not timid birds; around the parks and campgrounds of the North, they boldly steal whatever of an edible nature they can carry away. On our trail, they evidently subsisted mainly on the pine nuts. With long strong beaks, they would extract the nuts from the cones and fly to some favorite perch along the way, there placing the nut between their feet and, using the branch as an anvil, pound the nut with heavy strokes of their bills until the husk was breached and the nut meat was made available. They could always be found in the same general area. We saw them at the look-out only twice, and both times they spurned the offerings that attracted less-specialized species.

One day, without warning, they were gone. Our notes record that they departed on July 16, 1951. We wondered what triggered such a sudden desertion of an area that had apparently been perfectly satisfactory. The theory has been advanced that an invasion of these birds is spurred by a year, or several years, of generous precipitation resulting in a heavier than average crop of pine cones. If that be true, it seems logical that a dwindling of the food supply might trigger an exodus.

An invasion of a different kind of animal, which is destined to become a permanent part of our wildlife pool, occurred in the early years of the twentieth century. This was the coatimundi. It seems to have been first recorded in Arizona in the low mountains west of Nogales. We had seen their distinctive tracks in the dusty roads but had never actually seen one. Now we were seeing their tracks in the Huachucas, but my bad luck continued, and during the time that we were at the lookout, I never caught a glimpse of one. Irene proved to be more fortunate, however, and she several times ran across small bands of coatis.

They are unlikely creatures. Perhaps the most unique of their features is a disproportionately long, slim snout, which has a piglike pad of heavy cartilage at the tip. With this, they root through leaf mold and soft earth in search of insects and other small creatures that form their preferred diet. Their jaws are powerful and armed with long, sharp canines. It is said that no dog can be considered a match for a coati. They are not a bel-ligerent animal, however, and, unless cornered, are no threat to humans. Wistful brown eyes and small round ears complete a face and head that remotely resembles that of a raccoon, to which they are related.

The body is equally absurd. The front legs are short and have feet armed with long, curved claws; whereas, the hind legs are long with feet bearing short claws. Because of this novel arrangement, their tracks look as though a small barefoot child might be following some strange, clawed biped down the trail. At the rear of this improbable body is a matching improbable tail. As long as the body, it is slim and sparsely haired. Because the coatis frequently climb into the trees, many of the back-country people believe that the tail is prehensile like that of a mon-key. This is nonsense, of course; the coati probably does use its tail to some extent as an aid to balance when it is in the trees, but it cannot be used to grasp anything. The tail is carried straight up when the animal is traveling, and it is an interesting sight to see a troop moving through an area with their tails waving about. The Mexicans call these animals *chulas* (pretty ones), or *chulus*, for which I find no translation. I prefer the latter term, as they are definitely not pretty, in my estimation.

Interesting as these forays down the mountain trails proved to be, we continued to find much of interest in the relatively sterile environment of the rocky summit of the peak. Leading southward from the lookout was a path of about a hundred yards to an overlook with a commanding view of the mountainside to and beyond the Mexican border. Because much of this area could not be seen from the building, we made it our practice to saunter out to the overlook every morning and several times during the day to make a routine check of the grasslands far below. The path was narrow, and walking it was reminiscent of venturing out on the ridgepole of our barn when I was a child.

We had not been on the peak long when Irene came back from the overlook suppressing her excitement with difficulty. "Guess what I just saw?" she crowed with her eyes sparkling.

"Beats me," I replied. "What did you just saw?"

"Two turkey gobblers, right out there a little ways on the path."

"Fantastic," I said, "and what did they do?"

"They flew off the peak and flapped their wings until they got out a ways and then set their wings and sailed in big circles until they got down to the woods near the saddle," she said. These were the only turkeys we saw on the peak. Why they were there was a mystery. They are most usually seen in the mixed pine and oak belt around seven thousand to eight thousand feet in altitude.

On one of those red-letter days when Fred, our packer, arrived with our quotas of groceries, laundry, and mail, I received a small parcel from one of my friends who was in Denver at the time. In the package was a note that read: "I'm sending you some cactus plants which I was surprised to find this far north and at this altitude. I hope that you can identify them." Identification was no problem; there are only a few cactus species in the Denver area, but how to keep them in our situation was something else. I finally scrounged a one-pound coffee can from our "kitchen" and brought up some loam from the forest. I crowded the three small plants into the container and set it out on a ledge south of the building.

One morning a few days later, I picked up the can to see how the plants were doing and, low and behold, under it was a tiny rattlesnake curled up in a tight coil. It proved to be a Price's rattlesnake, one of three very small and very rare rattlesnake species to be found in the Huachucas. It was about eighteen inches in length and little larger in diameter than a lead pencil, but it had a well-developed rattle with six segments and a button. This species does not have the arrow-shaped head like most of the rattlesnakes and, if it were not for the rattles, could easily be mistaken for a nonpoisonous snake.

When we told Henry Van Horn what we had found, he said: "Yeah, I was bit by one of them little buggers once down at the diggins'. It made me a little sick for a while, but it didn't bother me much." He sounded real reassuring, but, in handling this snake and photographing it, I took great care not to get "bit" because I didn't fancy getting sick even for a little while. Anyway, it was an event of no great importance except that I'm sure that this was the highest altitude at which this species has ever been recorded.

One afternoon, some of the low bushes along the path seemed to have taken on an odd color. On closer inspection, we discovered that they were covered with ladybird beetles, or, as we always called them, "ladybugs." They were there by the hundreds. The next day, they were there by the thousands; on the following day, by the hundreds of thousands. This continued until selected shrubs and outcroppings bore coverings of the beetles several inches deep.

Henry was very unimpressed when we told him our story. "Yeah, I know," he said. "Happens every year on all the high peaks. Some lookouts collect them and sell them by the gallon. They send them to the orange growers over in California."

In spite of research on why this and some other types of beetles go through this strange performance, the full explanation seems to be eluding entomologists. It is known that the beetles collect together in the fall and winter in deposits of leaf mold or in rock crevices, and then, as spring returns, they emerge to cluster on shrubs and rocks in response to the changes that the season ushers in. Many factors seem to influence the urge to cluster. Variations in temperature, intensities of sunlight, and fluctuations of humidity all play a part. The advantages of this behavior are obscure as well. Foiling predation through sheer force of numbers can be one. The availability of partners during the mating period is doubtless important. At any rate, the tendency to gather on the high peaks has one final benefit: the winds of spring carry them far and wide as they disperse. They are truly scattered to the four winds!

The Little One

One balmy evening with supper finished and dishes done, we were relaxing—I seated on my bed with a book in hand, and Irene working at something or other while seated at the fire finder—when I sensed a movement at the open door. On the threshold, with one front foot raised while it surveyed the room, was an animated little bundle of black-and-white fluff. In a low tone I said: "Irene, don't move but look at the door. We have a visitor." After a long appraisal, the little skunk seemed satisfied that we posed no threat, and he slowly moved inside to inspect the premises.

This was a spotted skunk, the smallest of the four species of skunks native to Arizona. *Spilogale putorius* (rock weasel and "to stink") is also called civet cat and hydrophobe skunk. All of these names are derogatory, which is unfortunate because this little animal is sprightly, clean, and altogether charming. The term "spotted" is a misnomer, too, because its coat is more marbled than spotted. The only well-defined spots are on the face and head.

We were well acquainted with the species, having had one as a regular visitor while camping in Sabino Canyon some years before. Spotted skunks are great rummagers; they love to get into a cupboard and stir the contents about. Like other skunks, they prefer oily or fishy foods, and ours in Sabino was always trying to get into our butter dish. We were able to foil him in that effort, but it was disconcerting to wake up to the rattling of pots and pans in the wee, small hours.

Returning to this later visitor, he entered slowly and began to carefully work his way around the room, inspecting everything thoroughly as he went. Eventually, he climbed up on a pile of gear at the foot of

Figure 1.13
The "Little One" was a spotted skunk, the smallest of the four species in Arizona. He might better be described as marbled. These are agile little creatures, at home in the trees as well as on the ground.

Irene's bed and then upon the bed itself. Continuing on, he came to the place where my bed joined hers at right angles. Proceeding then in my direction, he reached the point where I blocked his further progress. He then looked over the edge of the bed, and it was plain to see that he was reluctant to take the jump to the floor for that was a long way to one of he size. He looked at me, and I returned his gaze. Then, realizing a solution to his problem, I very carefully uncrossed my legs and extended my left one to the floor. Without any hesitation, he climbed up on my thigh and then walked down the top of my leg to the floor. With his tour completed, he leisurely went to the door and left.

We supposed that was the last that we would see of him, but, just in case, we saved a piece of bacon for him from the morrow's breakfast. Sure enough, the next night he was back and went through the same performance except that, this time, he sat on my thigh and ate the bacon from my hand. Every night thereafter, he repeated his rounds with no indication that he had ever seen our belongings before. I did alter his feeding routine somewhat after he gained my confidence. I would break the bacon into small bits and hold one tightly between thumb and fore-finger. He would nibble it, oh so carefully, right down to the point where I would open my fingers and let him have the last small bit. I could feel his teeth working against my fingers, but he never bit me once.

Remarkably, although we grew to know the little skunk so well, we never assigned a name to him. The usual names in vogue for skunks are either crude or ridiculous and not in keeping with the affection that we held for our diminutive friend. We might have named him Tiny, for tiny he was, but, lacking that, he remained for us just the "Little One."

The Fire Season Winds Down

As the summer waned, we began to feel increasingly that we had become a part of the mountain's environment rather than a visitor to it. We realized that the birds and mammals that chose to live with us did so because of the food that we supplied; nevertheless, this came to be a small but constant element of their ecosystem. In addition, although at first they had a distrust of us human interlopers, that had given way to acceptance of our presence as the norm.

For our part, we learned how they reacted to various conditions and marveled at the accuracy of their biological clocks. Ours were regulated by the somewhat rigid schedule of duties that we performed. For instance, at 7:30 in the morning when I came out to hoist the flag, Tubby arrived at the door. By ten o'clock, Buck could be depended upon to be in close proximity to the lookout. Grabby came in after dark, but the "Little One" arrived just after suppertime. The birds followed a different schedule. They tended to arrive in numbers just after our breakfast, then they would disperse until shortly before noon. In late afternoon, they would return for a snack before retiring.

From noon to two o'clock nothing moved, following the custom of siesta as practiced by many of the desert peoples. Perhaps it should be said that the desert people follow the custom of siesta as practiced by the animals. All desert animals, humans included, have learned that the siesta is a necessary part of coping with the heat of midday.

Just before bedtime, weather permitting, one or both of us would walk out to the viewpoint for a final check. These nocturnal rambles were never quite the same. If the weather was windy, it was a cold and blustery ordeal from which we returned with haste to the warm shelter of the lookout. On the other hand, if the evening happened to be calm and warm, we dawdled along, savoring the spectacular panorama of sky overhead. During the dark of the moon, it was spangled with thousands of stars, with other thousands, even billions, unseen. At 9,500 feet of altitude, we were well above the desert haze, so they sparkled with a brilliance not known at the lower levels. On those evenings, it was an emotional experience to stand out there, alone, a mere speck in the scale of the universe and look into the immensity of space.

As the moon returned to the evening sky, our moods reacted accordingly. Surface features began to be more discernible and, finally, came the night when every shrub and rock stood out with almost the clarity of daylight, and a newspaper could be read, literally, by the light of the full moon. One night, in particular, stands out in my memory, when I could see the craters of the moon with the naked eye. Contrary to semi-scientific studies, however, our behavior on those nights continued on normal levels.

It was on just such a night that I witnessed a phenomenon that must have been displayed for my eyes alone, for I have never heard of its like. We had experienced a heavy rainstorm during the afternoon, and mist was rising from the saturated expanse below. There was not a breath of wind, and the grayish mass lay like a level sea a thousand feet below our island of rock. To the south, other mountaintops were similarly surrounded. The full moon was riding high in the heavens when I made my stroll to the vantage point. I stood there for a while enjoying the cool air and the unusual sight of a blanket of fog lying heavily over the desert. Turning to retrace my steps to the lookout, I thought I saw something in the mist to the east side of the mountain. Straining my eyes, I barely made out a faint, oh, ever so faint, rainbow on the surface of the vapor. I could see it for a few moments, then it would fade away, only to reappear once more. This happened several times and then it vanished, not to be seen again.

In my time, I have seen many rainbows, ranging from those of rainstorms and waterfalls to fog banks, but these have always been during the day, in sunlight, and standing in an arch vertical to the ground. This one was lying horizontally and curving around the side of the mountain. I have referred to it as a "moonbow," but, of course, it was created by the rays of the sun reflected down to the Earth from the surface of the moon.

The day arrived when our stint of fire watching was completed. The monsoon rains had saturated the forests, and the fire danger was low. We had reported a number of blazes during our tour, but Alex Gonzales and his crew had extinguished them with such dispatch that our losses were estimated at less than twenty-five acres. Bob Schmitt decided to leave us on the mountain for a few more days, during which time I would take down the telephone line as far as Miller Saddle. In the future, lookouts would communicate with the district ranger only by shortwave radio. In short order, this was accomplished, and Alex arrived one morning with two pack animals prepared to return us to the Reef. We had been on the mountaintop for ninety-three days, and, in that time, other than our packer and Bob, we had entertained but three visitors. These had hiked up the shorter but steeper trail from Montezuma Pass to the south.

Due to the intrusion of Alex and the pack animals, our animal friends stayed away while we loaded our belongings. The sky was overcast, and it was with heavy hearts that, when all was ready, we let down the shutters, locked the door, and walked down the steps for the last time. We were glad in a way that the animals were not there to watch us go. It would have made our parting that much more difficult. We had elected to walk down, so Alex and the pack train went on ahead, and we took our time trying to carry away as many as we could of the happy memories we had of the summer's stay. As we rounded the flank of Carr Peak, we spent a few minutes looking back at the lonely little speck on the tip of Miller Peak to which we were never to return.

The Desert Tortoise was none the worse for its three months of inaction. The tires were up, and, with a little coaxing, the motor sprang into life. Hurriedly loading our gear, we started down the mountain for the long ride into Tucson. We made haste slowly, however, for we were going down the switchbacks that we had climbed with so much concern on the night we had arrived on the Reef. Descending in second gear most of the way, we marveled at our good fortune in making the climb into the teeth of a raging storm. Even under good conditions, we were relieved to reach the valley floor without incident. With its wheels once more on an asphalt surface, the Tortoise made good time into Tucson.

There, the sudden contrast to the spartan life on the peak could not have been more complete. We entered into a round of ice cream, of fresh milk, of steaks and eating out, of showers and haircuts and clothes washed in a washing machine. Not so welcome were the traffic, the noise, the pressures of everyday living, and the noxious fumes that so irritated lungs used to the pure air of the mountains. Bob had asked me to do some work on the trail up Carr Peak, so, after a few days of city life, we forsook its "advantages" and headed back to the Reef.

This time we were more knowledgeable of the conditions there, so our load included an eight-by-ten-foot tent, cots, and a larger gasoline stove. We set the tent up close to the toolshed and installed the stove in the building, and, with these details accomplished, we were provided with the few amenities needed to exist for the month or so that would be required to do the work.

The trail was badly in need of maintenance. It climbed steeply in a series of switchbacks up the shoulder of Carr Peak for a thousand feet before it leveled off and headed for Miller Canyon Saddle. For most of that distance, it was exposed on a barren slope having neither trees nor shrubs to hold the sparse soil in place. In consequence, it had been badly rutted by the heavy rains of the summer storms.

It was now August, and, although the furious thunderstorms of June and July had subsided, an afternoon shower was an almost daily occurrence. The clouds would start to build up around one o'clock, and by two o'clock the familiar towering masses would start to level off into the formation called "the anvil." The first distant lightning strike would be my signal to head for pack base. Standing my tools against a ledge, I would strike out. The storm usually developed with terrifying speed, and, forsaking the trail, I would dash pell-mell down the mountainside with lightning splitting the air around me and thunder cannonading at my heels. Sometimes I would get to the toolshed ahead of the rain, but too often I would arrive soaked to the skin by the icy deluge. These showers were of short duration, but, by the time I had changed to dry clothes, the workday would be over.

Coati Neighbors

As soon as the trees had ceased to drip, we could expect the coatis to come in for their afternoon treat. Irene was quite familiar with the species, having met with several groups on the trails; however, this was the first time that I had been close to them. This group consisted of an old, rather dilapidated female with three small young—two females and a male. Contrary to usual coati behavior, she and her kits did not travel with a group but remained in the vicinity of the Reef Mine area, coming in every afternoon for the milk and cookies that Irene laid out for them. That the milk was of the powdered kind and the cookies of the poorest quality seemed to make no difference to them; they swallowed them greedily and looked for more.

Irene fed them on the floor in the toolshed, it being somewhat cleaner than the bare ground outside. It was interesting to see that their long, narrow muzzles, so well adapted for rooting through the humus and leaves of their normal habitat, were a distinct disadvantage on the flat, hard surface of the floor. To eat a cookie, they were forced to scrape it up on edge between their front paws, and then, by turning their heads to the side, they were able to take bites from the edge with their back teeth.

Drinking milk presented a somewhat similar problem. We learned that, if we served it up in wide, shallow pans, they were able to lay their lower jaws in the milk and, by much smacking and lapping with their tongues, get most of it down. As can be imagined, by meal's end they were far from being well groomed, with their hair and whiskers all bedraggled. Actually, this was but one more detraction in their general appearance. This is not to say that they are not beautifully adapted to the kind of lives they lead. Theirs is the beauty of a Sherman tank. Every ungainly line and awkward move spells efficiency in doing the everyday activities necessary for survival.

Among her attributes in this direction, the old female had a formidable set of long, canine teeth, which she bared if we came too close to her young. We were especially careful not to get between her and them. As is our custom with our animal friends, we did not try to touch the young—until one night when a situation arose that got completely out of our control.

The coati family had left at the usual time, and we were finishing our supper when we heard the distress call of a young coati outside. This is an unusual sound, more like a high, thin whistle than the guttural notes that one might expect from these creatures. We discovered that the little male had either been left behind or had become detached from the

Figure 1.14 The female coatimundi with two of her three kits. She was very protective of her young, and we were careful not to antagonize her.

family group, and he had returned to the shed hoping to find his mother and sisters there. What to do?

Darkness was fast approaching, and all sorts of dangers lurked in the forest surrounding the camp. It seemed best to put him in the toolshed for the night, where he might be very unhappy but at least safe until his family returned on the next day. We put cookies and milk out in the usual place on the floor and called him to come in and partake. How gullible we were! He divined our intentions at once, and would have none of our treachery, but stood outside complaining bitterly. This left us with but one course, which was to try to catch him. He was, after all, only a little larger than a kitten. So, donning a pair of leather gloves, I charged after him. He took off at once for a thicket of manzanita brush not far from the toolshed, with me in hot pursuit. Then ensued a game of tag, with me being "it."

Manzanita is a rather open shrub, but it has stiff, unyielding branches. The coati, being close to the ground, had all the advantage, while I was being held back by the heavier growth above. My struggles with these drawbacks were not aided by Irene's encouragement, as she circled the thicket, alternately shouting, "Here he is, there he goes, grab him," and so on. I soon decided that I was completely outclassed by my tiny quarry and gave up the chase. As soon as I abandoned the pursuit, he left the security of his thicket and scampered off into the darkening forest, whimpering his ridiculous distress call as he went.

The next day, the coati family arrived as usual, the little male showing no evidence that anything unusual had occurred. It all goes to show once more that usually the best solution in the event of a wildlife problem is to let nature take its course. Human intervention will often only aggravate the situation.

There was one other coati that enjoyed the hospitality of the Reef Ranch, if it could be called that. This was an old male that had given up traveling with a group. It sometimes happens, for whatever reason, that an old individual will do this. Why, no one seems to know; perhaps younger individuals force them out, or possibly old age renders them incapable of maintaining the strenuous activities that the pack goes through. The Mexicans call them *solitarios*, which can mean not only solitary, but also lonely, lonesome, and isolated, as well as a recluse or a hermit, all of which apply to these occasional outcasts. Ours, which we called El Solitario, was an inoffensive old patriarch who wanted only to be left alone and to be given a handout once in a while. He was a healthy individual with a glossy brown coat so dark as to be almost black, in contrast to the usual honey-shaded tan color of the species.

He became Hazel Seeman's special pet and would come to be fed at her call. He was a dainty eater and would carefully take the food from her hands, never touching her with his fearsome canines. One mark of his docile nature was his respect for Hazel's cat! She was a lean, gray virago, who barely tolerated Hazel and hated everything and everybody else. I soon learned to give her a wide berth. Sometimes in the evenings, when playing cards with the Seemans, I would look up and catch her lying in her favorite chair with her eyes fixed on me with a smoldering hate. At those times, I was glad that she was not as large as a leopard. She detested the coati and would go out of her way to attack him. Although he was several times her size, he would offer no resistance but would climb a tree and sit on a branch wearing an injured expression until she went away. I always wished that he would trounce her good, but that was not to be.

By September, our tour of duty with the Forest Service was over. High time, too, for the nighttime temperatures were crisp, and the trees were alive with the songs and rustlings of migratory birds gathering for their trip southward. Bob offered me a permanent position of grader operator for the Forest Service, but I declined. I was sorely tempted, for I had fallen in love with the Huachucas and the carefree life that we had enjoyed, but there was no future in following that daisy trail.

It was difficult to loosen the ties that bound us to those mountains all at once, so, before we went home, we decided to take a week's trip around the range, camping in the canyons over which we had watched so carefully through the fire season. We set off with great anticipation. Fall color was running riot over the peaks. Great patches of yellow-gold marked the groves of aspens that only a few weeks before had been a light green. Tongues of flame shot up the canyons where maples and sumac grew along the stream banks. In the lower reaches, sycamores and cottonwoods contributed a foundation of more somber yellows and deep reds. Even the Gambel oaks displayed their dark browns in the foothills.

The camping was delightful; calm warm days and frosty nights blended into one another with new experiences greeting us in every canyon we entered. At night we slept in the Desert Tortoise, and every morning we checked the dead ashes of our previous night's campfire to identify the unseen visitors of the midnight hours. We found the dainty paw prints of ringtail cats in Carr Canyon; coatis and skunks high up in Miller; foxes in the wide reaches of Ash; and, in Bear Canyon, a coyote came to our bait instead of the ursine for which the canyon was named.

Then it was back to our humdrum existence in Tucson; back to the problems that arise when people are too close together; back to a way of life dominated by time, in which schedules are all-important, and a clock informs you when to do what and how long to do it.

Part II

New Ventures in the Old Pueblo

Old Acquaintances

Altogether our return to urban existence might be characterized as underwhelming. It was easy enough to pick up the requirements of our eight-to-five jobs, but we felt imprisoned by the crush of thousands of our kind that surrounded us. However, "birds of a feather . . . ," and we took comfort from fraternizing with close friends from whom we had been separated. Foremost among these was William H. Carr. Bill had come to Tucson from New York City, where he had been an associate curator on the staff of the American Museum of Natural History. In Tucson, he had established a bookstore on Santa Rita Avenue, which provided him with a precarious existence.

Two other close friends were Ross and Florence Thornberg, an elderly couple from Iowa who spent their winters trailering in the Southwest desert. Ross was a skilled cabinetmaker and a former contractor whose boast was, "When I sell a house, it's the cleanest that it will ever be." Florence was a birder of national renown who fervently believed that Tucson needed a chapter of the Audubon Society, a belief shared by many local birders as well.

One of the catalysts that drew us together in that fall of 1951 was the action of the Arizona Game and Fish Department in placing the roadrunner on the predator list. Granted that this zany relative of the cuckoo will take eggs and fledglings of songbirds and young quail whenever it can, it is a part of the desert environment and should be accepted as such.

As I recall, our protestations to the Arizona Game and Fish Department were totally unsuccessful, but help came from another quarter. Made aware of our problem, the U.S. Fish and Wildlife Service took command of the situation by classifying the roadrunner as a migratory songbird and, thus, a protected species. This in spite of the fact that its song is a series of "coos" and it is migratory only to the extent that it crosses back and forth over the boundary line between the United States and Mexico. That settled a thorny problem that has not recurred and, in a way, helped speed the founding of the Tucson Audubon Society.

Bill, I think, had envisioned a natural-history museum in Tucson from the day of his arrival. His efforts to start one met with mixed approval but no financial support until he met Mr. Pack. Arthur Newton Pack was a businessman and philanthropist who also held a deep interest in natural history. He was active in promoting anything that might benefit the city of Tucson, and Bill's proposals caught his fancy. With his encouragement and the promise of some financial backing, Bill pressed forward with enthusiasm, and, as things developed, he suggested that I join him. This I was pleased to do; it seemed that exciting times lay ahead.

Finding a suitable site was our first concern. A ravine at the north base of "A" Mountain seemed to hold possibilities. However, the site presented difficulties in the construction of the buildings, and parking space was minimal. Several other sites were considered and rejected for various reasons. The availability of parking space was a main consideration. In retrospect, the volume of visitors at today's Arizona-Sonora Desert Museum was beyond our imaginations.

Mountain House

Eventually, our search led to the Mountain House at Tucson Mountain Park. It, along with several outbuildings, seemed ideal in many ways to house the natural-history museum that we had in mind. However, it, too, had disadvantages: it was fourteen miles from Tucson over a dusty unsurfaced road, the buildings were badly in need of maintenance, and the water supply was marginal. On the other hand, the main building, in particular, was in perfect harmony with its surroundings. With massive adobe walls and ceilings of ponderosa-pine beams covered with heavy lumber and, in one case, crisscrossed with saguaro ribs, it was representative of desert architecture during the Depression years. Designed by the National Park Service and built with ccc (Civilian Conservation Corps) labor during the Depression, it was meant to be the administrative center for a complex of areas to be known as Deserts National Monuments. These were Organ Pipe Cactus, Papago Park, and Saguaro. This never came about, and finally the buildings were returned to the Pima County Parks and Recreation Department as part of Tucson Mountain Park.

The setting could not have been more perfect for our purpose. The site rests upon a "bajada" (an incline) sloping down from the Tucson Mountains to the Avra Valley. This valley, bordered by low mountain ranges, drains southward across the U.S. border into Sonora, Mexico. Behind the grounds, short, rugged Kings Canyon penetrates into the steep, western wall of the Tucson Mountains. Ocotillos and paloverdes, interspersed with creosote bushes, soften the rugged contours of the bajada, and ironwood trees indicate that this is a frost-free area. Saguaros, chollas of various species, and barrel cactuses flourish on the rocky soil. Amidst all this luxuriance of plant life lives the amazing variety of animals native to this part of the Sonoran Desert. In essence, this was a perfect cross-section of desert environment, needing only the application of interpretive methods to explain its intricacies. When we realized that this might become our role, our enthusiasm knew no bounds. There was much to be done, however, before this was to become reality.

First was the need to convince the Pima County Park Board that we had the makings of a project that could really succeed in contrast to a number that had failed. With Arthur Pack's agreement to finance it to the amount of $1,000, the board consented to consider a plan for a natural-history museum, which was to be drawn up by Bill Carr. Board members stipulated that this should be done with no obligation, or cost, to the county. The plan, when submitted, was a simple one compared with what was to come in the future.

The larger of the two buildings of the Mountain House was to become the small-animals room, and the smaller would house the geology exhibits. A ten-acre area adjacent to the building was to be fenced and to contain enclosures for larger species of animals and a garden of native species of desert plants. This proposal won grudging approval from the board, and we set to work making models of what we had in mind.

Then ensued a hectic round of appearances before almost any group that would grant us audience. The models, augmented by a slide talk, fulfilled their purpose before civic clubs, chambers of commerce, schools, churches, and, of course, the Park Board. Bill was an accomplished and convincing speaker, and it was but a short while until we sensed that the indifference we had earlier encountered began to dissipate and drift away. The Park Board members also realized that public interest in the project was mounting, and, by the time winter was well over, they indicated that we should go ahead with construction. They still specified, however, that the project was to be funded by Mr. Pack and that progress was to be monitored by the Park Board to ensure that all was proceeding according to the plan that had been submitted. Target date for beginning was set at April 1, 1952. Encouraged by their acceptance of the plan, Mr. Pack donated $10,000 more toward financing construction.

Construction Begins

This resulted in feverish activity on our parts. Bill closed his bookshop, and we sold our house in Tucson. Bill took up residence in a caretaker's house somewhat removed from the Mountain House, and Irene and I moved into two rooms at the east end where the snack bar is now located. Irene took over the cooking chores, and Bill and I rolled up our sleeves and threw ourselves into manual labor. It was at that time that Bill began to consider what our wages should be. When he brought it up to me, I told him that, in view of our limited budget, we should hold them to enough to get along on and very little more. After some discussion, we decided on $300 a month. For this, we worked long hours for seven days a week through all that summer. If that seems a meager wage today, reflect that we had no time to spare for outside activities anyway.

Now that we were ready to begin construction, we were joined by friends who wished to contribute to the effort. The Thornbergs hauled their trailer out to the park and spotted it a little distance above the buildings. Ross, being an expert cabinetmaker, was put in charge of building the partitions and cages in the large room, which would now become the small-animals room. Julian Hayden, an archeologist turned contractor, insisted that we use his power tools. These were set up in the former kitchen, which now became a woodworking shop. Joe Carithers, superintendent of Tucson Mountain Park, contributed his great knowledge of the area and loaned the use of his truck and maintenance crew whenever available. With the necessity of keeping proper records, his wife, Hildegarde, became our secretary and bookkeeper. Even our old standby, the Desert Tortoise, was pressed into service hauling building supplies out from town.

Our first actual construction was to wall off a small room to serve as an office and library at the entrance to the small-animals room; next came the building of the partitions and the long frames supporting the cages. Outside on the patio, Joe's maintenance crew was engaged in tearing out part of the railing and installing a wide flight of steps leading down to ground level. As for the grounds, approximately ten acres were being encircled by a Cyclone fence designed to keep animals out, or to keep animals in, as the case might warrant. All of this was costing money, and we were using up Arthur Pack's latest donation of $10,000 at a rapid rate. However, Mr. Pack was watching this, too, and one day, having taken an inspection tour, he expressed himself as being delighted with our progress and promised continued financial support. Encouraged by his approval, we set forth on the most difficult project of all—the construction of the large-mammal enclosures.

It was important that these be as unobtrusive as possible to avoid the appearance of the usual zoos to be found along the roadside in those days. They were to be located on, and in, a low ridge running south down the bajada from the west end of the Mountain House. This ridge was composed of great rocks eroded from the mountain in the background and mixed with lesser stones and earth. Underneath it all was a layer of "caliche," a cementlike material that is the bane of all excavators in the Tucson area. This presented problems far beyond the capabilities of our staff. Obviously, outside aid in the way of heavy machinery was the only course to follow. Jackhammers, front-end loaders, and, eventually, dynamite were required to go to the depth necessary for the foundations of the structures.

The cooperation we received from the several construction companies we contacted was most gratifying. By this time, the business people of Tucson had come to the conclusion that the museum was to become a valuable asset to the community, and they were glad to further our cause in any way possible. Those who worked for us offered advice, drew up plans, and did everything possible to ensure that we received an outstanding job. Best of all, most did their work at cost or, in some cases, for free. There was also the important matter of finding a water supply sufficient for the project and the park headquarters as well. Pima County provided funds and manpower for a pipeline, and water was soon available.

Museum Collections

With all projects moving along smoothly, the next priority was to stock the small-animals room with living exhibits. The facilities were not yet completed, but we estimated that, by the time the animals had been collected, they would be ready. The man whom Bill had selected to capture these creatures was Dr. Charles Lowe from the University of Arizona. This big, jovial man, an authority on the subject of herpetology, fell to work with enthusiasm, scouring the desert in all directions, mainly at night during the period of the animals' greatest activity. His success kept us busy trying to stay ahead on accommodations for his collections. Bill Woodin, another herpetologist, who was later to become director of the museum, made the labels and descriptive materials for the cages.

We, too, provided specimens that we encountered in the course of construction. Our first acquisition was a Harris ground squirrel, which one of the men saw run into a pipe lying on the ground. The pipe was plugged at both ends, it was brought into the building, and the squirrel was released into a cage, thus becoming our first exhibit. This was a fortunate circumstance; our capture of some other potential display creatures was not always so successful.

Joe Carithers's maintenance crew often ran across interesting creatures in the course of their work. Living in Tucson, the crew members came to work early in the morning. Their vehicle was an old truck, and some of the crew rode in the back. On this particular morning, they spied a badger foraging a short distance from the road. Jumping out of the truck, they soon surrounded it. A badger is a formidable creature in any circumstance, and this one was growling, and gnashing its teeth, and charging at one or another of them. Having no other means of capturing it, one of the men took off his belt and, forming a noose, dropped it over the badger's head and carried it, snarling and struggling, to the truck. When they arrived at the museum, it was still full of fight.

This posed a problem. It was a fine specimen, and we wanted it but, as yet, we had no enclosure that would hold it. Finally, Bill said: "Take it up

to the tack room. We can keep it there until we can build a cage for it."
The tack room had been built to store riding gear at the time that there
was a riding stable at the area. It had thick adobe walls and a cement
floor and seemed an ideal place to confine our unwilling prisoner until
we could provide quarters befitting its strength and truculence. What a
surprise that evening, when we went up to check on it, to find that it
had clawed a hole through the wall and then, to add insult to injury,
dug a burrow underneath the concrete floor. We carried food up to the
burrow for a few days, hoping to recapture it later, but it soon wandered
away, and we never saw it again.

We had better luck with a baby jackrabbit that the men discovered
while putting in a water line. It was the same blacktail jackrabbit that is
so common in the Southwest. Properly speaking, it is not a rabbit at all
but a hare. One of the distinctions is that little rabbits are born blind and
naked, while jackrabbits at birth are fully furred and sighted. They are
precocious little creatures so that, within a few days after birth, they no
longer depend on mother's milk but are able to subsist upon the adult's
vegetable diet.

Ours did very well on a diet of salad scraps from the table, augmented
by rabbit pellets and an occasional vitamin pill. Within a short time, our
little ball of fluff began to assume the lanky, long-legged proportions of
an adult. More to the point, it had outgrown the cramped confines of the
small-animals cage in which we kept it. It was obvious that something
had to be done at once.

Bill suggested that it be liberated in his front patio, where it could be
fed and protected until it was fully adult and could exist on its own. It
seemed an ideal solution. The yard was in lawn, surrounded by an adobe
wall. Several shrubs around the perimeter offered protection from sun
and cover at night.

So . . . one evening after dinner, we carried the cage up to Bill's quarters. Setting it on the lawn, we opened the front and retired to the ve-
randa to see what would develop. The sun was almost down, and the
recently watered lawn lent a coolness to the surroundings. At first, the
occupant of the cage, bewildered at all of the unaccustomed activity
of moving its quarters, crouched motionless in one corner. Eventually,
when all remained quiet, it slowly moved to the open front and surveyed what must have seemed to be the whole wide world. It sniffed

at the moist grass, something entirely new to its experience, and then, suddenly, in the realization that freedom beckoned, it exploded from its prison.

Then occurred a performance that we never could have imagined. It leaped, it danced, it raced around the patio like a thing demented, while we sat entranced, laughing in sympathy over this pathetic joy in being free. Eventually, it quieted and began to explore its new surroundings. As Irene and I returned to our quarters, we realized full well that we had witnessed something to be forever unique in our experience. This jackrabbit was eventually released in the fenced area below the museum, where it became a great favorite of the visitors because of its winning disposition.

As summer came on, and with it the rainy season now popularly called the "monsoons," animal activity in the desert increased. As the Desert Museum was by then becoming generally known, what better place for people to bring the wildlife that invaded their yards and homes in the Tucson area? Invertebrates were the most plentiful offerings—with scorpions, centipedes, and tarantulas the most common of these—followed by reptiles, including snakes, lizards, and sometimes a desert tortoise. Some of these we kept for display, while most were released into the surrounding desert. Mammals and birds presented problems. Taking care of the birds was especially troublesome since, at that time, we had no aviary. One such incident I remember very well.

Redtail Hawks

On this day, a prominent rancher who was on his way to a foreign assignment stopped by with a pair of baby redtail hawks, which he wished to leave with us as his "contribution" to the museum. We really had no alternative but to accept them. Few things are as unlovely as little hawks. These had big heads, scrawny necks, and awkward legs, with pinfeathers just beginning to appear through their baby down. They had received no food for a day and were in the last stages of malnutrition and dehydration.

Obviously, food and liquids were of the highest priority in caring for these unfortunate mites. In nature, both food and liquid are supplied by the diet of rodents and snakes that the parents bring them. Our only source in this respect was a small stock of mice that we were building up for snake food, and we had none to spare. In desperation, we mixed up a concoction of ground beef and cod liver oil and force-fed them. This could be only a temporary measure since the raptors must have roughage, just as we humans must, to help move food through the digestive system. The only medium we could think of that might substitute for hair, skin, and bones was plumbers tow. This is a fibrous material that plumbers used to pound into bell joints of sewer pipe to render them leak proof. When molten lead was poured on top of the tow, the joint was believed to be watertight (they hoped).

A courier was sent post haste to Tucson to get a supply, and this, mixed with ground beef and augmented with whatever we could salvage from road kills along the highway, became their diet. It seemed to suffice; at any rate, they developed at a normal rate. Strangely, neither bird bonded with us, but they remained very tame. We especially liked the female. The female of a pair of redtails will be the larger, and, in this case, the more gentle.

When these two outgrew their cage, we had an ideal outdoor home ready for them. At an early age, raptors begin to use their wings to strengthen them for a life in the air. They will stand in their nests and flap their wings vigorously while hanging onto the nests. In this case, Irene and I had a dead tree in an enclosed patio back of our living area. It was not a large tree, only ten or twelve feet high, but it had horizontal limbs ideal for this stationary flying exercise.

Here they lived twenty-four hours a day. At night, we would check on them with a flashlight and see them hunkered down and fluffed up against the chill. During daylight hours, they might be hanging on for dear life while a summer storm buffeted them with wind and rain.

The day arrived when they began to make experimental flights to adjacent rooftops. However, they always kept a sharp eye on what went on in the patio and would fly down at once when we brought out their food. We fed them twice a day, and, as they gradually ventured farther away into the desert, these times became the most thrilling to Irene and me. At our whistle, they would sail down from their lazy circles in the sky to swoop into the patio. The male would go directly to his usual perch in the tree and take his food from our hand, but the female preferred to come to our outstretched arm to be fed. As her skills improved, she would come in faster and faster and set her talons to fasten on my arm. Then it became necessary to wrap a gunnysack around my forearm for my own protection. What a thrill it was to see her descend at increasing speed until, at a hundred feet away, she set her wings and came in like a bullet with her legs and talons extended for the strike.

Arch-predators that they were, instinct took over, and gradually they became wild in all respects but one. They hunted their own food, wandered over vast sections of desert, stayed away all day at times, but, as evening approached, they would come home to roost on the dead tree in the patio.

Another perch they enjoyed was the cross-arm on a high pole that brought power into the area. The highest point in the immediate vicinity, it gave them a good view of all that went on. One afternoon, just at sundown, Irene and I happened to be outside when the hawks came home. As the female settled toward the cross-arm, the tips of her outstretched wings made contact between two wires. A loud snap and a flash of light and it was all over. Her body fell to the ground, a mass of singed feathers and charred flesh. We buried her there where she fell, and buried with her all our hopes for her normal life in the wild.

The male stayed around for a while, but he was uneasy without the company of his sibling and gradually drifted away. We wished him well.

At the end of five months, it was time to evaluate our progress toward opening on Labor Day, as we had agreed. Much remained to be done, as is usually the case with any healthy, growing organization, but the basics were in place. The small-animals room was completed with animals and labels installed. The geology room was filled with mineral displays. On the grounds, the large-animal enclosures were completed but, as yet, not fully occupied. Paths led through the area and were dotted with a token number of labels describing the most prominent features. In short, the foundation of a desert museum had been laid and now provided a solid base for future development. We had given our best to give something unique to Tucson. Did this community in the desert care enough about its environment to learn about it? Had we created something fine and useful just to see it die on the vine through public neglect? We had to hope not!

Opening Day

Labor Day, September 1, 1952, dawned bright and clear and full of promise. Early morning found a sizable group gathered on the patio of the Mountain House. Founders, donors, staff and friends, County Park officials, contractors, and others—not necessarily in that order—were on hand for this opening. The same question was on everyone's mind: Would they come? The next three hours would tell the tale!

The parking lot filled up early. The patio was abuzz with visitors asking questions, offering congratulations, and making favorable comments. They filled the small-animals room, viewed the geology exhibits, lined the paths in front of the large-animal enclosures and, in some cases, did it all over again. Latecomers, unable to get into the parking lot, lined the park road for a half-mile in each direction. It was estimated that between two thousand and three thousand visitors attended the Desert Museum that day.

At sundown, when the last car had left the parking lot, we were all exhausted; exhausted but convinced that it was all worthwhile. On that day, Tucson took the Desert Museum to its heart, and there it remains.

We are pleased to have been members of the task force that established a secure beachhead for the fledgling Desert Museum. From that start, it has expanded in so many disciplines that it has a reputation as one of the best. Now known as the Arizona-Sonora Desert Museum, it has never lost the unique manner in which it explains the ecological associations of the desert environment. That has been, and will continue to be, its greatest contribution.

With the opening of the museum, Irene and I decided that it was time to move on. A nomad at heart, I did not relish the prospect of a permanent job as a curator. Even at that late point in life, I harbored visions of someday being a writer. The first trip we took was one I had long planned. It was to follow the boundary line between the United States and Mexico from Columbus, New Mexico, to Yuma, Arizona, on the Colorado River. This line had originally been defined at the time of the Gadsden Purchase of 1854. Later, the government decided to survey it more critically, and a party of surveyors accompanied by a United States Army detachment was detailed to that task in the late 1800s. The line today is marked by stone monuments at irregular intervals joined by fences, many in disrepair. A two-track road of sorts follows the line on our side. It is for the use of the U.S. Immigration and Naturalization Service. Most of the way, the line traverses wild, rough, desert country, uninhabited for the most part.

Our guide for this trip was a book, *Mammals of the Mexican Boundary of the United States* (Washington, D.C.: Smithsonian Institution, 1907), by Edgar Alexander Mearns, M.D., a major and a surgeon in the United States Army. It had an excellent map, and we followed it up and down mountain ranges, across rocky plains and dry lakes, through sand dunes, and even through a few towns. We followed his diary: we camped where he had camped, hiked where he had gone, and saw many of the animals he had listed. We had a wonderful time, and we owed it, for a good part, to Dr. Mearns and the Desert Tortoise, which, as usual, had never let us down. Our return to Tucson was anticlimactic—we bought a house.

Nature Trail at Saguaro

I was hard at work at my desk in Tucson on the afternoon that the phone rang. The voice at the other end said: "George, this is John Lewis. I would like to take you and Irene to dinner tomorrow night with Lucy and me. Can you make it?"

I thought: "That's John, directly to the point." But I said: "That sounds great; we would be pleased to join you."

"That's settled then, we'll pick you up at seven o'clock." And he hung up.

I had known John for the year since he had transferred from being chief ranger at Bryce Canyon National Park to superintendent of Saguaro

National Monument (the "Cactus Patch") at Tucson. He was a big man of boundless energy, with a ribald sense of humor, a photographic memory, and an insatiable appetite for practical jokes—all attributes that endeared him to some but kept him in hot water with the Park Service, for he was not noted for "going by the book." On several occasions, he had used me as a straight man for his nefarious schemes, so I determined to be on my guard for whatever intrigue he might propose on our dinner date.

On the following evening, he picked us up on the dot, and we headed north out of Tucson to El Corral, a popular steakhouse in the foothills of the Catalina Mountains. When we were comfortably seated with drinks in hand and a beautiful view of the lights of Tucson spread out below the picture windows, John came to the point at once.

"As you know," he began, "the director usually picks out some goal every year which will draw attention and good will to the [Park] Service. This year, he has decided to stress cooperation with the Boy Scouts, so the word is out to encourage them to carry out meaningful projects in the Park Service areas."

"And so now you have got some Boy Scouts under your wing," I interrupted.

"Yes, in a way I have," he replied. "There are two fellows in South Tucson who head up an Explorer troop, and they are all gung ho to start a project at Saguaro."

"An Explorer group. That means that their boys are all teenagers; they ought to be able to take on a pretty important assignment," I said. "Do you have anything in mind?"

"Well, yes, in a way. . . . These fellows are all Eagle Scouts so there isn't much in awards to shoot for except the Hornaday Award."

"The Hornaday Award? That's one I haven't heard about. What is it?" I asked.

"I understand that it's an award given by the New York Zoological Society to honor William T. Hornaday, the great naturalist. The qualifications are high, so high that it has never been given in Arizona, although several groups have tried to snag it. It stresses conservation, combined with public education. We thought that a nature trail somewhere along our Loop Road might meet the requirements."

"That sounds great," I enthused. "When do you start on it?"

"Well," he said slowly, and he looked at me, "that depends on you. I want you to head it up."

"Oh, I couldn't, John! I appreciate your confidence, but, no, I just couldn't. I'm sorry."

"Why not?" he persisted. "I'll give you full charge of the project."

I said: "Well, it's this way. I've led a pretty carefree life, as you know, and it's really past time for me to settle down and make some preparations for the future. I've tried to get into the Park Service, as you know, but the educational requirements have foiled me, so now we have bought a house and are settled for the foreseeable future. Things are going well for me in the writing game; I've produced a book and several articles that have sold, and I just can't interrupt all that."

"But this won't take long," he protested, "and I need you. It isn't just anyone who can do this job. I'll give you your choice of area, leave the interpretation up to you; I can't promise you much money, but I'll guarantee you a good time and the satisfaction of doing a worthwhile project."

I considered this for a bit. "How long do you think it might take?"

"Oh, about six weeks," he said, sensing my softening attitude.

"Well, I shouldn't do this, but let me come out and meet the group and discuss the matter further, and we'll see."

"I knew you would do it," he said with a sly grin. "Now that that's settled, let's eat."

The introductory meeting went well. The two Scout leaders clearly had the group well disciplined, and the boys seemed to anticipate that this would be a serious undertaking that would take time and effort to accomplish. We drew up some guidelines and then went out on the Loop Drive to select some locations suitable for the trail. We settled upon one that embodied wash, plain, and hillside features within a fifteen-minute hike and contained the plant and animal features appropriate to interpret.

Building a nature trail would seem to be a simple matter, but there is more to it than meets the eye. Some rocks must be removed; others can be placed unobtrusively to guide visitors on their way. Some plants must be removed; others emphasized as specimens. Interpretive material must be prepared and placed, and a parking area must be constructed. And all of this done under the blazing heat of a Sonoran summer.

We started with a group of eleven boys, but gradually that number dwindled as the heat and the drudgery took their toll. By the time school started in the fall, we had only seven left. However, the physical work was completed. Next to be accomplished was the instruction in environmental matters as required by the guidelines given us by the New York Zoological Society. All that winter we met every Wednesday night at the visitor center to listen to lectures delivered by experts in the fields of ecology, game management, botany, and mammalogy. Professors from the University of Arizona were very helpful in this regard.

During this time, too, the Scouts placed several exhibits stressing ecology in store windows in Tucson, and an exhibit they entered in the Pima County Fair captured first place in the educational division. Finally, each boy was required to make two talks on environmental matters to outside groups. These were well received by service clubs, church groups, and school assemblies, all of whom were impressed by the competence of these lads. Each boy was required to keep a scrapbook of events in which he participated. These, together with my report, were forwarded to the Zoological Society by the Catalina Council of the Boy Scouts. On the night of January 16, 1957, I was given the honor of pinning the gold medals on each of the seven, the first to win the award in Arizona.

Saguaro National Monument

With that project finally completed, it was time to assess my priorities once again. In spite of John's optimistic estimate, the projected six weeks had lengthened into a year and a half. The rhythm of my writing had been completely disrupted, with dubious prospects of ever being resumed. My status as seasonal park ranger stood little chance of improving, since all permanent positions in the park were filled. But . . . Saguaro National Monument was a desert naturalist's dream: ninety-nine square miles of southwestern desert encompassing parts of four life zones and ranging from three thousand feet to almost nine thousand feet in altitude. So, in defiance of any logical choice, I elected to stay!

This "Cactus Patch" to which I had committed myself was established as a national monument by proclamation of President Herbert Hoover on March 1, 1933. At that time, it contained what was considered to be the finest stand of saguaro cactus in the United States. In some areas of greatest density, it was estimated at twelve thousand plants to the square mile. These were plants of varying age, the preponderance being mature individuals. In the decades that followed, it became noticeable that an unduly large number of the plants were dying. An investigation by the U.S. Department of Agriculture indicated that an organism identified as *Erwinia carnegieana* was killing the saguaros. It became apparent to the department that, should the spread of this infection continue unabated, there could come a time when Saguaro National Monument would be without this cactus that it had been established to protect. Stringent measures were called for.

First, it was decided that, as far as was possible, all infected plants should be destroyed. Long trenches were dug, into which these plants were dumped and buried. Then a series of studies followed to determine the causes and effects of the decline of the saguaro forest. These went on until shortly before the time when I became involved at the park. At about that time, Dr. Stanley Alcorn was appointed by the Department of Agriculture to further pursue the studies. We became close friends, and he was kind enough to include me, partly as a friend and partly as the naturalist pro tem at the park, in some of his projects.

A number of problems were of concern at that time. One of the most serious was the paucity of young plants to take the place of those that were disappearing. Some of the reasons for this were obvious. For many years before the establishment of the monument, people visiting and picnicking in the area had dug up many of the young plants and carried them home to be planted in their yards. Other factors were less well known, and, in theory, there were still others yet to be discovered.

In order to survive, a young saguaro must have the shelter of a tree or a shrub to protect it during its tender years. Normally, there are grasses and weeds under these trees, too, and the seedling saguaros, amidst this clutter, are sheltered against the cold of winter and the heat and aridity of the summer. Grazing had been allowed in the monument since its inception, however, and most of this ground cover under the trees had been eaten or trampled into extinction where the cattle had also sought shelter. The same circumstances also applied to the saguaro seeds. In order to germinate, they should fall into the duff under a tree, where, during the summer rains, they are washed free of inhibitors that prevent them from germinating until they are kept moist for several days. Lacking such conditions, most of the seeds of the monument cactuses lay on the packed surfaces of the bare ground until they were picked up by rodents and birds or carried away by ants.

It seemed clear that only a long-term ecological study of the plant and its environment would provide the answers to the problems with which the Park Service was concerned. Moreover, such a study held out fascinating possibilities of other discoveries as yet unknown. It was an exciting prospect, and I entered into it with enthusiasm.

Baboquivari

In our second summer at the monument, Irene and I took advantage of a Fourth of July weekend to take a trip into the Papago Indian Reservation west of Tucson. Our destination was Baboquivari Canyon at the south end of the Baboquivari Range; Kitt Peak at the northern end was destined to become the site of the world-famous observatories to be built on its summit. At that time, the range was known mostly as the eastern boundary of the sprawling Papago reservation and was otherwise largely ignored as just another series of low desert mountains.

Baboquivari Peak was another matter. It reared up over the desert floor to an altitude of almost eight thousand feet. The name is Papago in origin, and various translations are attributed to it. One is "with its beak in the air." Another is "water on the mountains." The true meaning matters little; the mountain is the sacred mountain of the Papagos, and a more impressive symbol would be hard to imagine. Visible from all parts of the reservation, its sharp, pointed "bill" dominates all of the plains and lower mountains to the west. Papago legend is said to have taught that, at one time, the mountain was shaped like an hourglass and that, because of an ancient upheaval, the upper half fell off. It's a fanciful tale that, when one is in the neighborhood of the peak, seems even logical.

When we set off at midmorning, the temperature had already reached a hundred degrees Fahrenheit. The heat of the Sonoran Desert in July is not to be taken lightly. The Tortoise was not equipped with air conditioning, so, cracking the windows just a bit to allow for some circulation of air, we steeled ourselves for the trip of a little over a hundred miles. The first sixty miles were on pavement that led us to tribal headquarters at Sells, Arizona. It was a dusty little village with a trading post, a gas station, and a collection of functional, but unlovely, government buildings. The Catholic mission church and a few private dwellings made up the rest of the town.

Leaving the pavement at that point, we proceeded southward on a graded dirt road for the next twenty miles to the even smaller town of Topawa. The road was "washboardy," making our progress slow, while dust rose in clouds around us and settled on our belongings. The temperature by now had risen to well over a hundred degrees, but we had no alternative but to grit our teeth (literally) and push on. We were relieved when at last we reached Topawa and exchanged the washboard and dust for a two-track trail that headed east for Baboquivari Peak, which now loomed high above the desert haze.

This was a road fashioned in the Indian way, winding back and forth as it avoided obstacles in its path. These desert roads are a joy to drive, as one goes slowly enough to check items of interest along the way. We climbed gradually as we wound our way among the low foothills at the base of the range. The heat subsided as we ascended the bajada, and when at last we entered the dappled shade of the sycamores in the canyon, we were almost comfortable.

The contrast of this cool, wooded canyon to the arid, almost barren, desert we had just traversed could hardly have been more complete. A little way inside the entrance, the Forest Service had built a stone building. It had been unused for some time but was still in a good state of repair. A well near it had water in its depths, but the nearby stream was dry at that time of year. We had the area to ourselves, which, of course, was much to our liking. It was the perfect spot to camp for a few days while we searched the canyon for several rare plant species that were known to be there.

By the time we had set up our cots, the shadows were lengthening. and a cool breeze began to waft down the canyon. Supper was quickly prepared over our gasoline stove. I have an aversion to standing over a campfire on a hot desert evening. It seems wasteful of fuel and wholly inappropriate in ninety-degree weather. Supper finished by dusk, we settled ourselves at a card table with our books and waited for whatever might develop in the way of wildlife.

As darkness descended over the land, the breeze died, the leaves ceased to rustle, and the only sounds were the soft hiss of the gasoline lantern, the distant (bouncing-ball) call of a screech owl, and the fluttering of an occasional bat as it circled above us capturing moths attracted to the lantern light.

The owls arrived almost without a sound. A family of elf owls, little larger than sparrows, chose to perch on the lower branch of an oak tree just within the circle of our light and sat there solemnly staring at us. All owls, even these little gnomes, have the facility of staring unwinkingly at whatever attracts their attention. There is no hint of what goes on behind those glassy orbs, ever ready to see what might transpire. So it was with these mites. Probably never having seen a human before, they sat there like a number of first-nighters in the front row waiting to see what might take place on the stage. We did little to entertain them beyond talking to each other, and, after ten minutes of this inaction, they slipped away as silently as they had come.

For some time after their departure, I tried to concoct some scheme to get pictures of them in this unusual setting. Elf owls are ordinarily denizens of the saguaro forest, but occasionally, as in this case, they will nest in wooded canyons adjacent to the desert if they find a hollow snag or an abandoned woodpecker nest to their liking. We had a camera and flashbulbs with us, but a picture of four or five tiny, wide-eyed birds in a tangle of branches had little appeal for me and surely still less for anyone unacquainted with our situation. No alternative seemed to present itself, so I put the matter out of my mind and gave myself over to the sheer pleasure of being outdoors on a night in the canyon.

Morning dawned bright and clear, but the radio warned of possible afternoon thundershowers. We had expected this when we started out. July and August are the months when the Thunderbird shakes its wings over the arid land, and all the desert and its creatures rejoice in awakening as the spell cast by heat and drought is washed away. Because we had planned to climb part way up Baboquivari Peak to take some photographs, it behooved us to do this in the forenoon, while it was still relatively cool, and return before the showers set in during the afternoon. I was not at all enthusiastic over this project. I am not an avid hiker who feels compelled to climb a mountain just "because it is there." Far from it! As far as I am concerned, it can stay there undisturbed by my presence.

So, as we set off up the trail, I carrying a tripod and heavy camera case, my feeling was one of "this has to be done, so let's get it over with." This negative attitude moderated somewhat as we went on. The trail might more accurately be described as a path, and more than likely it dated back to prehistoric times. I was told that it ascended to the very top of the peak, improved in recent times by a cable attached to the wall in a dangerous section close to the summit. I certainly had no plans to climb anywhere nearly that high, so, when we judged that we were approximately one-third of the way up, we stopped to take stock of the situation.

At this point, we were in the Upper Sonoran Zone, and the plants around us were quite different from those that we had left in the canyon. Agaves, sotols, and yuccas were all around us, and numbers of them were in flower. Of these, the most prominent species was *Agave palmeri*, a so-called century plant. It bears flower stalks out of all proportion to the size of the plant, some of them reaching heights of ten or more feet. The upper part of the central column of this massive inflorescence bears a number of short, lateral branches, each one, in turn, supporting a number of upright tubular flowers. Each chalice contains a generous supply of nectar that makes them attractive to many species of insects and some birds, especially the hummingbirds. I must say, however, that these animals have poor taste, in my estimation; having sampled the nectar, I found it to have a vile taste reminiscent of the nicotine that collects in the stem of a tobacco pipe. To each his own. However, perhaps this very characteristic screens out the undesirables and encourages the more efficient pollinators.

The clouds then beginning to form warned us that, if we wanted pictures, it would soon be time to take them. Selecting a vantage point a little way from the trail, we set up the camera and waited for the best effect. The tan-brown Sonoran Desert stretched away as far as the eye could see. To the south, it joined the plains of northern Sonora in Mexico, the general drainage being to the southwest toward the Gulf of California beyond the horizon. Thin lines of yellow-green trees outlined the washes, dry now but discernible because of this growth along their banks. Here and there, a glint of sun upon water indicated a *charco* (an impoundment for collecting floodwaters for cattle) still not entirely dry.

Of other marks of civilization, there were few. Topawa and Sells lay close beneath us, easily seen because of their White Man's developments, but the Indian settlements, composed of homes built of saguaro ribs and ocotillo branches and plastered with adobe mud, blended almost perfectly with the earth of which they were built. A few low mountain ranges were within our view, but their names were more interesting than their appearance: the Quijotoas, the Comobabis, the Sierra Blancas, and, far off to the northwest, the Silverbells. The only discordant note in the scene was the gray plume of smoke rising from the smelter at Ajo seventy air miles away. It flattened out and masked the western horizon for many miles before it finally dissipated. This was the picture that I was striving to get.

A desert panorama spread before us with blue sky, white clouds, and dark cloud shadows upon the plain. In the foreground was a rugged outcrop of dark rock with two agave plants helping frame the composition with their showy flower stalks. While waiting for the proper cloud effects, we were entertained by the hummingbirds and sphinx moths that worked the agave blossoms. Suddenly, I realized that this was just what I needed to get some owl pictures down at camp. I would cut off a stalk, carry it down with us, and set it up under the branch upon which they had perched on the previous night. Then, when they had flown down among the flowers to catch the moths, the flash would catch the little rascals in a perfectly natural setting. On our way up the trail, I had noticed a particularly nice specimen close to the path, and, on our return trip, the upper six feet of the inflorescence was sacrificed on the altar of posed wildlife photography.

I had my problems getting to camp as Irene would not participate in this nefarious scheme, so I then had tripod, camera case, and the heavy shaft of flowers to carry. To add to my difficulties, I had to carry the inflorescence upright so that the nectar would not shower down upon me and be wasted. Once in camp, I leaned my troublesome burden against a bush and went looking for a base. Near the old headquarters building, I found a rusty five-gallon can, into which I placed the stalk and filled in around it with small rocks and gravel from the streambed. When placed against the old oak tree, it looked very acceptable to me, and I hoped it would satisfy the owls as well. As soon as we had moved away from it, insects began to gather around it in the usual fashion.

The promised shower having failed to materialize, we spent the afternoon exploring up the canyon. We were looking for *Lysiloma thornberi*, a shrub that had been discovered in Chiminea Canyon (its only known habitat in the United States) in Saguaro National Monument. Rumor had it that it had also been found in canyons of the Baboquivari Range. We were unsuccessful in this effort, so it may well be that this species, which since has become a popular landscaping plant, is still known in the wild from only the one locality.

Upon our return from this unprofitable foray, I set the camera on a tripod and arranged the flashbulbs in preparation for what I expected to be an interesting evening with the owls. I was gratified to see that, as the dusk deepened and the lantern was lighted, the moths gathered to the light as they had on the previous evening and that numbers sufficient to attract the owls settled on the agave flowers as well.

As time went on, no owls appeared. I began to wonder if I was giving the party to which no one came. As I was about to give up, a dark form fluttered into the light, flew up to the flowers, and disappeared as swiftly as it had arrived.

"Did you see that?" I whispered to Irene. "That bat took a moth!"

I tensed myself for another visit, but it was so long in coming that again I was unprepared when it occurred. This happened several more times, and, eventually, I abandoned any thought of pictures. I was not focused on the right spot, and, beyond that, the bat's flight was so swift that flashbulbs would not have frozen the action and a blurry picture would have resulted.

I was not too disappointed because, after all, I had witnessed an event that probably no one had ever seen before: a bat in the wild taking moths from an agave inflorescence. Somehow, a small doubt crept into my mind upon thinking it over. Why should a bat come into a lighted area with two humans close by in order to capture moths when there were probably a greater number flying about in the open air above us? Probably just an aberrant individual that did not conform to the norm, I supposed. The owls never did appear, and we left the next day without pictures, but with lasting memories of them perched among the branches and watching us with those unblinking eyes.

Bats

Shortly after our return to Tucson, I became involved in what I thought was a totally unrelated matter. Sometime previously, I had written an article on the bats of Colossal Cave. These caverns are located only a few miles from the park boundaries. Dr. Lendell E. Cockrum of the University of Arizona had been kind enough to participate in the venture and had checked my manuscript for accuracy. He had several studies going forward in the cave, and I volunteered my help if and when another pair of hands might be of use. Two of his studies involved the homing instincts and the longevity of bats. In both instances, the bats used had to be first captured and then banded so they could be readily identified at any time, and I was enlisted to help in both activities.

Banding is a simple procedure, but it requires painstaking accuracy in documentation of the species, date, and place. The band is a small tube of aluminum that is split down one side and has identification numbers stamped into the metal. A bat's wing compares with the human arm and hand, the fingers being greatly elongated. A thin skin is stretched over this framework. In the banding process, the open band is slipped over what would be the upper arm of a human and then is closed with a specially made pair of pliers until it slides freely back and forth along the bone. The number on the band is entered into the record, together with the species, sex, date, location, and whatever other information is pertinent. As with banded birds, there is a National Registry record of the numbers.

It was relatively easy to catch the bats at Colossal Cave. There were two entrances opening out upon the hillside. The larger was the visitor entrance and was developed with a gate and stairs leading into the depths. The other was more like a mine tunnel that, after forty feet or so, led directly into a large room where most of the bats congregated. On those nights when bats were to be banded, Dr. Cockrum would stretch a mist net across the outside entrance of the tunnel, and we would then go into the cavern where the bats roosted. A number of them would fly into the tunnel thinking that they might escape. When we thought there were enough in the tunnel, we would stand at our end of it. The bats, being unable to get outside because the net was blocking their way and equally unable to reenter the big room because we were blocking their way, would fly back and forth from the net to us.

It was relatively easy to capture them with a butterfly net just as they were making a turn in front of us, then to reach in to the net and grasp the bats, carefully, for they are delicate little creatures, and put them into the collecting bag. They bit very enthusiastically but, except for the larger species, seldom drew blood, for their teeth, though sharp as needles, are very short. Were I to be doing that sort of work today, I would wear gloves when handling bats, but in the late 1950s, when this took place, little thought was given to the possibility of contracting rabies from bat bites. In the intervening years, much research has been pointed in that direction, and much more is surely needed.

Several of the species thus collected were used in the homing experiment. Dr. Cockrum and his students would band a number of bats and put them into containers for release in different directions at five-mile intervals from the cave. We volunteers would then sally forth with our captives and note the mileage from the cave and the time at which we opened each container. At the cave, a crew would be waiting to, if possible, recapture the returning bats and note the time of their arrival. Times varied, of course, depending on, among other things, the velocity of the wind and the anxiety of the individual bat to return to its roost. However, the results clearly indicated that the bats, like their diurnal counterparts, the birds, had a well-developed homing instinct and experienced no difficulty in returning to their home turf.

Of the several species of bats then frequenting Colossal Cave, my favorite was the long-nose *(Leptonycteris nivalis)*, later to be called Sanborn's long-nose bat *(L. sanborni)*. There were several reasons why I was more interested in it than the others. At that time, it was considered to be a fruit-eating species, a trait that it shared with only one other species in the continental United States. It is a migratory species, coming north from Mexico, or possibly Central America, in early summer and leaving again in early fall. The colony in Colossal Cave was a nursery colony consisting of gravid females, no mature males having been collected there.

The young were born in the cave, and, when they were old enough to endure the trip, the whole group migrated south again in the fall.

These bats were thought to subsist mainly on the pollen and fruit of the saguaro, together with such insects as might be ingested at the same time. Analysis of stomach contents and the pollen adhering to their faces indicated that this was the case. As can be imagined, field studies of this nocturnal creature feeding at night on the flowers and fruit of a towering plant like the saguaro would be difficult, to say the least. So this aspect of the studies on the long-nose rested for the time being. A theory persisted, however, that this mammal might, like the hummingbirds, feed on the nectar of the saguaro flowers. Dr. Stanley Alcorn asked us all to look for any signs that bats might have scratched the petals or otherwise damaged saguaro flowers while feeding, but none of us ever detected any such damage. The verification that these bats did, indeed, feed on nectar came about more by accident than design.

A mammalogist from the West Coast had made arrangements to give a program about bats on a local television show in Tucson. On the day before his presentation, he had collected a half-dozen bats in a mine tunnel in the Chiricahua Mountains of southeastern Arizona. These were of the long-nose variety, and, after twenty-four hours without food, they were in a sorry state of dehydration and hunger. Certainly, they could not be shown on the program in their condition. He contacted Dr. Cockrum and related his problem. Dr. Cockrum told him to "take them over to the Olins; maybe they can do something with them."

When he arrived at our home, the bats were lying on the floor of the small, screened cage, apparently in the last stages of exhaustion. Leaving them with us, he hurried away, saying that he would be back later that afternoon and pick them up if, by chance, they could be revived.

Proceeding upon the assumption that these were, indeed, fruit bats, we cast about looking for something in that line that might tempt them to eat. All that we could find about the house was a can of sliced peaches in heavy syrup. Taking a slice of the fruit, we offered it with no success. We rubbed their noses in it, tried to open their mouths and force small pieces in them, all to no avail. Finally, in desperation, I picked one up by the hind feet and, with a spoonful of the syrup in the other hand, dipped her nose into the liquid, as she hung from my fingers. To my surprise, her tongue dipped in and out of the syrup, and, in no time at all, the spoon was emptied. As one spoonful after another disappeared, her belly swelled until it seemed as if it might burst. With her hunger appeased, complete animation returned, and, in a short time, we had them all revived to the point that they were flying around the room and clinging to the drapes. When they were returned to the cage, they hung on the screened sides without difficulty.

This experience satisfied us that nectar, if not the chief food of these bats, was of great importance to their diet. At the same time, we had no proof that they depended on the saguaros for this food or that, in the act of feeding from the flowers, they cross-pollinated the blooms. It remained for another experiment to provide the answers and finally prove the theory.

One of Dr. Alcorn's associates at the University of Arizona was Sam McGregor. Mac was a small man of boundless energy and a sunny disposition. His specialty was honey bees, a study that occupied most of his time and from which he had gained an international reputation. He was a frequent visitor at the monument, especially during the time of the flowering of the saguaros. I recall one early morning when, having heard music coming from one of our study plots, I went to investigate and found Mac reclining in a lawn chair on the roof of his motorhome, which he had parked alongside a flowering saguaro. With notebook in hand, he was tabulating bee trips to and from the flowers at his elbow, while at the same time luxuriating in the shade of his umbrella and listening to his portable radio. This was nothing out of the ordinary for Mac. He was always finding new and far-out ways of accomplishing his research. To our good-natured ridicule of his methods, he would only smile and observe that work was what you made it.

At this same time, Dr. Alcorn was checking on the influence that birds were exerting on the pollination of the saguaro flowers. Both men knew that these two vectors (pollinators) had much to do with this matter, but it was difficult, if not impossible, to satisfactorily document this in the field. Fortunately, in the winter of 1959–1960, circumstances developed that made it possible.

Theories on Pollination

West of the city, in Tucson Mountain Park, a series of winter rains had so saturated the soils that a heavy windstorm had blown down a number of saguaros. Once a saguaro is windthrown, it is virtually impossible to salvage it because of the damage done to its succulent tissues when it strikes the ground. However, the arms, especially the shorter ones, are sometimes undamaged, and, if these are removed from the prostrate trunk, they may be kept for several years, flowering and fruiting until their stored supply of moisture is depleted.

Taking advantage of this "windfall," Dr. Alcorn activated a project that he had planned for some time. First, he constructed a cage in the study area of the monument. The metal frame was twelve feet by twenty-four feet in area and nine feet high. To make the enclosure, the bottom third of the frame was wrapped with wire window screen, which was partly buried in the ground so as to exclude rodents and other mammals, and the remainder with twelve-mesh-per-inch plastic screen. Within the cage were a small mesquite tree and a young saguaro about seven feet tall. These were included to serve as perching places for the birds that were to be involved in the experiment.

When construction was complete, Dr. Alcorn put on his heavy welding gloves and brought in forty-five saguaro arms from the windthrown plants. Most were in the three-to-four-foot range, and all were in heavy bud. Two large pans of water completed the setup for the first pollinating agent, which was to be the honey bees. The situation was ideal for the research for which it was intended; the bees could not escape, other possible pollinators could not get in, and the flowers were at a convenient height for observation.

The saguaro, in common with most of the tall, columnar cactus species, blooms at night. The buds arise from small sunken areas called "areoles," which are scattered along the ribs of the plant. These small organs are all-important to the cactuses. Spines, roots, new branches, flowers, and fruit all have their source in them. The buds appear in rings

Figure 2.1 The metal-frame screen cage built by Dr. Stanley Alcorn kept study plants and pollinating agents in and all others out.

encircling the tips of the branches in the spring after the weather has warmed sufficiently; this is usually from April into May. At first, they are inconspicuous green knobs, but, under the influence of rising temperatures and sunny days, they rapidly develop into fleshy tubes up to four inches in length. The outside of the tube is covered with leaflike scales that merge with the sepals and the petals of the flowers. The petals are white; when fully opened, they lie out horizontally and form a wheel-like corolla. A thin ring of stamens lies against the inner edge of the tube, and within all this, in the very center of the tube, stands the style with its six stigma lobes.

Only a few flowers open each night, so, in a year when there are abundant flowers, the flowering season may extend over several weeks. To the casual observer, the opening of the flowers seems a commonplace happening, but, as so often occurs in nature, appearances can be deceiving. There are certain stages and processes that must occur in proper order so that the flowers receive the fertilization that will produce a fruit containing ample seeds.

Depending somewhat on the temperature, the flowers begin to open about nine o'clock in the evening. By ten o'clock, they are fairly open but are not yet ready for pollination. The stamens tightly clustered around the throat of the bloom do not as yet have pollen available. The stamen consists of two parts: the "filament," which attaches it to the inside of the floral tube, and an "anther," which it supports. The anther is a sort of capsule tightly packed with pollen grains. As the flower continues to open, the pollen "ripens," and the top of the anther ruptures, allowing the pollen to spill out in a powdery mass around the opening of the floral tube. While this is going on above, nectar is being produced at the bottom of the tube. Finally, at around eleven o'clock, all is in readiness for a vector, or pollinator, to transfer this pollen to some other flower.

The saguaro is a "self-sterile" plant. This means that it will not set fruit from its own pollen, but only from that of another. The animals that feed on the nectar provide this service. As they move from flower to flower, pollen, which adheres to them, is transferred to the stigma lobes of the various blooms that they visit. The stigma lobes are carried at the top of the style; at the bottom is the ovary that, when fertilized by the pollen grains, will produce the fruit. This, in the case of the cactus family, is characterized as a one-celled berry, meaning that it is not compartmentalized but that the pulp and the seeds are contained in one mass about the size of a golf ball. When ripe, the walls of the fruit split and allow the pulp and the seeds to escape. This starts another cycle in the ecology of the saguaro that is as intricate as the pollination of the flowers, if not more so.

On May 28, 1960, a hive well stocked with bees in all stages, honey, and pollen was placed in the cage together with Mac, who spent the mornings of the following week with his charges. On that first morning stationed at the hive, he counted a total of 943 bee loads of pollen brought in from forty-one flowers that had opened on the previous night.

It was my job to photograph the activities of the bees among the flowers. As can be imagined, with a full hive of bees in an enclosed space even as large as the cage, there was always a cloud of bees buzzing about our ears. I was not disturbed by this as I had several stands at home and enjoyed having these industrious little insects about. Bees have one of the most structured societies in the insect world, and the division of labor could not have been more apparent than there in the enclosure.

We had essentially only two classes of bees to work with among the saguaro flowers: the pollen gatherers and the nectar collectors. While at work, they were easily identifiable. The honey collectors went directly to the flowers and dived immediately into the depths of the tubes to get at the sweet liquid. The pollen gatherers approached more deliberately. If the pollen lay thickly on the ring of stamens, they first would hover above it, creating a current of air that lifted the pollen grains up to them. They then gathered them while the grains were airborne and stuffed them into pollen baskets on their hind legs. When this method no longer sufficed because of a diminishing supply, they settled down upon the flowers and assiduously collected every grain remaining.

At times, the numbers of bees competing for the relatively few flowers became bothersome for my photography. Mac noticed this and said: "If you are bothered by too many bees, send some of them home."

"How do you do that?" I asked.

"Just touch the ones you don't want lightly on the back, and they'll return to the hive and stay there. But don't do this to too many, or they will tell the rest not to return, and you won't have any." At that time, Mac did not know how they communicated this information, but he assumed that it might be through body movements, as in the case of the well-known "honey dance." (In the honey-dance sequence, scout bees are sent out to find a source of honey. When one does find such a source, it returns to the hive, and, with certain movements of its body and wings, it somehow indicates to the hive where the source is located.) Later he discovered that it was transmitted by the sound of wing vibrations. In any event, it worked, and we were able to control the numbers at our picture setup very well.

The commercial honey bees, such as we used in the experiment, had little to do with the long-term ecology of the saguaro because they were introduced into the Southwest only in 1872, but, in the intervening years, they have become a familiar associate of the giant cactus, even at times building hives in old woodpecker holes. However, because they are diurnal in nature, they might be viewed as secondary pollinators of the flowers. Under normal conditions, night-flying insects and, as we hoped to prove, night-flying mammals (the bats) would have first chance at the nectar and pollen provided.

Nevertheless, the bees represented an added factor in the pollination process, and, as the days passed, the flowers in the enclosure were tagged with the date and other pertinent information. After fertilization, some days elapse before the swelling of the ovary at the base of the tube becomes apparent. If pollination has not taken place, the flower tube withers and falls to the ground. Final results were encouraging: more than 50 percent of the 193 flowers exposed to the bees set fruit. Bearing in mind that the blooms are self-sterile, this proves that the bees moved the pollen from flower to flower. On May 8, after the bees had spent ten days in the cage, the hive was removed and the enclosure left vacant for a day.

Next to occupy the cage were white-wing doves. These handsome birds spend the winters in Mexico and return to Arizona about the time that the saguaros come into bloom. This being the dry season of the year, the doves depend to a considerable extent on the nectar of the saguaro flowers. Capturing the six doves desired for the experiment proved to be no great problem. In front of the administration building at the monument is a small pool kept for the convenience of the wildlife. At that time of year, there were usually a number of white-wings close by. We covered a large frame with chicken wire and propped it up with a stick on one side. A string led from this trigger to the inside of the building. A few handfuls of rolled oats thrown on the ground under the frame attracted our quarry, and, on our first effort, we captured exactly the six doves we required. When first placed in the cage, they flew against the netting a few times, but they soon became accustomed to their prison and quickly tolerated our being in with them.

The white-wings are admirably suited to a role as pollinators of the saguaro flowers. The dove-pigeon group has been described as drinking like a horse—that is, they thrust their bills into a liquid and swallow without raising their heads. To reach the nectar at the base of the saguaro flower, they must necessarily thrust their heads through the ring of stamens encircling the corolla, and their faces and the tops of their heads become covered with pollen. They proved to be somewhat less efficient than the bees, however: only 44.7 percent of the open flowers set fruit during their stay in the cage.

Photographing the Bats

Finally came the day that we had all been waiting for—the testing of the long-nose bats! There were several problems incidental to observing and recording the activities of the bats among the flowers. Most important was the requirement that they be kept cool during the days in the blistering heat of May in the Sonoran Desert. By contrast, the temperature in Colossal Cave is a constant seventy-two degrees Fahrenheit. Then, too, we had to provide controlled lighting so we could see what was going on, but the cage was in an isolated spot in the cactus forest far from any source of electricity. We would need to use high-speed flash to photograph the bat activities that we hoped to record on film. This called for strobes, which at that time were just becoming available to amateur photographers and were still an unfamiliar tool to me.

We had anticipated these difficulties early on and tried to prepare for them as best we could. We knew, of course, that the best-laid plans "gang aft agley," and we were later surprised that things went as well as they did. First was the matter of providing comfortable quarters for our guests. We built a box measuring two feet square by one foot high and lined it with screen wire so the bats could cling wherever they chose. We fastened a gallon can to the roof inside the box in such a way that we could fill it from the outside with ice cubes, and we installed a door in one side of the cage so the bats could go in or out at will during the night. Once the bats were in the box, it was to be kept in the air-conditioned administration building during the day, and taken down to the study cage and hung in a corner of the enclosure at night. We had no idea if this would prove successful, but, with this attempt, we took a "shot in the dark."

Lighting was to be obtained by the use of storage batteries with switches and a rheostat so that it could be dimmed or intensified as the situation demanded. Lighting for photography was another matter for which we had no guidelines or previous experience. I had a little Ultrablitz unit and was able to borrow another from a friend. These operated on self-contained batteries that had a limited use life. They could also be plugged into 110-volt, 60-cycle current for continuous use. Our only substitute for this commercial current was to use two 12-volt direct-current car batteries and to convert that voltage to 110 through the use of an inverter built for an electric razor. It was too small for the job and heated up badly in preliminary tests, but we hoped for the best. On all counts, the bat experiment got off to a shaky start, but we hoped to adapt to circumstances as we went along.

On May 27, we accompanied Dr. Cockrum on a trip to Colossal Cave and were successful in capturing nine long-nose bats. During our return to the monument, we gathered an armload of blooming agave stalks. Pollen from this agave, the shin-dagger or amole, had been found on the faces of long-nose bats, and it was supposed that this and perhaps the nectar as well were standard fare for the long-nose. If this were true, it might have been a factor in attracting these bats to Colossal Cave. for it grew in profusion on the limestone hills thereabouts.

Later that afternoon, we checked out the lighting system, placed the flower stalks in buckets of water, and hung the bat box with its occupants in a corner of the enclosure. Then Dr. Alcorn and I went home, leaving Mac on the scene to record what might take place in the cage that night.

Upon my return to work next morning, I found the bat cage on top of the air conditioner and a cryptic note from Mac that said simply: "Have we got data, or have we got data?" I knew that he was goading me, but I resisted my first impulse to rouse him from his hard-won rest after his long night in the cactus forest. He did call me as soon as he got up that afternoon, and his news was wonderful!

He had opened the door of the bat cage as soon as it began to get dark, and, as soon as it was completely dark, the bats had emerged. Since the saguaro flowers were not yet fully opened, they went to the agave flowers. It was evident that they were after the nectar rather than the pollen.

They employed several methods: they hovered in front of the flowers; sometimes they also alighted on the stalks and worked an individual bloom; other times they clambered awkwardly up and down the stalks, working a number of flowers before taking again to the air. Whichever method they employed, the pollen was liberally powdered over their faces and heads. Their actions were much the same with the saguaro blossoms later.

It was interesting, too, that they accepted the box as their quarters. As was their routine at the cave, they emerged early in the evening, returned to the box around eleven o'clock, came out again in the early morning hours, and retired before dawn. It seemed that we were to have an unparalleled opportunity to get some pictures of a hitherto unknown, but suspected, association between this mammal and a plant.

That evening Bruce Hayward, one of Dr. Cockrum's graduate students, and I took the box of bats and headed for the study enclosure. With us, we took tripods, the strobes, batteries, and cameras for 4×5 black-and-white and 35mm color pictures. We accepted that we would have to adjust to problems as they unfolded, for we had no idea of what they might be. After hanging the box in a corner of the enclosure, we set about covering the tips of the saguaro branches with cheesecloth, leaving uncovered only those that we had selected for photographs. We did the same with the agave flowers. Then we set up our lights, cameras, and strobes and checked out the electrical circuits. We then opened the door on the box and, believing that we had prepared to record anything that might happen, sat down on our stools and waited. Daylight waned quickly, as it does in the desert, and all was quiet.

A few streaks of color still lingered in the western sky when the bats emerged. We turned up the viewing lights to the point where we could see them as they fluttered around the enclosure, apparently familiarizing themselves with their surroundings. They seemed unafraid of us, sometimes flying past our heads so closely that we felt the breeze of their wings against our ears. It was not long until they discovered the agave flowers that we had left uncovered. When the first bat fluttered up to a flower, hovered there a second, and then flew away, it carried my memory back several years to the time in Baboquivari Canyon when I had seen (I thought) a bat fly up to that other agave bloom and snatch up a moth. I now realized that what I had seen was a long-nose gathering nectar as this one was doing. It taught me once again that it never pays to jump to conclusions concerning the activities of our animal neighbors.

We had no difficulty getting the pictures we wanted. Pictures of bats hovering and gathering nectar, of bats clambering up and down the agave stalks and working each open flower as they went. They seemed oblivious to our equipment and even to our close proximity. The flashing of the strobe lights seemed not to affect them in the least.

As the first flowers became drained of nectar, we removed the cheese-cloth from fresh supplies; by ten o'clock, we were likewise providing access to the saguaro blooms. These heavier flowers seemed to be more to the bats' liking. They hovered before those that projected horizontally from the arm, but, if the flowers arose at an angle from the stem, they plunged their heads deeply into the flower tube and rested the front part of their bodies on the corollas while their flapping wings maintained their position upon the flower.

As the evening wore on, we began to be concerned about whether there was a sufficient number of flowers to supply the needs of our nine bats. Studies have shown that the average saguaro flower produces ap-proximately 4.5 cubic centimeters of nectar and that, if this is drawn off, it will produce another half as much. Anticipating that there might be a shortage, we had brought along a supply of sugar water that we hoped would be acceptable to our mammalian hummingbirds. As midnight ap-proached, the activity in the cage slowed, and, in a little while, all the bats had reentered the box and all was quiet once more.

We turned up the lights and, using an eyedropper, filled all of the flowers with sugar water. We rearranged our camera equipment in order to take advantage of certain activities that we had not recorded initially. Then we sat down once more to wait. Time passes slowly on a hot desert night. An occasional far-off "chewk" of an elf owl as it keeps in touch with its group or the distant bark of a fox may be all that breaks the silence. One's ears ring with the very absence of sound. We were busy with our thoughts, however, arranging and rearranging what we had seen to match what we hoped that we had captured on film. We knew that what we had was a first, and, unimportant as that might seem to the uninitiated, it was extremely important to us. As Mac had stated: "Have we got data, or have we got data?"

About two o'clock in the morning, the bats again left their temporary home and made the rounds, this time mostly among the saguaro flowers we had filled with sugar water. They seemed to accept this synthetic nectar without question, and we felt satisfied that when they returned to the box they had received enough food to sustain them through the following day.

Figure 2.2
The pollination study.

A: These worker bees are of two types: a nectar collector is disappearing down the corolla of the left flower, while the pollen gatherer is circling above the stamens of the other and filling its pollen baskets with grains wafted up by the currents of air produced by its wings.

B: White-wing doves must thrust their heads deep into the flowers to reach the nectar; when they do so, their heads become dusted with pollen.

C: A long-nose bat takes nectar from an agave flower while on the wing; its nose becomes liberally dusted with pollen in the process. Long-nose bats have extremely long tongues with which they can reach the nectar while on the fly, but at times they may land on the flowers as well.

Table 1 Results of Pollination Study

| Vector | Flowers | | Avg # Seeds | |
	Exposed	Set	Per Fruit	Germination
Doves	338	44.7%	2,634	83.5%
Honey				
Bees	193	51.8%	1,751	90.4%
Bats	186	61.6%	1,887	80.2%

Dawn was breaking over the Rincons by the time we had loaded our equipment, and it was full daylight when the bat box was back on the air-conditioning unit in the administration building. Two days later, when the bats had been returned to the colony at Colossal Cave, the fieldwork of the project was, to all intents and purposes, finished. There remained the long hours in the laboratory to determine the relative abilities of the various vectors to cross-pollinate the flowers as indicated by the numbers of fruits set, the numbers of seeds per fruit, and the viability of those seeds through germination tests—all done under Dr. Alcorn's supervision. The accompanying table summarizes the results.

In the published paper, Dr. Alcorn summed up the experiment this way: "The results show that viable seeds were produced in considerable quantity by both night and day pollinating agents. The effectiveness of similar pollinators in the area would indicate that failure of the saguaro to repopulate is not due to lack of cross-pollination. . . . To our knowledge, this is the first experimental proof that honey bees can pollinate the saguaro or that white-wing doves and *Leptonycteris* bats can pollinate any plant." Couched in the precise language of the scientist, the report conveyed little of the earnest planning that went into this project or, indeed, the exhilaration that comes to one when theory blossoms into reality. This was a small contribution, perhaps, but the cause of science is advanced by great numbers of small experiments no more important than this.

A Park Naturalist

In 1960, Superintendent John O. Cook succeeded in getting the position of park naturalist established at Saguaro National Monument, and I was fortunate enough to be appointed to the job. Actually, this took me away from some of the field activities and threw me into more contact with the visitors. Not that I had not already been involved to some extent ever since I had been at Saguaro.

Manning the information desk was the best of the many duties of the naturalist at Saguaro. Visitors spanned the widest possible spectrum of knowledge concerning the desert. Some were amazed to find that, contrary to their expectations, the desert was not a barren waste of rocks and sand infested with rattlesnakes but instead supported a considerable cover of shrubs and low trees and many species of wildlife. Others, experts in their fields, knew much more about the Sonoran Desert than we. Those who fell between these extremes, especially if first-time visitors to Arizona, could be expected to ask three opening questions at the desk. They were in this order: "How old are they?" "They," of course, being the saguaros. "How tall do they get?" And, finally, "What about snakes?" This referring only to rattlesnakes.

I'm sure many of them were disappointed with our answers. "Well, we don't know how old they get to be; there are no annual rings in saguaro ribs, you see. We estimate that an old saguaro might be as much as two hundred years old or even more. How tall are they? Not as tall as they look. We have records of several in the monument that are slightly over fifty feet in height. This is exceptional, though—most will be in the twenty-five-to-forty-foot range. Now, about the snakes; we have a large number of snake species in the park. At least five of them are rattlesnakes. You probably won't see a rattlesnake during your visit, but, if you do, avoid it. Rattlesnakes are dangerous creatures; however, they occupy an important niche in the ecological pattern of the desert. They are protected, as are all forms of wildlife in the monument."

I, among many naturalists, have been puzzled at the hostility exhibited by a great many people toward snakes. This same degree of antipathy is not held toward others of the reptiles; in fact, some, such as the lizards, are often admired, and tortoises are frequently kept as pets. No doubt much of this bias stems from the serpent being responsible for the Fall from Grace in the Garden. Other cultures than our own, in some cases, deify the serpent, and our Native Americans accept snakes for what they are—an element of their environment. This, unfortunately, did not extend to many of the early pioneers and their progeny, who detested snakes, especially rattlesnakes, and eliminated them whenever they could.

Black Rattlesnake

Such a one was our packer, Frank. A tall, lean Texan, he lived at Madrona ranger station at the mouth of Chiminea Canyon. From that point, a trail led up the Tanque Verdes to Manning Camp and Mica Mountain. At Madrona, the corrals and barn housed the four mules and several horses belonging to the Park Service, as well as Blaze, Frank's personal mount. Frank would sometimes tell me of his encounters with rattlesnakes on the trail and how they "spooked" his pack string. He singled out one big bay gelding that "went crazy" whenever he was astride him at such a time.

I used to tell him: "Frank, your animals are only reacting to your fear of the snakes. Next time you see a snake, stop your string, get off your horse, and walk up and ease it off the trail. You'll find that the string will watch what you're doing and won't spook."

"I'll help it off the trail alright, with a few rocks," Frank would growl.

I turned the tables on Frank, though. Before my appointment to the naturalist position at Saguaro National Monument, I spent some time working on various construction jobs in the Manning Camp area. The camp itself is located at about nine thousand feet, at the end of the ten-mile trail leading up from the ranger station at Madrona. It consists of Manning Cabin, built in 1905 by Tucson industrialist Levi Howell

Manning as a mountain retreat and now a historic structure, and a fire tower. The Park Service maintains a fire crew there during the summer months when the fire danger is at its peak.

One of the problems, as in many mountain settings, is lack of water. My assignment on this occasion was to superintend the construction of a small dam to impound enough water for the dry spells. I would ride up from Madrona early on Monday morning and come down on Friday afternoon. I usually rode the bay gelding that Frank had warned me went crazy at the sight of a rattlesnake.

One Friday afternoon, when I was but a short distance down from Manning, I spotted a black rattlesnake some ways ahead in the middle of the trail. Here was my chance to test my theory, I thought, and I took a firm grip on the saddle horn, just in case the gelding might spook. He had seen the snake at about the same time as I, and I could feel by his gait that he was wondering what I might ask of him. Urging him on with slow words of "let's go now, old boy," and "don't worry, everything's all right," we came down to about fifteen feet from the snake. There I stopped him and considered what we should do next.

The black rattlesnake is a dark phase of the Pacific rattler and is found at higher elevations in only a few mountain ranges in southern Arizona. I needed a picture for the records but had no bag or snake stick with me. Meanwhile, the snake calmly remained where it was. Finally, a solution to the dilemma came to me. Taking my jacket down from back of the cantle, I severed a leather thong from the saddle skirt and tied it tightly around the cuff of one sleeve. Then, cutting a forked branch from a shrub alongside the trail, I had a reasonably acceptable capture outfit.

Feeling sure that my horse would stay where he was, I threw the reins down in the dust and approached the snake. The black is not an aggressive rattler, and I had little trouble in catching it and lowering it into the sleeve of the jacket. Then, folding the body of the garment around the arm, I had a bundle that I could again tie behind the cantle. The horse had watched all of this going on, almost beneath his nose, with interest but with no evidence of fear. I presented the bundle to him for his inspection, and he sniffed at it carefully with his ears cocked forward. Still no uneasiness on his part, so I rubbed the bundle against his flank and then tied it securely behind the saddle. The rest of the trip down the mountain was uneventful.

Figure 2.3
This is the black rattler that came down from the mountain on horseback. I released it in the same area where I found it.

Frank came out of the barn as I rode into the corral. "Have a good trip down?" he asked.

"Oh, as usual," I replied casually. "We did run into a black rattler about a mile and a half out of Manning."

"Aha," he said. "Give you some trouble, did he?" and he nodded toward the horse.

"Not at all. I rode him right up to the rattler, within fifteen feet," I boasted.

"I don't believe it," Frank stated flatly.

"Then believe this," I said. "That snake is alive and right there in that bundle behind the saddle, and the horse knows that it's in there, too."

Frank hastily retreated several steps. "Man, you is crazier than I thot you wuz," he pronounced in his Texas drawl.

The episode went a long way toward proving my theory, as far as I was concerned, but its significance was probably lost on the locals at the bar where Frank customarily stopped to imbibe one for the road on his way home from work. As for the snake, I released it at the point where I found it on the following Monday morning when I next went up to Manning Camp.

I have never made a practice of handling venomous snakes with my bare hands. Snakes and lizards have a troublesome trait of alternately relaxing and then suddenly making convulsive efforts to escape or to bite, as the case may be. Their reactions are so swift that human responses cannot match them even when one knows that they are about to occur. Therefore, it is my opinion, often stated, that anyone who is foolish enough to handle dangerous reptiles will, sooner or later, get bitten by them. One might argue that circumstances alter cases. Actually, they do not; the risks are not worth the gamble.

Rattlesnake Bite

This was borne out in my own case on Election Day in 1960. My day's work was scheduled to my satisfaction. I would stop by the polls and cast my vote on the way home from work. I had not missed voting in a presidential election since the Hoover-Smith contest in 1928 and was rather proud of exercising my civic obligations. It was a little after twelve o'clock noon, and Superintendent Cook had gone home for lunch. I was alone in the Saguaro visitor center. A monthly report was occupying my attention when an elderly couple came in and reported that there was a snake in the cactus garden. They thought that it might be a rattlesnake. I supposed that it might have been a gopher snake or a racer but went out with them to check it out.

It was, indeed, a rattlesnake: a middle-sized Mojave about two feet in length. Venomous reptiles and visitors do not get along well, so it was our policy to catch the reptiles and release them several miles away in the cactus forest. We had a snake stick and sacks in the building for just that purpose, but this was only a little snake, so I decided to catch it by hand. The visitors were all attention as I looked about for an appropriate forked stick. The only thing available was a clump of brittlebush, which is a low-spreading forb with short, brittle branches. The branch I selected was hardly adequate. It was about eighteen inches long and little larger in diameter than a pencil, but I thought that I could make do with it. I approached the snake carefully, and it remained quiet until I pinned it down just behind the head. Then I made my mistake!

Catching a rattlesnake is somewhat analogous to defusing a bomb. It should be done "by the numbers," for any deviation can result in disaster. One chooses whatever method suits his capabilities best and, depending upon the circumstances, varies it as little as possible. I am not partial to using a forked stick because, unless care is exercised, it can injure the snake. However, in many situations it may be the only way available.

Being right-handed, I use the superior dexterity of that hand to pin the snake down, placing the fork on the neck just behind the triangular-shaped head. At this point, the snake may react violently, and who can blame it? When it has quieted down, I shift the stick from my right hand to my left and then, oh so carefully, slide my right hand up the snake's neck to just back of the fork. When I get a firm grip around the snake's neck, I discard the snake stick and use my left hand to pick up most of the snake's weight about midway of the body. The snake is now under control and can be put into a sack. This is the preferred container, as the snake cannot injure the delicate skin on its nose against the fabric, as it might if put into a box or a cage.

This particular day, my miscue took place just after the first step of capturing the snake. I had pinned it down with the makeshift forked stick when, instead of transferring the stick to my left hand, I reached down with it and grasped the snake by the neck. I compounded my error by not sliding my hand far enough toward the fork, so that, when I removed the stick, the snake had slack enough to twist its head about and strike. One fang slid into my thumb halfway between the first joint and the base of the nail. It was as if a hot needle had been jabbed through my flesh. My first reaction was disbelief that this had happened. I remember saying: "Ouch! It bit me." I laid the snake down before it had another chance to strike and went through the capture sequence once more, doing it right the second time. The visitors were appalled at what had happened, but I assured them that, since I was a large person, and the snake was small, and it had bitten me with only one fang, the situation was in no way life threatening. We took the snake into the visitor center, put it into a bag, and, after some discussion, the visitors departed.

As soon as I was alone, I sucked the puncture and then went to the lunchroom, where I found an empty half-size peanut-butter jar. Filling it with crushed ice, I put my thumb into it and went on filing my report. I felt little pain at the time. John Cook returned from lunch at one o'clock. At his questioning look when he spotted the peanut-butter jar decorating my left hand, I confessed.

"John, I've just done a stupid thing. I've gone and got myself snake bit."

When I had given him the details, he said: "What do you think we had better do about it?"

"I'm not worried about it," I replied, "but perhaps if complications should occur, it might be best for insurance purposes to have it attended to."

"Good idea," he said. "I'll drive you down to the Tucson Medical Center."

By the time we had driven the fifteen miles to the center, it was close to two o'clock. There were several people ahead of us at the emergency entrance, where we were handed some necessary forms. After filling them out and getting into line again, I finally arrived at the admission desk, still with my peanut-butter jar. The nurse at the station had evidently had a hard day. "And what is your problem?" she asked wearily.

"I have a slight case of snakebite," I informed her. I could see her tense.

"What kind of snake?" she asked.

"A rattlesnake," I told her.

"A rattlesnake!" she shrieked, and bedlam let loose. Buzzers shrilled, lights flashed, and a bevy of nurses descended upon me. Despite my protestations, I was thrown upon a gurney and wheeled into an operating room. My peanut-butter jar disappeared, and, in its place, my arm was thrust up to the elbow into a deep pan of crushed ice and water. I continued to tell them that I was doing just fine and had no intention of dying on their hands, and they were equally adamant in telling me to lie still and relax because the snake-bite specialist was on his way and would soon be there.

When he did arrive, I was allowed to escape their well-meant ministrations and to discuss the situation with him in a less highly charged atmosphere. He looked at the site of the bite, asked the species of rattlesnake, and the time that I was bitten. He agreed with me that my size, and the fact that only one fang had struck me, lessened the seriousness of the bite but shook his head at the species, saying that it had the reputation of having the most potent venom of any of the local rattlesnakes. He said that I seemed to be getting along just fine but that I should have a shot of antivenin, even though several hours had elapsed since I had received the bite. I demurred at taking the shot, and he asked me if the reason was because I was allergic to protein serum. I said that I didn't know if I was. Eventually, I gave in and received the shot. He asked me to check back with him in three weeks if no complications occurred in the meantime. John took me home, and, as I was beginning to feel rocky, I missed voting.

By five o'clock, I was hurting—I mean, really hurting! My thumb swelled until it seemed as though it would split open, and my hand resembled a ham. Ice water made my hand ache, but without the cold it ached even worse. I slept fitfully that night with my arm elevated on a pillow. By the next morning, a large black-and-blue spot appeared on my left side, but I felt much better. The next two days were my days off, so I was quite well recuperated when I returned to work.

On the evening of the third day, I noticed some bumps appearing on my left arm. Their itching was intolerable, but after a couple of hours they went away. This became a routine happening for a week or more. Every evening at the same time, the hives, for that was what they were, would appear and drive me practically insane for several hours. They disappeared eventually, but the memory lingered on; when I mentioned them to the doctor on my checkup visit, he said: "You are evidently allergic to protein serum. If you ever have occasion to take such a shot again, mention it to your physician."

"Now you tell me," I responded. My levity notwithstanding, I felt fortunate to have escaped so easily from an episode in which, had the snake been larger, or had both fangs entered my flesh, the aftermath might have been serious, indeed. I have worked with a number of poisonous creatures since that time and, so far, have used great caution. "Once burned, twice careful" was coined for my situation.

Spring in the Desert

Spring! That period between the vernal equinox, March 21, and the summer solstice, June 21, is unique in the Sonoran Desert! In most climes, spring is a time of seeds sprouting, of leaves bursting forth, of buds coming into flower, of birds returning, and of all Nature rejoicing that the shackles of winter have been loosed. It all goes forward at an accelerating pace so that, as spring eases into summer, there is no break in continuity. Spring in the desert is less of a prelude to summer than a finale to winter. The annuals that spangle the landscape with color in March and April are borne on plants that rose from seeds germinated through plentiful fall and winter rains. Theirs is a race against the time when searing heat will crisp their petals and parch the soil upon which they stand. Precious little rain will they receive from "April showers." If they have not set seed by May 1, they will have failed their purpose. The grasses that, after a good winter, have carpeted the plain with lush green will turn brown and sere when the rains have ceased.

The perennials carry on in better fashion. Some of the trees and shrubs sink their roots deep into aquifers below the dusty desert floor and carry on in spite of surface conditions. Cactuses and some other succulents are already prepared for the cessation of their water supply. Their pores are sealed against the evaporation of their hoarded stores of moisture. Ocotillos drop their leaves, as do several other xerophytic (water-storing) desert shrubs, and stand naked, patiently waiting for the time when summer rains will come and clothe them once again.

Animals prepare for the coming drought as suits their needs. Tortoises browse on flowers and forbs and drink from temporary pools until the reservoirs beneath their carapaces are filled. When the drought begins, they retire to their burrows deep beneath the surface and estivate until the summer rains call them forth again to wander the desert. Roundtail ground squirrels spend two long resting periods under ground: winter hibernation and summer estivation. Larger mammals take to the shade or rest in burrows during the days and move about their businesses in the relatively cool evening hours. The migratory birds that have spent the winters in the desert leave for higher altitudes or more northern latitudes. Human visitors follow their example, clogging the Interstates with recreational vehicles. Permanent residents hunker down for a long hot spell, and the song of air conditioners is heard throughout the desert land.

Daily temperatures in the Lower Sonoran Zone rise to one hundred degrees and sink to thirty degrees lower at night. Humidities are low, often no more than 25 percent and sometimes as low as 2 percent. Under these conditions, evaporation is great; in some of the more arid places, it amounts to as much as eleven feet of water over a year's span, with most of it occurring during May and June.

In early June, clouds begin to form over a land gasping for relief.

Great, beautiful cumulus clouds pile high in the heavens and float to the north like a fleet of celestial galleons on a voyage to nowhere. They drop no rain unless it be the trailing veils of moisture called "virga," which are swallowed up by the superheated air before ever reaching the ground. Lightning flashes over the mountains, but no rain falls there, either. Eventually, June 21 arrives.

San Juan's Day

The summer solstice does not signify much weatherwise to old desert hands. It is overshadowed by a later date, June 24, the feast day commemorating the birthday of the martyred apostle St. John. To the largely Catholic population of Mexicans and Indians in the Tucson area, the date has held a special significance. San Juan is enshrined as the patron saint of running water. Lacking a living stream since the Santa Cruz River dried up, the devout would gather at the irrigation ditches for their morning ablutions on that day. On that evening, the night-blooming cereus, *La reina de la noche* (the queen of the night), is reputed to bloom, and very often it does. Finally and most importantly, it is supposed that the first rains of the monsoon season will arrive on San Juan's Day. Actually, that is a couple of weeks earlier than the rains normally come to Arizona. In all of my years in the desert, I have seen it happen only once, and that under unusual circumstances.

In the latter part of June 1954, a lightning-caused fire started in the Rincon Mountains of Saguaro National Monument. Later named the Turkey Creek Fire, it rapidly spread out of control, and we, in Tucson, watched aghast as the huge clouds of smoke increased in size hourly. A call went out for help from the Forest Service and other agencies. One of those that responded was the Zuni Indian Reservation. Several of the Indian tribes maintain cadres of well-trained firefighters whose services are on call during the fire season. These are tough, hard-muscled men proud of their ability and jealous of their reputations as being the best at their specialty. In due time, a busload of Zunis pulled up in the parking lot at Saguaro, and the men got out and looked up at the huge billowing clouds of smoke rising from the mountain. Superintendent John

Lewis came out of the visitor center and advanced to meet their foreman. As they shook hands, the foreman said: "Don't worry about your fire, Mr. Lewis. The Zuni Red Hats are here!"

We were told that, having arrived at the site of the fire, they held a rainmaking ceremony that evening. The next day, which was San Juan's Day, a heavy rain soaked the mountain, and the entire Tucson valley as well. It effectively ended the Turkey Creek conflagration. Coincidence? Perhaps. *"¿Quien sabe?"* (Who knows?)

We Leave Saguaro

All of these activities made the time pass quickly, and, before it seemed possible, I had spent seven years at the monument. The last three had been under the tutelage of Superintendent John Cook. John was a Park Service man par excellence. He went out of his way to groom us for the time when we might be transferred to other areas. As he explained, it is healthy for transfers to take place. Too often when an employee gets everything arranged to his or her satisfaction, there is a tendency to sit back and let further improvements slide. This is bad for the area as well as for the employee. Nonetheless, we were all distressed when we learned that John had accepted a transfer to a military area in the eastern United States. Then, in quick order, the administrative aide was transferred to a site in Oregon.

Some days before John was to leave, Irene and I had spent my two days off on a short desert trip. Upon our return, John called and said: "I've been trying to get ahold of you. You've been offered a transfer and promotion to chief naturalist at Mammoth Cave National Park." He paused a moment to let this sink in, then asked: "Are you going to take it?"

"I guess so," I answered. "Where is Mammoth Cave?" When I found that Mammoth Cave was in Kentucky, I was not too pleased. A greater contrast to the bright, open spaces of the desert could hardly be found than the damp, gloomy caverns under the hardwood forest of an eastern state. However, as I told Irene, "We'll probably hate it, but no doubt we will be transferred to the West again in a couple of years or so."

In thirty days, our house was sold and the ties that had bound us to the Tucson area were severed. Our going-away party emphasized that our departure was, indeed, a fact, and so, on a bright day in late January, we left for a different environment, hoping that we could adapt to it easily and with grace. The saguaros were left behind as we drove into the Chihuahuan Desert of southern New Mexico and thence northeast over the Sangre Christos Range at Ruidoso. Then it was out across the Llano Estacado (the staked plains) of northern Texas.

On we went, with the reflection of Sierra Blanca's snowy summit sinking ever lower in the rearview mirror. When it vanished below the horizon, we were no more than a tiny speck in the immensity of the plain; the road stretching away before us and patches of dirty snow here and there the only indication that we were moving ahead across that wintry land. Darkness falls early in January, and the lights were on when we drove into Lubbock. The day was done, and so was the life we had led for those pleasant years in the desert Southwest. There was now no turning back!

Part III

The Return to Tucson

Back to the Desert

The two years I had programmed for Mammoth Cave stretched into four. They were followed by a transfer to the post of chief of interpretation and visitor services at the national memorials in Washington, D.C. Life inside the Beltway was exciting, but we longed for the desert. In 1970, after four years in the nation's capital, we decided that eight years spent east of the Mississippi was enough. I retired from the Park Service, and we made preparations to return to Tucson. We rented a twenty-foot van and hitched my car behind it. Irene was to follow in our station wagon loaded with twelve hundred pounds of books. Our first day was a hard drive over the winding roads of the Blue Ridge, but at Knoxville, Tennessee, we picked up Interstate 40 and struck out in more of a straight line for Arizona.

There were incidents along the way. East of Memphis, we found ourselves in the path of a fearsome bank of jet black clouds moving at us with express-train speed. I could envision a tornado spinning down from that inferno, and we sought shelter under an overpass where we cowered until danger had passed, leaving drifts of hailstones and streams of rainwater in its wake. We became separated in Memphis due to some stupid maneuvering on my part, and we both spent a nerve-wracking hour until I caught up with her parked along the roadside west of the city, waiting for me, according to our game plan. Once we got across the Mississippi, the character of the people changed with that of the country, and, as we worked our way westward, the nasal twang of the Ozarks gradually gave way to the broad accent of the Oklahoma plains.

Now we encountered wind, honest to goodness prairie winds that, unfettered by mountain or forest, battered us with unceasing pressure. Mile after mile and hour after hour, it held the van in its grip, keeping our speed to just under high gear and just over third gear. It blew all night at El Reno, Oklahoma, and all the next day through Amarillo, Texas, and not until we reached Santa Rosa, New Mexico, did it abate. That night it died away completely, and, as though this were a good omen, we made good time up the long grade and past the Sandia Mountains into Albu-querque. Then it was down the Rio Grande, through Socorro, and into Lordsburg for that night.

The next morning we entered what, to me, was the promised land. We crossed the Arizona state line, with Cochise Head marking the Chirica-huas, and continued past all the familiar ranges we had known so well: the Dragoons, the Mules, the Huachucas distant in the blue haze to the south, the Santa Ritas, and, finally, the Catalinas behind Tucson, our journey's end. Home to the desert at last!

With her customary foresight, Irene had placed an ad in the Tucson newspaper requesting rental of a two-bedroom house. We were de-lighted to find eight responses and, from them, chose a very comfort-able dwelling on the far east side of the city. Within a few days, we were well established and ready for action. It is an axiom that retirees can find themselves busier in their retirement than in their workaday jobs. I found this to be especially true in my case because it was early August, the beginning of the monsoon season when the most activity occurs in the desert environment, and I was in a fever to be a part of it.

One of my fantasies during the years in the East had been to choose an unfrequented area in the huge Tucson Mountain Park west of the city, divide it into quadrants and nightly, over, say, a two-year period, observe and record the activities of its flora and fauna. To achieve any significant success, the area would have to be undisturbed by anyone but myself. My presence would be bad enough, but at least it would be a constant that could be computed. I found such a project to be what I had dreamed—a fantasy. In the intervening years since Irene and I had left, Tucson had grown enormously, and, with the increase in population, pressure had mounted on all of the recreational area adjacent to the city. There were no undisturbed areas to be found in Tucson Mountain Park.

Night-Photography Equipment

Abandoning that specific project, I decided that some sort of research on the desert at night was still needed, since it was a comparatively un-touched field. To make it really meaningful, however, would require pictures. Remembering our difficulties during the bat experiments of years past, I set out to get some adequate photographic equipment together.

Naturally, a light source was the first requirement. By 1970, stroboscopic lighting had largely replaced flashbulbs in nighttime outdoor photography. Strobes, as opposed to flashbulbs, give a soft, even light that might be described as wrapping around the subject instead of the harsh, flat effect of the bulbs. However, strobes had the disadvantage of depending on either self-contained batteries, which had a very limited use life before they required recharging, or a source of constant 110-volt, 60-cycle current, each of which presented difficulties in the field. Eventually, I solved the power-source problem by determining that I could use car batteries hooked up to an inverter that converted the 12-volt DC current to the household current, which the strobes required.

I selected three strobe units: two on a boom that would be at a forty-five-degree angle above the subject, and one low on the ground to take out any shadows beneath. I had to figure the exposures by trial and error, since the manufacturer's recommendations were for average conditions indoors, while photographing outdoors at night would require much more light than that. As for the cameras themselves, I would use three: a 35mm for slides and two 4×5s: one for color and one for black and white. I fixed them so that I could trip the shutters, by remote control, singly or all at once, depending on the merits of the situation. The controls were in the car, which would serve as a blind, and a very good one, too, as most animals seem to have come to an acceptance of the automobile simply as a mobile part of the landscape.

Choosing and preparing a site for a good picture is not always easy to do. I would need a site that was far enough from a traveled road so that neither I nor my subject would disturbed. It should have a background of rocks or shrubs or other recognizable features of the animal's habitat. After I found a promising site, I would have to bait it with food for a few nights. Then, once the animal or animals started coming regularly, I would introduce some objects, such as cartons and assorted junk, at the site to accustom them to the cameras and lights that would come later. The next move would be to park the car nearby and survey the site through binoculars to determine the species and the condition of my subject. If all that was to my satisfaction, then I would mount the cameras and position the lights for a night or two. Only after all that would

I proceed to photograph my animals. If this sounds like it takes a lot of time and trouble, it does, but it yields good results and is well worth the effort.

Having worked out all these generalities, I decided it was time to put them to the test. Where else than in Sabino Canyon?

Sabino Canyon

Sabino Canyon is one of the stellar attractions of Tucson. Said to have been named after Sabino Otero, an early pioneer, it has its beginnings in a basin high on the south side of the Catalinas. Water collected in this basin spills into the upper canyon, providing that rarity in the desert land, a living stream. It meanders down the floor of the canyon for several miles, finally losing its waters under the sands of Rillito Wash, which crosses its path at the base of the mountain. A surfaced road penetrates up the canyon for about six miles, crossing the meanders of the stream on picturesque stone bridges built in the Depression days by the ccc (Civilian Conservation Corps).

Normally, Sabino Creek is a sedate little stream with raccoon and heron tracks patterning the silt along the edges of its placid pools. A visitor hears tinkling sounds as it cascades down little falls and murmurs down the rapids. All of this can change if a rapid snow melt or a summer cloudburst should occur. Then sound fills the canyon as the current charges down its course, swirling waist high over the bridges, roaring down the rapids to discharge its accumulations of leaves and debris into the Rillito.

At one time, the Forest Service maintained several picnic areas that existed along the stream and two public campgrounds. Now access to the canyon is only by foot, bicycle, or on a tram operated by the Forest Service. It was necessary to apply these restrictions because the public was literally wearing the canyon out. None of this was the case in 1970. Visitation to the upper canyon was restricted to the hours between eight o'clock in the morning and eight o'clock at night, however.

In common with most deep canyons opening into desert valleys, Sabino provides a "breezeway" for the fluctuating air pressures resulting from the scorching heat of the summer sun. In the mornings, it is relatively cool in the lowlands. As the sun rises, it begins to heat the ground and air. As the air warms, it expands and begins to force its way up the surrounding canyons. This upward flow continues from midmorning to late afternoon. As the setting sun approaches the horizon, the air again cools, and, while it does, the land begins to radiate its latent heat toward the sky. The cooling air contracts, and the vacuum this creates sucks the upper air back down the canyons into the valleys again.

The changes in temperature are considerable. During the day, the breeze rising upward is hot and dry, but, as the day wanes, the air wafting downward from the heights is deliciously cool and moist. The fauna is attuned to these fluctuations. Most strident, and for that reason most noticeable, are the sounds of the cicadas.

As spring merges into summer and the hot winds ruffle the leaves of the cottonwoods along the creek bank, the air throbs with the shrill sounds made by these insects. Their stay in the canyon is short; the larvae come up out of the ground, climb up on tree trunks, and their skins split down the backs. The lacy-winged creatures, now adult through the emergence from their larval form, climb into the leafy canopy, and there the males sing their raucous song. The sound is produced through vibrating a diaphragm under the abdomen. In some way as yet undiscovered, they perform in concert, all following some invisible conductor. For a time, the chorus will go on fortissimo with an enthusiasm that is deafening. Suddenly, the baton drops, and it all stops with a silence, equally deafening. Their engagement is a short one. At the end of two weeks, the females have laid their eggs, ensuring that a similar performance will again go on at some time in the future.

I could not have found a more favorable environment for nature study. The canyon floor is covered with sycamore, ash, and cottonwood trees, which yield to mesquite and paloverde trees on the arid slopes. A thick stand of saguaros and barrel cactus clings to the lower walls of the canyon. The understory growth is equally abundant. White-thorn, acacias, and creosote bushes vie with other shrubs that have descended from higher on the mountain. Ocotillo, brittlebush, and fairy duster claim the drier hillsides. Annuals brighten the scene throughout the summer, gilias and penstemons run riot in spring, and the xerophytic species follow more sedately later in the season.

It follows that the canyon is celebrated for its wealth of bird life. In winter, when the snows lie deep upon the heights, jays, Lewis's woodpeckers, and other high-ranging species descend to the warmth of the desert. Throughout the year, the desert species luxuriate in the unaccustomed humidity along the stream. Several species of hummingbirds come there to nest, and one of the most exotic birds that could be imagined in a desert area, the water ouzel, has been recorded in years past.

Gray Fox

The mammalian fauna is equally rich in species, and these were highly interesting to me because of my project, for a number of them are nocturnal. Some, such as the raccoons, the ringtail cats, and the four species of skunks, are seldom found away from the water, the trees, and the rocky habitat that a canyon environment supplies. Foxes, bobcats, and coyotes are adaptable enough to succeed in almost any kind of habitat.

I decided to first try my luck at photographing a gray fox. The Arizona gray fox is a beautiful animal—silvery gray with a rufous area around its neck and a black stripe down its back that extends to the tip of its tail. For this first attempt, I chose a little cove adjacent to the road leading to the lower campground. In this grotto, framed by drooping mesquite branches, lay a flat granite boulder that offered a splendid place to pose the subject. Laying a few steak bones on the rock, I went home to dinner anticipating what might develop from this offering. The next day when I returned, I found the bones where I had placed them and the area swarming with ants. Retrieving the bones, now bare of meat, I swept the rock free of the annoying ants and returned home to devise a bait station that was ant proof.

Among other things I learned in those first weeks was that, to do night photography in the desert, I had to carry everything I might need with me. Rocks are never the right size or shape, sticks are always too short or too crooked, and nothing suitable can be found in the dark. In consequence, my car soon looked like the proverbial junkman's, loaded with pieces of lumber, lengths of wire and rope, and even rocks of various kinds and shapes.

Figure 3.1 This gray fox was my first photographic subject in Sabino
Canyon. Many species of animals roamed the area in search of scraps.

My next attempt to establish an ant-proof bait station at the same site
was successful, and, in a few days, I was ready to stake out and observe
what was coming to it. It was a beautiful night with a full moon shining when I settled myself in my car some forty feet from the grotto and
trained my binoculars on the rock. Binoculars at 7×50 magnitude gather
a lot of light, and, with the full moon, I could see almost as well as in
daylight. All was quiet, not a breath of wind stirred the mesquite fronds,
and I was beginning to feel that I might be in for a long night, when,
suddenly, there was a fox in my view! I have always marveled at the way
a fox can materialize so suddenly and completely. At one moment the
scene is empty, and in the next instant he is there.

This one took his time at eating the bait, stopping frequently to look
and listen. He seemed to completely ignore the car, but I have no doubt
he knew that I was there. When he had finished, he placed his mark at
several points in the close vicinity and then vanished as silently as he

had arrived. For the next few evenings, the fox and I made rendezvous at the same time, each night adding different pieces of rubbish around the picture area. To these, he paid little attention.

It was in the dark of the moon when we were ready to begin shooting. I installed a light over the site, controlled by a rheostat in the car so that I had a good view of the setup. The fox showed little alarm at the click of the shutters and the flare of the strobes, and I took a good series of photographs. I was disappointed when I saw the prints, however. The exposures were good, but the shots might just as well have been taken of a mounted fox in a taxidermist's shop. The poses were wooden, frozen by the instantaneous flash of the strobes, and the stone base looked highly artificial.

Sabino Skunks

Trying for a fresh approach, I moved up the canyon to one of the upper picnic areas and selected another bait station, this time with plants and surroundings more in keeping with the purpose. This picnic area was a walk-in situation, and I was forced to park my car along the roadway. I carried in a low, three-legged stool, which, being close to the ground, kept me as inconspicuous as possible while I waited to observe what might come to the bait. I had not long to wait. Dusk had barely begun to deepen when here they came!

"They" being skunks! Light ones, dark ones, striped, hooded, and hog-nosed, they drifted in until a dozen or fifteen were combing the area for whatever scraps of food the day's picnickers might have left. Beyond giving a start and raising their tails if they happened to come too close, they paid no more attention to me than if I were something forgotten by one of the visitors. The bait vanished early on, and I could see that it would take a lot of victuals to satisfy that bunch. Skunks use up more bait for fewer usable pictures than any other small mammal I have worked with. Nevertheless, I was pleased to have such a fine selection at my disposal.

On the next night, I was back with a gallon can full of cheap mackerel packed in oil. I hoped that these might be acceptable, and they exceeded my expectations. Then a problem arose: when the picture site was baited, several skunks immediately pounced on the food, and the ensuing struggle promised to smell up the whole area.

My own situation was no less perilous. Their keen noses told them that I was the purveyor of that delicious smelly food they loved, and, although I placed the can under my stool, I was surrounded by a circle of black-and-white bodies and waving tails with all noses pointed expectantly toward that hoard. I was a Gulliver surrounded by an army of Lilliputians smaller than I, but with infinitely more firepower. That night gained me nothing as far as pictures were concerned. I simply acquired a group of fair-weather scroungers who accepted me for what I had and, in the process, lost respect for what I was.

The skunks and I eventually worked out a system, after numerous revisions, that was satisfactory to the point that it produced some pictures. With the cameras trained on a setup against a rock ledge on one side of the area and the bait hung in a tree out of reach, I would take a position against the ledge on the right side of the picture format. Squatting there with a can of bait and a fork, I would call the skunks to me and, when they were in the right pose, move back out of the picture area and trip the shutters by remote control. At first they were reluctant to come to me, suspecting in some way, perhaps by my actions, that they were being lured into some sort of a trap. They would advance a few steps, stop and stamp their feet and woof a few times, and then come on again. I would talk to them and return their woofs, meanwhile holding out a piece of mackerel, and it was but a few evenings until we were on more friendly terms.

Raccoons and Ringtails

Before long, these evening get-togethers attracted the attention of two raccoons that sensed that food was available but were too cautious to come to me for it. I selected a large, flat rock with a catclaw shrub behind it for their table. A deep crevice running across it provided a good

Figure 3.2 When a raccoon and a skunk arrived simultaneously at the same bait station, push developed into shove. Each was careful not to press the other too hard, however. The ultimate weapon was never used.

place to put the bait so that it was within reach of their clever fingers but hidden from camera view.

Of course, the skunks discovered this alternate source of food at once and, although unable to reach it with the same success as the raccoons, decided to claim it for their own. This led to shoving matches for rights to the strategic spot. The raccoons, being larger, had the physical advantage; the skunks, the superiority in chemical weapons. Both were reluctant to trigger the unpleasantness of outright battle, so the struggle would continue until, eventually, the raccoons got away with all of the bait.

Secretly, I was rather pleased at this outcome because skunks are so pushy in their attitude; however, it seemed to me that the raccoons left much to be desired as photographic subjects. The western race is much paler in coloration than the eastern population and somehow lacks the personality of those that Irene and I had met and enjoyed at Mammoth Cave. So, after a few picture sessions with these, I began to watch for their cousins, the ringtail cats.

The ringtail cat *(Bassariscus astutus)*, "sly little fox," is well named. Native to a large part of western America, it is not common anywhere. Also called "miner's cat," because in earlier days prospectors tamed them and kept them around their cabins to rid the premises of rodents, they are doughty little predators. Though classed as carnivores, like the raccoons, they are omnivores and will subsist on a great variety of foods, both natural and artificial.

I had heard reports of seeing them in Sabino but had not sighted any myself until one night, as I rounded a curve on my way home, my headlights picked up a small form with the characteristic banded tail jumping out of a trash barrel and running down the embankment. This new development brought my work in the upper canyon to a halt at once. Spring was coming on, and, as the days grew longer, I had less time to spend with my subjects before the eight o'clock hour when I must be out of the canyon. Leaving the skunks and the raccoons to their own devices, I concentrated on establishing relations with these less well known creatures.

I soon learned that there were four of them in the group: an old battle-scarred female, a young male in splendid condition, and two kittens about half-grown. In the short time left to me, I managed to get passable photographs of the adults, but the kittens, although I sometimes saw them, stayed away from my bait. Their den was evidently in a jumble of huge boulders on my side of the stream. I stayed in the canyon all night on one memorable occasion just to watch them. On that night of full moon, they romped and played within feet of me with all the abandon of a couple of Siamese kittens.

On my last evening for that season in the canyon, I had a good illustration of the omnivorous character of the ringtails. Partly, I suppose, because of the abundance of natural food, I did not see the ringtails at the bait that evening, and I folded up my equipment and left earlier than usual. On my way out, I stopped to chat with an entomologist from a West Coast university who had been collecting insects for several eve-

Figure 3.3 The old female ringtail cat was a battle-scarred veteran. The older animals frequently have their ears torn in fights between themselves.

nings. Making a trap for catching night-flying insects is a simple matter. A bedsheet is stretched tightly between two uprights and lighted from the rear by an electric bulb. The insects fly into the light and land on the sheet, where they are easily captured according to the collector's needs. I casually mentioned that I had been working with the ringtails.

"I've got one of your friends here," he said, pointing to a nearby mesquite. There, stuffing himself with young, tender mesquite pods, was the male. Evidently, he preferred this natural food to my offerings of fish and beef scraps. I have to agree that the sweet, nutritious mesquite pods were better for him.

Later that summer, Hal Coss, the naturalist at Saguaro National Monument, called me. "George, I've got a man from the *Geographic* that's interested in getting some desert pictures. I'm sending him over to see you. Okay?"

"Of course," I replied. This was an opportunity to make contact with one of the nation's most prestigious publications, which I was eager to do.

A short time later, a van pulled up in front of the house, and a couple got out and came up the walk. The man was Walter Meayers Edwards, and the woman, Mary, his wife. Mr. Edwards was of middle height, of middle age, and impressed me immediately as being in full command of whatever he chose to accomplish. Mary was petite and dainty but had a hint of steel under her demure demeanor. Irene and I liked them at first sight, and they apparently returned our regard, for they came in and were at ease immediately.

It turned out that Mr. Edwards (he preferred to be called "Toppy") was the picture editor for *National Geographic*, the popular journal of the National Geographic Society. He was approaching retirement age and had prevailed upon his superiors to let him go out and pursue his first love—taking pictures in the field. His present assignment was to procure the pictures for a book on the American deserts. Obviously, he would not be able to take all of the pictures himself, so he was checking all possible sources as he went. We discussed the possibilities in general terms all afternoon and found several subjects in the Lower Sonoran Zone surrounding Tucson that seemed appropriate for his publication.

As our conversation wound down, he asked me if there might be some special thing that intrigued me and could be illustrated by an arresting photograph. After some thought, I agreed that there was. It was that wood rats, which had their dens in the vicinity of teddy-bear cactus, always had quantities of the joints of this horribly spiny cactus piled on top of their mounds. I had wondered how they could carry these dangerous burrs, which are avoided by most animals, without being impaled by the barbed spines.

"Do you think you could get a picture of one carrying a joint?" he asked.

"I don't know how," I replied, "but I'm sure willing to try."

"Suppose you do that; you've got me interested now," was his final comment.

When they were leaving, Irene and I walked with them to the van. It was wonderfully fitted out with all the necessities for a photographic safari of long duration. I especially liked the refrigeration provided for the film and other heat-sensitive materials. Long and low like household freezers, the two units supported mattresses and sleeping bags. As we bade them good-bye, we had no intimation that we were to see them in the future; in fact, from their retirement until the present day.

Following their departure, I began to evaluate the difficulties involved in taking the wood-rat picture, which I hoped to provide for the book. My only previous attempt at photographing a wood rat had occurred years before when packer Frank Stansberry and I had been quartered at Manning Camp on Mica Mountain after a forest fire. We had ousted this rat from his home in the cabin, and every night he returned, hoping no doubt that we had left. Disappointed in that, he rummaged about in our foodstuff and regularly inspected the sink and the drain board, looking for the source of the appetizing odors that lingered there.

I resolved to get a record shot of it for the Park Service files and sat up several nights with my finger on the cable release of the camera shutter but to no avail. The wily animal would run out on the drain board, take the bait, and leave without giving me a satisfactory pose. I finally tired of this variation of a cat-and-mouse game, and, taking a stale piece of American cheese, I nailed it to the wooden drain board with a ten-penny nail. I got my record shot and, while in a way I suppose it had its merits, in no way did it help me in planning a course of action at this later time.

My first plan was simple, cheap, and gave promise of being successful. It was to use an electric eye in the same way as those that announce a customer entering a store. I would install it alongside a runway used by the rat; when the light beam was broken, the apparatus would trip the camera shutter. One of my friends who lived in the north part of Tucson had a huge yard, most of it covered with native vegetation. In two clumps of prickly-pear cactus were wood-rat mounds, and to these I arrived loaded with equipment and filled with high hopes. We ran an extension line out to the closest mound and set the electric eye at a well-traveled runway. We soon found out that wood rats were highly intelligent beasties that knew full well that something out of the ordinary was going on. The only pictures we got were a few of obviously frightened rats that, under those conditions, were carrying nothing. It was clear that the electric eye was not the answer to the problem, so we bent our efforts in another direction more mechanical than electronic.

After several trips out to Saguaro National Monument, I found a large wood-rat nest along the road that led to the dump. Built in and around the base of a creosote bush, it was close to a prickly-pear clump, the only cactus within a hundred yards of the mound. Deprived of the usual spiny materials, this unfortunate rat had piled up a heap of bits of branches, wood chips, small stones, and such refuse as had blown in his direction from the dump ground. It seemed to me that here was an opportunity to remedy the situation to our mutual satisfaction. I returned to town with plans that became more elaborate as time passed.

At home, I scrounged a wooden dynamite box, which had served us on many a camping trip, and cut a hole six inches square in one end. On my next trip out to the monument, I loaded it, an empty five-gallon pail, and a pair of tongs into the car. Unloading the box at the wood-rat mound, I went on to a rocky knoll about a mile distant where there was a thicket of teddy-bear cactus.

This plant, so named from its deceptively fuzzy covering of light yellow spines, is the most feared on the desert. The spines are as sharp as any needle and have barbed members along their length, which makes them difficult to extract. The joints, or burrs, bearing these spines are easily detached from the plant and lie about on the ground, where, in time, they may take root. Using the tongs, I gathered a pail full of the joints and returned to the wood rat's home. Placing the box about six feet from the den, I filled it with the cactus joints, closed the lid, and left the area to the recipient of my philanthropy.

On the following day, I was delighted to find the box completely empty and the cactus burrs scattered over the top of the mound in the best wood-rat tradition. As I was carrying the joints back to the box, I gave some thought to varying my contributions to his cause. On my next trip, I brought some peanuts in the shell, some plastic spoons and forks, and some small plastic cars and boats. These were all accepted in the same grateful spirit as the cactus burrs. I was surprised to find the peanuts uneaten, but, as I discovered later, some species of desert rodents are highly selective in their food patterns. This is not necessarily a matter of taste but more likely a response to the stern environmental factors that govern their existence under the severe conditions imposed by the desert.

At any rate, after a week or so of transferring these items to and fro, I decided to find out how my adversary carried the cactus joints to his home. Placing a dim light over the area, I surveyed the scene with binoculars. The wily animal would not stir from his mound as long as there was any light at all over the scene.

My next move was to construct two treadles sensitive enough so that his weight would close an electrical circuit. One of them lighted a small bulb on my control board in the car, and the other, governed by a two-way switch, would trip either the camera shutter or light a bulb, depending on the position of the switch. I placed the first treadle close to the mound and arranged the area around it to provide a good picture. I positioned the second one at the entrance to the box that contained the cactus burrs.

They worked well. As the rat emerged from his mound, his weight closed the contact in the treadle, and it lit a bulb in the car. When the light went out, I knew he was on his way to the box. When he went across the treadle located at the box, he lit the other bulb. When it went out, he had entered the box. When, after a short interval, it lit once more, it meant that he was on his way home, presumably with a cactus burr. At that time, I quickly flipped the switch on the other treadle so that, when he stepped on it, the camera shutters tripped and set off the strobes.

This arrangement worked like a charm except that, after four pictures, the canny creature had learned that the treadle at the mound somehow flashed the lights, and, from then on, he went around rather than step upon it. The results of these few pictures were good enough to merit further work, though, so I fabricated a more sophisticated apparatus from a section of cholla wood and arranged it so that it offered the smoothest pathway through some obstructions along the way. As before, my subject learned my stratagem after four pictures, but with these I hit pay dirt. Three were of the rat carrying cactus, and the fourth, through extraordinary good luck, showed him with a little blue plastic car held high as he scampered for home.

The important thing was that we learned how the wood rats carried the cactus joints. They pick them up by clamping their teeth on several of the longest spines and then charge ahead with them as confidently as though they were not the most dangerous booby traps around. Since that time, I have seen these clever little animals repeat this procedure many times, always in the most nonchalant way, while I, with painful memories of past encounters with these vicious burrs, cringe at their au-

Figure 3.4
The white-throated wood rat carries a joint of a teddy-bear cactus at a full run. It seems incredible that they can do this. The vicious barbed spines of this cactus will impale human flesh at the slightest touch.

dacity. Oh, yes, and by the way, Toppy got his picture, which appeared some months later in *Great American Deserts* (Washington, D.C.: National Geographic, 1972, p. 124), written by Rowe Findley, with photographs by Walter Meayers Edwards.

Tucson, in the meantime, had begun to pall on us. Dubbed "the Old Pueblo," it had charmed us in earlier days with its sleepy Mexican character. Now it was the Old Pueblo no more, with all of the problems of big-city life becoming more acute by the day. Traffic overwhelmed the narrow streets, and its smog, augmented by pollution from several mines around the edge of Tucson, enveloped the city in a brown haze. Irene and I had not discussed these matters to any great extent, but it was our unspoken feeling that there were better alternatives to be found. We had purchased a travel trailer shortly after our return from Washington, and frequent trips to the desert in this, our home away from home, provided a welcome release from the noise and pollution of the city. One such outing happened to mark another turning point in our lives.

Organ Pipe Cactus National Monument

It was in the middle of April in 1972, while the spring annuals were still in bloom, that we decided to take a trip to Organ Pipe Cactus National

Monument. Organ Pipe is about 135 miles west and a little south of Tucson. Its more than 300,000 acres border on Mexico to the south and lie at altitudes of from less than two thousand feet to more than four thousand feet. Although the lowest elevations are only a thousand feet or so below Tucson, they provide an environment suitable for a considerable number of plant and animal species not found elsewhere in the United States.

The roadsides were bright with colors of lupines and purple mat as we drove westward. In many open areas, gold poppies and evening primroses spread a variegated carpet of yellow and white under the creosote bushes that, though vastly outclassed by the colorful annuals, still contributed to the general picture with tiny yellow flowers sprinkled among their minuscule leaves. The washes we crossed were lined with paloverde and ironwood trees in yellow and purple shades, and, more rarely, a desert willow would treat us with a glimpse of orchid flowers dancing within its lacy canopy.

As we penetrated deeper into the plains of the Papago Indian Reservation, native grasses began to take their places in the scheme of things, their dark green colors attesting to the bountiful winter rains of that year. It seemed incredible that all of this lush color would vanish within another month and that this Cinderella desert would return to its drab appearance when the clock struck May 15.

At the little settlement of Why—why, indeed, travelers muse as they view the motley collection of buildings and trailers bunched together around the intersection. Simple enough: this is where a road branches off to the south, forming a "Y," later corrupted to Why. We turned left here toward Organ Pipe and the Mexican border. As we proceeded south, Montezuma's Head, a volcanic plug, reared its black form at the north end of the Ajo Range. These low mountains are also of volcanic origin and consist of mixed basalt and the solidified volcanic ash known as "tuff." Far off to the right, the parallel Growler Range forms a similar barrier.

Before long, the organ-pipe cactus, from which the area is named, begin to make their appearance. They are impressive plants, their columns branching from the base and reaching heights of eight to twelve feet. They prefer to grow on the rocky bajadas that slope up to the base

Figure 3.5 Irene stands dwarfed by a massive organ-pipe cactus. This specimen is larger than the average found in Organ Pipe Cactus National Monument.

of the mountains. Growing with them are the usual saguaros and ocotillos, as well as paloverdes and ironwood trees, for, at this low altitude, the area is virtually frost free.

A few miles of this and we arrived at the administrative building. Long and low, it sits unobtrusively in a small rincon (the point at which two mountain ranges join at an angle) among some low hills. We were assigned to a site in the campground and hastened there because it was beginning to get late. This campground is one of the largest in the National Park system. Situated on a bajada sloping gently to the south are two hundred sites with facility centers placed strategically among them. Our site was close to one of these and bordered by the loop road on one side. We had no close neighbors; although the grounds had been filled to capacity all winter, most of the "snowbirds," as winter visitors are called, were gone by April. Because of their departure, the small creatures that had come to depend on them for their winter food descended upon us to see what we had to offer. We broke out some birdseed—which found favor as far as the linnets, blackthroat sparrows, and doves were concerned—but we put the cactus wrens, thrashers, mockingbirds, Gila woodpeckers, and flickers on hold until the following morning, when pancakes would be on the menu. We have found that flapjacks are relished by most birds, and mammals, too, and we believe that this food in moderation is not harmful to them.

At suppertime, we received exciting news on the radio. It was April 16, and Apollo 16 had blasted off that day for the moon with John Young, Charles Duke, and Thomas Mattingly on board. All was proceeding according to plan, and we, as well as the whole country, breathed sighs of relief, for the trouble-plagued mission of Apollo 13 had brought home to everyone the ever-present possibility that, in spite of the most meticulous preparations, the astronauts were ever subject to a calculated risk of disaster.

After supper, we went out into the warm desert night and there, in the west, hung the thin crescent moon, which was their goal. A good omen, perhaps, Venus hung below the lower horn, closer than I had ever seen it. I got out my 600mm lens and, setting my tripod on a picnic table, took several record shots of the phenomenon. They turned out well and, because of the circumstances, have always seemed of special significance to me. We sat outside for a long time, then, when the moon had sunk below the horizon, turned in with the pleasurable feeling that marks the end of a perfect day.

In the morning, we awoke at first light to the sounds, as Irene described it, of birds stomping on the roof. There was also a great variety of bird talk going on around the spots where we had put food out on the previous afternoon. After breakfast, we joined our feathered visitors outside and, stretched out on our lawn chairs, began to check out the species. Most of them were old friends we had met on trips past. We had little trouble in recognizing them.

Desert birds, by and large, are not your retiring kinds inhabiting the deep forest; rather, they tend to be bold and, after only a short acquaintance, become outright demanding. Around a campground such as this one, they become very tame, and, if the doors of the vehicles are left open, it is not unusual to find cactus wrens or thrashers inspecting the interiors. This delights most visitors, and the resulting handouts only encourage these feathered opportunists to repeat their intrusions from one site to the next.

We gave "our" birds no such opportunity, keeping the door and the windows tightly closed during our absences. Upon our return from touring the roads of the park, we would find tracks everywhere around the trailer and upon the picnic table. Not all of them were bird tracks; two small species of ground squirrels came in for their share of food as well. We divided our time between watching this abundance of wildlife and touring the two loop roads through the park. We found both experiences fascinating. The park and its wildlife are magnificent examples of Lower Sonoran Desert environment unmatched on this side of the border.

We Visit Ajo

I was relaxing under the awning one morning after experiencing new delights on these pasears (journeys) when I told Irene: "You know, I believe that I would enjoy living somewhere down here. I could never get tired of all it has to offer."

"I've been thinking the same thing," she said. "Why don't we go up to Ajo and see if we can find a place?"

"Oh, I don't know," I demurred. "It would be a pretty drastic change from Tucson."

"That's exactly the point; maybe it's just what we need. Let's go up there tomorrow and look around," she insisted.

Impressed by her enthusiasm, I agreed. "It won't hurt to see what the town is like at least; sure, let's go up tomorrow."

Turning the matter over in my mind for the rest of the day, I realized that Irene was right. Tucson was getting more polluted all the time, and the traffic problem was increasing by the month. As far as my night photography was concerned, I had worked over the most promising areas. A move to this area held promise of more and better opportunities in that field. Yes, a move down here might be exactly what we needed, as she said. I began to anticipate the possibilities with increasing approval.

So it happened that, on the morrow, we were on the road to Ajo, some forty miles to the north. *Ajo*, pronounced "AHH-ho," is the Spanish term for "garlic." The town is named after the Ajo Range, which, in turn, was so named for the "wild garlic which grows all over the hills in good seasons," according to Charles D. Poston, one of the early historians in Arizona. This quote evidently refers to the wildflower commonly called Ajo lily (*Hesperocallis undulata*, from Greek and Latin for "evening beauty: wavy," referring to the ripple-edged leaves). It belongs to the onion family, and its bulbs are said to have been relished by the Indians and the early Spanish explorers, who named it. The town owes its existence to the New Cornelia Copper Mine, which has been operated since 1855. Ajo had a population of approximately five thousand persons in 1972, mostly of Hispanic extraction.

Retracing our route of a few days before, we turned west when we reached the "Y" at Why. Very shortly thereafter, we picked up the plume of dirty gray smoke from the mine smelter as it drifted slowly toward the northeast. Next to come into view was the "tailings pile," its light tan color extending several miles to the north from the town. A long, flat-topped ridge to the left of the highway soon became recognizable as a man-made mountain of overburden and waste from the open pit. Past it, the huge gray steel of the mill came into view, climbing the steep slope behind it in orderly steps. To the right of the mill, the offices of the Phelps Dodge Corporation occupied the top of a small knoll, which held a commanding overlook of the town. Passing under a tramway, which

Figure 3.6
The Ajo lily, from which the Ajo Range and the town of Ajo take their names. It flowers only during those years in which the winter rain and temperatures meet its requirements. Ajo in Spanish means "garlic," a reference to the pungent flavor of this plant's bulbs.

led from the mill to the tailings pile, we circled the front of the office complex, bumped over a railroad crossing, and suddenly found ourselves in the middle of Ajo!

As in most of the Mexican towns south of the border, the cultural life of Ajo revolved around the plaza. A rectangular area of about two acres in size, it is surrounded by business establishments, several of them company owned. At a respectful distance from one end is the Catholic church, dazzling white and built in typical Mexican architectural style. At the other end of the plaza is the station of the Tucson, Cornelia, and Gila Bend Railroad, a company-owned operation. On the plaza is a bandstand. With tall trees shading the lawn and a scattering of tables and chairs about, the plaza is a pleasant place to spend an afternoon or evening. At the station end are a half-dozen ancient oleander trees, which must be a century old, judging by the trunks that are upward of eighteen inches thick and as gnarled and distorted as those of old olive trees.

Clustered around the plaza are the various sections of the town, each more or less distinct by reason of age, affluence, and architecture. The oldest part of Ajo lies between the plaza and the entrance to the mill. It consists of small company-owned houses crowded closely together and having tiny yards filled with shrubs and flowers. To the west is a long street lined with large homes, occupied mostly by company executives. On the north side of town live many of the people who do not have any connection with the mine. This was the area to which we went to investigate. We liked what we found there.

Upon inquiry, we learned that there was a real-estate agent in town, and, after following several false leads, we found her in a tiny office near the station. Millie Davenport ran it more or less as a sideline under the tutelage of the parent company in Tucson. She was helpful, but, when we told her what we had in mind, she told us that she had nothing that we would be interested in and doubted that she would have. She explained that, between company-owned houses and old-time residents, there were seldom any available properties on the market. However, she took our names and said that if anything came up, she would get in touch with us.

We left in a rather subdued mood because, actually, we had seen enough of Ajo to have moved there had the opportunity offered itself. Nevertheless, I am committed to two principles that have shaped our lives to a degree, to how great an extent is hard to say. The first of these is the law of averages, and the second is fate. Of these, fate is the least considerate, and the law of averages the most inexorable. In my experience, if one is meant to attain certain desires, they will be forthcoming; if not, all efforts will avail for naught. There is no such ambivalence in the law of averages, which is as precise as a mathematical formula, which, indeed, it is. In this case, as I told Irene: "If it had been ordained that we should live in Ajo, we would have found a place. We did not, so let's just put the whole matter out of our minds."

Quitobaquito

The following day (our last on that trip), we had reserved for Quitobaquito. This name, said to be Indian in origin, meaning "many springs,"

Figure 3.7 The oasis of Quitobaquito looking west. A favorite resting place for migrating birds, it supports a large resident population as well. The ancient cottonwood tree leaning out over the water makes an excellent platform from which to take pictures of the birds, as well as to view the aquatic life beneath the surface.

refers to an oasis in the southwestern corner of Organ Pipe Cactus National Monument. We got off to an early start. Our road followed along the north side of the international boundary line, crossing wide, sandy washes carpeted with flowering purple mat and sand verbena. The low ridges between the washes supported a sparse growth of bur sage and salt bush mixed with the ubiquitous creosote bushes. All of these plants are adapted to the deep, sandy soils on this, the outwash of several low mountain ranges to the north. To the south, only a little distance from the boundary line, flows the Sonoyta River; following the line even more closely, and separated from the United States by only a barbed wire fence, is Mexico Highway 2, which runs west to the town of San Luis on the Colorado River.

The oasis becomes visible at some distance. A spot of bright green, it lies below the end of a low chain of hills. The "many springs" of Quitobaquito issue from the base of these hills and are channeled into the reservoir. The water issues at a temperature of eighty degrees Fahrenheit, and the thick mineral incrustations on the surrounding soils attest to its origin from deep underground.

The lake thus formed is small by most standards; only some seventy feet in diameter, it would be considered a tiny pothole in Minnesota, but, in this desert setting, it represents a precious resource. It is roughly circular in outline, with low banks and a thick growth of reeds around the edges. On the south side, an ancient cottonwood tree leans out over the water at a precarious angle, its massive trunk making an ideal perch from which to view the aquatic life in the clear waters below. Close to it is a small wooden platform bridging the outlet that guides the overflow to the south toward the Sonoyta River. This surplus is not inconsiderable: the combined flow from the springs is estimated to average several hundred gallons per minute, season in and season out. It is this abundance of water in an otherwise arid environment that makes the place so extraordinary, a sparkling jewel in a massive lead setting.

History of Quitobaquito

This very uniqueness has led to a long and interesting history and prehistory. Artifacts found in profusion around the area indicate that this was an important gathering place for the Sand Papagos. These were a nomadic branch of the more numerous and sedentary Papagos of southern Arizona and northern Sonora. They wandered from these springs to the Colorado River and from the northern shores of the Gulf of California to the Castle Dome Mountains. They went wherever and whenever experience told them food was available. Their camping circles are found from around the beaches of the Gulf, where seafood was plentiful and the climate was mild in the winter months, to the edges of the dunes, where, in the springtime, bulbs of the wild onions and the succulent stems of the parasitic sand food plants were to be found. In summer and fall, they fed upon the seeds and nuts that only they knew where to find, all the time keeping on the move as these sources waxed and waned. Animal food was equally varied, consisting mostly, no doubt, of the smaller forms that were most easily captured.

Quitobaquito became known to modern civilization at an early date. It is of record that, in 1699, Father Eusebio Kino founded a mission supposedly at Santo Domingo on the Sonoyta River only a few miles south of the springs. At this mission, he established the first cattle brought into the region. It seems unlikely that an able husbandman such as Kino would not have checked out the source at Quitobaquito as a watering place for his herd, so he must be considered one of the earliest white visitors to the area. It was Kino who established the famous route from the Sonoyta area to the Gila River, later named the Camino del Diablo (Devil's Highway).

For the next hundred years, there was little activity in the area. Then, in 1830, the Mexicans drove the Sand Papagos away, and various squatters utilized the waters of the springs for irrigation. At the time of the California gold rush, Quitobaquito saw streams of prospectors heading west on the Camino del Diablo, which now went to the Colorado River by way of Tinaja Altas, a group of natural rock pools in the mountains east of Yuma.

Later in the nineteenth century, several buildings were erected by the pool, and, at the time of the Gadsden Purchase of 1854, the surveying crew camped there at Monument 172. In 1894, on a resurvey of the boundary line, Major Edgar Alexander Mearns and his assistant, Mr. Frank X. Holzner, were encamped at the springs from January 25 to February 18. At that time, Major Mearns wrote: "The settlement consisted of 3 adobe dwellings, a warehouse and a corral at the springs, and a small house at the garden. From Quitobaquito Springs, several streams flow into a shallow artificial lake, the overflow from which is conducted by an acequia [an irrigation ditch or canal] to an extensive field of wheat and white clover, bordered by fig trees and surrounded by a brush fence. This proved to be an excellent collecting ground for birds and mammals. A few ducks and waders, and one pair each of the white-bellied swallow, black phoebe and vermillion flycatcher frequented the lake."

On this, the last day of our stay, we had the area to ourselves for most of the time. From our vantage point at the base of the cottonwood tree, we could look across the pond to a place where a portion of the bank had caved in, making a shallow-bottomed cul-de-sac, ideal for birds to drink and bathe. We did not see the ducks or the waders mentioned by Major Mearns, but several coots swam busily about, clacking their metallic calls. The vermilion flycatcher was there, however, perched like a spot of flame on the tips of the swaying reeds. Many of the species we saw at that time of year were migrants, dropping in for a drink and a bath before proceeding on their northward journey. Our most memorable sight was that of a flock of western tanagers flashing their varicolored plumage as they splashed happily in the shallow area of the pond.

Along in the afternoon, a lone visitor drove up and took out a tripod and a movie camera. We relinquished our viewing point to him, and he set his tripod on the wooden bridge and put on a long-focus lens with which to shoot across the pond. As the sun began to sink in the west and the shadows lengthened, he folded up his gear and left us alone once more.

As the light faded, I began to see in my mind's eye the ghosts of the multitude that had preceded us to this remarkable oasis. First was an Indian gathering insects in the tall grass around the springs, while his mate was crushing mesquite beans in a mortar hole sunk in the rock above. Then came a black-robed friar accompanied by several Spanish soldiers who acted as his bodyguard while he evaluated the number of cattle that the springs might supply with water. Some Mexicans followed, eager to irrigate the small amount of arable land in the vicinity. Hard on their heels were the prospectors on their reckless journeys to the gold fields of California. Ignorant of the dangers presented by the waterless desert ahead, they hurried on, pursuing a vision that for many would never materialize, ending only in death. In this place camped the boundary-survey teams with their mules and wagons. Not only did they fix the boundary line, they also made collections of the flora and fauna of many species new to science. Then, in recent years, came the cattlemen with herds far beyond the capacity of the range. Finally came the visitors, including us and the man with the camera.

As I thought of the vast numbers who had used and/or abused these springs over the ages, it occurred to me that not one had ever repaid the benefits that they had received from this miraculous wonder in the desert. One might say: "How can man repay a gift of nature?" I can't answer that; I only know that it is man's instinct to wrest whatever he desires from the environment, with seldom any thought of repayment.

Crepusculars

We started back to camp at that witching hour between daylight and dark. Man should be classified as a diurnal creature, active by day and sleeping during the hours of darkness. This is the norm; anyone who departs from this pattern by necessities of work or by choice is viewed with solicitude. This is just not the ideal way for a person to have to live, is the thought. Creatures of the desert are somewhat more selective than humans in the way they adapt to the demands of the environment. Likening the desert to a factory that operates twenty-four hours a day, we discover that there is a day shift, a night shift, and, between them, a third, which corresponds to a swing shift. Creatures active by day are known as "diurnal"; those by night, "nocturnal"; and the swing shift is a smaller group known as crepuscular (from the Latin for "twilight"). It draws its numbers partly from the other two shifts, some coming in early and some working late to pick up some overtime. These latter were conspicuous on this evening.

The gilded flickers and the Gila woodpeckers were taking their usual leisurely way to bed. Having started life in nests in the saguaros, it seems appropriate that, as adults, they should choose to sleep in old nest holes in the massive trunks. They make quite a performance out of this matter. It starts with the bird taking up a perch on the tip of one of the various stems of the saguaro. There it surveys the area minutely, occasionally calling to others of its kind in the neighborhood. After ten minutes of this, it seems to believe that all is safe, and it works its way to the nesting hole that will serve as its bedroom. There it hangs for a while, looking alternately into the hole and then around the area with jerky movements of its head. Eventually, it enters the hole, from which still come muffled cries, then sticks out its head, surveying the area once more before finally disappearing for the night.

While this is going on, another bird of the saguaro forest is making preparations to get up and go to work. This is the tiny elf owl, which sleeps through the day and nests in the abandoned woodpecker nests in

Figure 3.8
The Gila woodpecker is responsible for drilling most of the holes in the saguaro trunks. It uses them for sleeping purposes, as well as nesting sites. When the woodpeckers abandon them, other species of birds, bats, and bees move in.

the giant cactus. It is a true nocturnal, spending its nights hunting the scorpions, centipedes, and moths that share the darkness with it. It will appear at the entrance of its nest hole at sundown and, like the wood-peckers, will sit there for some time surveying the surroundings as the darkness deepens.

As we proceeded toward camp on the sandy road, a hardly seen shape skittered across the way and headed for a barrel cactus. Stopping the car, we followed its course and found a horned lizard, which had taken up a position by an anthill at the base of the plant. It was difficult to see, as its color matched almost exactly the sandy terrain on which it lived. Ants are one of the favorite foods of this lizard, which is commonly known as the horned toad, and this was an ideal situation for this one. An unending supply of them issued from the nest and increased as the colony became aware of this attack upon their numbers. The horned liz-ard deliberately snapped them up one by one with flicks of the tongue

Figure 3.9
The horned lizard, commonly known as the horned toad, lives principally on ants. This species, called the regal horned toad because of its prominent "crown of horns," prefers to live in the sandy portions of the Sonoran Desert.

too fast for the eye to register. The enraged ants swarmed over the surface of this enemy, but its scaly armor was proof against their bites, any one of which would have given me serious trouble, as I have learned to my sorrow. We left the lizard there, knowing that, as darkness fell and it had eaten its fill, it would return across the road to its chosen sandbank and work its way down into the soft warm sand, there to sleep until the sun signaled the arrival of another day.

Now it was almost completely dark, but the headlights picked up several more creatures of the twilight zone. These were tarantulas, the big black spiders of the western desert. They are slow-moving creatures that hold their bodies well off the ground as they walk deliberately along, as though they were up on eight stilts. Actually, they are nocturnal animals, but they are out so often in late afternoon that they fit the classification of being crepuscular as well. Their purpose in these late afternoon ramblings is unclear. They may be hunting prey or, which seems more likely, searching for a mate.

The coyotes were serenading the departure of the day when we reached our campsite, and Venus was already visible in the western sky. The moon was overhead, and much more robust than the thin crescent that had greeted us on the night of April 16. The astronauts had arrived, performed their experiments, and were on their way back. They had had a momentous journey, and, in a less important way, so had we. It seems

Figure 3.10
Tarantula spiders are often seen on the sandy roads in late afternoon and early evening during the summer months. Despite their forbidding appearance, they are not aggressive creatures and should be left alone to continue their quest for who knows what.

paradoxical that we race to explore and understand other worlds when we really don't begin to know our own. This is not to denigrate space exploration—far from it! Nevertheless, our blue planet is unique in this solar system, and it behooves us to cherish and protect its values by word and deed.

Sonoran Summer

Our return to Tucson was in marked contrast to our trip down to Organ Pipe. In the mere ten days that had elapsed, the heavy hand of a Sonoran summer had been laid upon the land. A haze distorted the outlines of the mountains against the sky. On the road ahead, illusionary pools of water appeared and then disappeared as we approached them. The lacy crowns of flowers that had graced the trees along the washes now lay in windrows of faded yellow and lavender petals at their feet, where the careless winds had drifted them. The verdant green of the grasses on the creosote plains had returned to the parched brown of summer. The brilliant patchwork of annual flowers that had delighted us then was now no more; its plants withered and dry, but with their mission of producing seed for future seasons fulfilled. The onset of heat and aridity had affected the perennials as well. Many of them were shedding some of the leaves they had too optimistically produced during the time of plenty. Only the saguaros seemed unaffected by the onset of summer. Fat and distended with the water they had stored away, every arm wore a crown of buds. The white-wing doves were already gathering in anticipation of the nectar that would soon be available.

Part IV

Life in Ajo

Quijotoa Trading Post

We remained in Tucson through the long, hot days of midsummer. The city sweltered under a filthy blanket of brownish haze, while, high above it, great white clouds drifted slowly northward, never deigning to bestow one drop of rain upon the suffering land. Day followed day with a deadly monotony until, one afternoon, a call from Ajo raised us out of the doldrums.

It was from Millie Davenport, the real-estate agent whom we had contacted on our Organ Pipe Cactus National Monument trip in April.

"Are you still in the market for a place in Ajo?" she inquired.

"Affirmative!" was our answer.

"I think I have a property you would like," she said. "Would you be able to come down and see it?"

"We'll be down tomorrow, if that's all right?"

"That would be fine."

"We'll see you about one o'clock then, at your office?"

"I'll be waiting," she promised.

We set off on the following morning with a feeling of anticipation. It was hot; hot as only the desert can be on a July day. The air conditioner hummed full on, while, up ahead on the pavement, the usual shimmering mirage of water retreated before us. Sixty miles out, we stopped briefly for a cold drink at the general store in Sells, the headquarters of the sprawling Papago Reservation. Another twenty miles and we dropped into the Quijotoa Trading Post for a look at their stock of the distinctive baskets fashioned by the Papagos. These are made of split yucca leaves, decorated by black designs made from fibers from the devil's-claw plant.

These trading posts, scattered about the reservation, are always fascinating to visit. Their stocks consist of items seldom found in the urban markets but indispensable to the primitive way of life still practiced in the isolated settlements. Hard by the refrigerator and its adjacent cases of carbonated drinks are coils of rope, tools, kegs of nails, horseshoes, and all of the paraphernalia associated with the raising of range cattle. Clothing on racks and piled on the counters in confusing array contrasts with the more orderly displays of jewelry, watches, transistor radios, and cosmetics kept in locked glass cases as a precautionary measure. Bolts of cloth, notions, hats, and shoes are to be found in one section for the convenience of those who cannot get to Tucson or Ajo for these items. In the grocery division, the rich aroma of bulk beans, rice, cornmeal, cheese, and chilies attests to the Mexican influence on these desert peoples. Dried and canned fruits, as well as various vegetables never cultivated in the arid conditions of this land, offer exotic supplements to an otherwise spartan diet. Over all hangs the heavy odor from the many items that meet the needs of the past and provide the luxuries of this electronic age to several generations of Papagos.

We would have loved to tarry a while and watch the action as customers shopped in the deliberate way that is traditional with most Indian tribes, but we still had many miles to go. So, after purchasing several baskets, we threaded our way between the pickups parked in front of the building and continued on our way.

Only a mile or so beyond Quijotoa, we passed the settlement of Covered Wells. A scattering of small adobe buildings, most with ramadas, surrounded a small Catholic mission. Due, no doubt, to the heat, no one was visible outside; probably all were indulging in the customary siesta. Would that we all could do the same in the desert Southwest.

We now entered upon the wide, gently sloping plains in the southwestern portion of the reservation. Occasionally, a primitive road would turn off, marked with a weathered sign with lettering that was barely legible. Pisinimo—11 miles, the first one read. Much later, we went to Pisinimo (Bear's Ears) and found that it, too, was a little settlement like Covered Wells, its tiny houses gathered around a mission like baby quail around a mother hen. It had one outstanding building, however: a large, circular structure built in the Papago way, with tall mesquite posts supporting a roof of saguaro ribs and ocotillo branches over walls of interlaced ocotillo branches and sacaton grass. The Father told us that the chief function of this building was to contain the annual Deer Dance, and, if we were interested, he would advise us as to the time of the next performance.

Nearing the western boundary of the reservation, we came to a crossroads. Here a miscellany of dilapidated signs proclaimed that to the north, at varying distances, might be found Hickiwan, Vaya Chin, and Ventana, while to the south Gu Vo, Pia Oik, and Menager Dam were responsible for some thirty miles of roadway. With the exception of the two at the ends of the roads, these names meant nothing to us. Ventana was near Ventana Cave, an important archaeological site, and Menager Dam impounded an impressive body of water, a rare sight in this land of little rain.

Leaving the reservation, we rounded the south end of a low ridge of black basalt covered with paloverde trees and occasional organ-pipe cactuses, then passed the entrance of Coyote Howls Campground. It might be classed as a suburb of the town of Why.

The campground, like Topsy, just "growed." First, a few winter visitors squatted on the site with their trailers. The word spread, and, in only a few seasons, the winter population had increased to the point that it became necessary to elect officers and draw up a simple charter to administer the area. Coyote Howls is an appropriate name, inasmuch as it parallels the Indian way of identifying a given area.

The ever-present plume of smoke at Ajo was now in sight, and, fifteen minutes later, we crossed the railroad tracks and pulled up in front of the cafe across from the plaza. Mexican food is the specialty of every eating place in Ajo; since it is risky to order anything else, we were properly "fired up" when we presented ourselves at Millie's tiny office. She greeted us enthusiastically and proposed that we go at once to view the property. Locking the office, we headed toward the northeast section of town, the area that had impressed us the most favorably when we had been in Ajo that spring. The property was located a block up from the main highway going north from town.

We parked in front of a two-bedroom bungalow with a huge bougainvillea vine hiding much of the front of the house. The lot was huge and accommodated two smaller dwellings behind the main house. It sloped enough to ensure good drainage, and, across the street, a deep ravine ensured that flooding would be no problem. Inspecting the houses, we found them to be well suited to our needs. The main house was not large but had two bedrooms and boasted two baths. Of the two smaller houses, one was an ideal guest house, and the other, with some alterations, would give Irene a studio, and me a darkroom and a library. All in all, it seemed that this would be an ideal opportunity for us to escape from Tucson and live in the desert.

"The mills of the Gods grind slowly," but no more so than the wheels of the realty machinery. Nevertheless, the transactions went forward smoothly enough, and, by late summer, our belongings had been transferred and we were ensconced in our new home. When the dust had settled, we began to evaluate our new surroundings and assess our significance in the scale of this new environment.

Ours was a corner lot facing east and south. Across the street, on the east side, we had no neighbors, and, to the south, the aforementioned arroyo precluded any development. Across the fence to the north side were our good neighbors, the Martinezes. Francisco was an elderly gentleman of my own age, retired from work in the mine. He had been born and reared in Sonora, Mexico, and we spent many an hour reminiscing about our younger days. Across the alley in the rear of the property lived another retiree who was equally companionable.

From our vantage point on the rising ground west of the highway, we could look across the valley to the great tan tailings dump spawned by the mine mill. A hundred feet or more in depth, it must have covered a square mile in area. Along our edge ran the track upon which, usually in the evening, a small locomotive hauled out the molten slag from the smelter. This intensely hot liquid was contained in great ladles mounted on cars and poured out over the embankment, where it cascaded down in fiery red streams to collect along the base of the dump. There it settled in glowing pools, slowly darkening as it cooled until it solidified into a vitreous material as hard as stone and as black as coal. This pouring of the slag is an impressive sight somewhat akin, in a small way, to the outpouring of lava from a volcano but, in this case, under human control.

The smoke from the smelter pours out twenty-fours hours a day from two tall stacks and usually floats away to the northeast, driven by the prevailing southwest wind. It poses no problem to the local population except on those days of calm when an inversion layer forces the sulfurous fumes down to ground level. Then it behooves one to stay indoors until the winds return and clear the area. This smelter smoke, when combined with the surrounding air, produces a weak solution of sulfuric acid, which is extremely irritating to breathe and destructive to the finish of automobiles.

The mine from which this incredible amount of tailings, slag, and smoke issues is in the top of a mountain on the outskirts of Ajo. Surface workings date back to Spanish days, but it was not until early in the twentieth century that it was developed into an open-pit operation by the Phelps Dodge Corporation. Eventually, it became a huge hole six thousand feet long, five thousand feet wide, and eight hundred feet deep. It is obvious that a company with such a large operation has almost total control over a town with a population of only seven thousand or so. These people don't owe their soul to the company store, as the song goes; however, there is a company store, and many of the miners trade there.

The water system is controlled by the company. The wells, six miles from town, are six hundred feet deep in a lava formation, and the water is hot when brought to the surface. Transported through a surface pipe, it can increase in temperature on the way to town. In summer, the ground temperature frequently reaches 160 degrees Fahrenheit or more. During the first summer, we learned to do as the natives do—that is, to use the cold-water tap for all uses requiring hot water, and to turn the heat off under the hot-water tank and bathe and shower with that water relatively cool at air temperatures only slightly more than a hundred degrees Fahrenheit.

There were other annoyances as well, but none of them serious enough to dim our interest in the polyglot society of Ajo. It was an unusual mix of Hispanics, Indians, and Anglos, each with their distinctive ways. The Hispanics, whom I prefer to call Mexicans—I see nothing derogatory with the term—are a deeply religious people who adhere to many of the customs practiced below the border. They celebrate the religious holidays of the Catholic Church, and Cinco de Mayo, and Mexican Independence Day (September 15) with equal fervor. The Indians maintain an inscrutable aloofness until one gains their friendship, but then a glimpse of their rich and fascinating culture is revealed.

The Anglos were divided among mine officials, "old-timers," and newcomers of our ilk. The company people formed the nucleus of an upper crust in the social order, leading to the establishment of a country club with a primitive golf course. It is admittedly a golf course, even granted that one might have to chase a sidewinder or two off the sandy greens during an early morning round. The old-timers viewed this refinement with disdain, and most of the newcomers did not have the money, nor were they invited, to join this exclusive group.

Interesting as this potpourri of cultures might be, we had not moved to Ajo to be absorbed into its society, so, as soon as necessary changes to our new property had been made, I began to explore the geography of the surrounding desert. Ajo, plus its neighboring settlements of Childs and Why, is completely surrounded by federal lands of one kind or another. To the east lies the great expanse of the Papago Reservation. On the south, Organ Pipe Cactus National Monument extends to the international boundary line. To the north, the Goldwater Air Force Bombing Range controls the area from Ajo to Gila Bend, thence west along Interstate 8 almost to Yuma and south to the border. To the west of Ajo, and contained within the bombing range, is the Cabeza Prieta National Wildlife Refuge.

This vast composite of federal lands lies like a great wedge in southwestern Arizona. The eastern, and widest, portion borders on the Baboquivari Range in the east. The southern edge is bounded by the international boundary, which runs northwest. The northern leg follows close to Interstate 8 in a southwesterly direction until it meets the southern leg. The distance from east to west is approximately 150 miles.

Scattered about over this great expanse are a considerable number of short, low, mountain ranges, some granitic and some volcanic in origin. Most are precipitous, their flanks cut by deep arroyos. None is high enough to support any but growth typical of the Lower Sonoran Zone. The foothill paloverde is the most common tree on their steep sides; in the western portion of the tract, occasional elephant trees (*Bursera* sp.) are found. Mesquites, blue paloverdes, and ironwood trees are common along all of the washes, and, in the western portion, smoke trees are to be found. On the open plains, the lowly creosote bush grows everywhere, spaced according to the availability or scarcity of water.

For the plants and animals of this great wedge of natural history, there are no boundary lines. For humans, however, there are such limits and areas set aside for specific purposes. They all concern restrictions on travel and visitor activities of various kinds, but, upon request, permits may be obtained. The United States Air Force is the most restrictive, with good reason, as anyone who has witnessed the awesome bombing runs by attack planes from Phoenix and Tucson will attest.

It did not take long for me to learn when and where I might be allowed to enter these areas, but, notwithstanding this great reservoir of wildlife surrounding Ajo, I found all of the opportunities for photographic subjects close at hand.

I took this opportunity to pursue my study of what went on in the desert at night. This was a matter that had intrigued me ever since my early days at Saguaro National Monument, but one that was inconvenient to pursue in the urban conditions around Tucson. Here there was little activity outside of town, and I was seldom disturbed on my nightly rounds.

I began by laying out two loop routes: one paved and north of town, and the other a graded dirt road that circled the open-pit mine. Each was about fifteen miles in circumference, and traffic, as a rule, was light, especially in the late hours of the evening. At first, the sheriff's patrol would stop and question me as to what I was doing, but they soon accepted me as being harmless and, when they passed, would flick their lights in greeting.

Creatures of the Night

Observing the ecology of the roadway is not as simple as it might appear. First to consider is the human factor. Meeting a car is no great problem, merely a matter of dimming the lights and staying close to the shoulder on your side of the road. It is the car that catches up with you that presents the danger. It is best to pull entirely off the road and let it go by.

When I first undertook to cruise the roads in a search for small animals, it seemed reasonable that, on a dark night with the bright lights on, I should be able to proceed at a slow speed of, say, fifteen miles per hour. Such was not the case, however; a little experience taught me that a rate of four to five miles per hour was much more productive. This can vary, though; small creatures are much more easily seen on dark pavement than on dirt roads, where their protective coloration renders them almost invisible unless they move.

The abundance of animals on the roadways during the hours of darkness may seem unusual but, actually, these are the times when many desert creatures are abroad going about their business of hunting, perhaps for prey, perhaps for each other. Searching for a mate is a necessity that may be best accomplished at night, when it is safest to be about. To all of these creatures, the roadways are just another of the varied kinds of terrain on the desert in which they live. So it is that, when the sun has gone down and the heat radiates to the sky, the animals emerge from burrows, from crevices, from all of the hidden places where they have escaped from the glare of day, and some of them happen to cross the road.

Careening down the roads at the dizzy pace of five miles per hour, I was to see much, and learn much, about the animals that are almost never seen by more speedy drivers. They may catch a fleeting glimpse of a coyote or a fox momentarily caught in the headlight beam, or perhaps the reflections from the eyes of a deer along the shoulder, but they miss all of the tiny creatures at close hand while their eyes are focused on the forward limits of their headlights' penetration. I was to see tarantulas delicately manipulating their eight black legs in perfect coordination as they wandered slowly along. This contrasted to the haste of the giant centipedes, which rippled along with rhythmic convolutions of their supposed fifty pairs. The big hairy scorpions made better time, holding their pincers up out of the way as they hurried along. The solpugids (commonly called "sun spiders"), were the speedsters of the arachnids, drifting across through the light like windblown leaves.

Reptiles, being cold blooded, were not out for about half of the year. In summer, especially during the high humidities of the monsoon season, I might see several in a night. Rattlesnakes were the most numerous, consisting of sidewinders, western diamondbacks, and Mojaves, in that order; while the nonvenomous species were mostly gopher snakes and racers, which, it seemed to me, were chiefly diurnal and were abroad after dark only on those nights after or during a rain. I saw no lizards on these rounds, although I have on several occasions encountered Gila monsters on off-road situations at night.

Rodents, pale in color to match the soils of their environment, showed up especially well against the black asphalt of the surfaced roadway. They were most numerous in the area encircled by the lower loop, which was a plain covered with creosote bushes and bur sage. They consisted of two classes recognizable by their ways of running. The kangaroo rats, of which there were two species, large and small, bounced across the road with a series of leaps, while the smaller mice moved like children's toys pulled by a string.

It was rare to see a cottontail or jackrabbit on these forays. Evidently, the vegetation was unsuitable for them. Kit foxes and coyotes were common, however, as one might expect from the numbers of rodents.

Occasionally, I met with a screech owl on the roadway dining on a scorpion or a centipede. Strange as it might seem, I encountered nighthawks, too, their eyes glowing like jewels in the headlights. These unusual birds would play a game with me, waiting until the car was almost upon them and then fluttering up and away, landing upon the road some distance ahead to repeat the exercise. I would return home in the wee hours of the morning with red eyes, too. However, there was much to be learned on these rounds.

It soon became clear that animals are part of an ecosystem that dictates what they do, how they do it, and when. This once held true throughout the twenty-four-hour day, but we humans have injected ourselves into this complex so that, during the daylight hours, wherever we are present, normal activities are not possible. However, our disruptive pressures on the ecosystem are greatly lessened at night when we are indoors.

Then, on the darkened desert, activity waxes and wanes in response to all of the obvious, as well as the many unknown, conditions imposed by this demanding environment. There are many of them, a bewildering array of variables, some of them ranging over the full gamut of favorable to unfavorable in the length of a single night. One of these is moonlight.

You might think that the moon is like the sun of the night, providing in a limited way some of the beneficial services of that blazing star. Often the opposite is true. Some animals of the night are adapted to darkness, not that semidarkness under a full moon, when, on a clear night, you can read a newspaper by its light. Under these conditions, rodents are reluctant to leave the protection of their burrows, and their predators mark time until conditions improve.

The moon rises approximately fifty-one minutes later every twenty-four hours, so, in a few days, it rises well after dark has fallen. At the same time, it diminishes in light, becoming a quarter moon, then a crescent moon, and, finally, the dark of the moon occurs. As the light wanes, a mammal's activity increases until it is carried on under starshine, which is adequate enough for creatures used to living in the total darkness of a burrow.

Wind is another variable that inhibits animal activity in proportion to its force. On those infrequent nights when a gale sweeps across the land, it "ain't fitten for man nor beast" to be out. The rustle of leaves being swept across the ground and the thrashing of bushes under the blast are totally distracting to predators and prey alike. On the other hand, a light movement of air after a hot day is very pleasant and seems not to disturb the usual activities of the animals.

Whereas bright moonlight and wind are negative factors on animal activity, summer rain and humidity are positive in their effect. Although it may be August on the calendar, it is spring on the desert for flora and fauna alike. The unaccustomed humidity of this season brings out most creatures during the nights. Its effects are noticeable on the human species as well. On those cool evenings, when the odor of wet creosote leaves proclaim that the rains have arrived, desert people get into their cars and drive around just to enjoy.

The Kit Foxes

With the close of the monsoon season and the shortening of the days as fall came on, it was time to plan some nighttime photography. I had noticed on the lower loop that sometimes I saw a kit fox crossing the road in the vicinity of the rodeo grounds. This was appropriate because of the rodents attracted by the grain spilled around the horse stalls. Scorpions and centipedes also frequent the nooks and crannies under the straw that collects in those places. These small creatures are all relished by this little carnivore, which preys upon large insects as well. It is this wide diversity of food that enables the foxes to exist in some of the most inhospitable areas of the desert. These are tiny creatures, actually no larger than a house cat, a full-grown individual weighing no more than five pounds. I was to find that they are not at all suspicious, coming readily to any bait that their keen sense of smell locates.

The site I chose for this photography was a place across from a turnout along the road where I could sit in the car and observe a bait station at a distance of about thirty feet. There, a small gully about three feet deep and four feet wide ran parallel with the car. By chance, there were also several creosote bushes, part of a number scattered farther back upon the plain. Among them grew the usual low shrubs of bur sage. The summer grasses were already parched by the scorching heat of fall. Issuing through the grass were trails leading to a few kangaroo-rat mounds. The soil was typical alluvium of a fine texture and tan in color.

With some improvisation, I found that I could mount my lights in the tops of two creosote bushes and set my cameras up on my side of the gully. I placed some bait in an abandoned burrow that afternoon, and, when I passed the site several hours after dark, it was gone. Fresh scats and claw scratches near the burrow indicated that the visitor had "claimed" the area as his own.

It is characteristic of the dog family to "mark" territory boundaries and possessions by leaving scats, urine posts, and scratch marks in strategic places. This not only lays claim to these spots but, by scent, serves to identify the owner to others of his kind. Any unusual or prominent object in their areas is likely to have been marked in this way by these little foxes. Sometimes this leads to situations amusing or perhaps aggravating as the case might be.

In Organ Pipe Cactus National Monument, rain gauges are placed in various places out in the field. They are built to satisfy the requirements posed by the isolated desert environment. The gauge itself resembles a 2.5-foot length of stovepipe closed at the bottom. A funnel is set into the upper end. The gauge stands in an upright position and is surrounded by a square wooden housing anchored so that it cannot be tipped over by the wind. A thick film of oil in the bottom rises above any rainwater that collects and prevents its evaporation. A graduated measuring stick thrust down through the funnel to the bottom will give an accurate reading of the amount of precipitation that might have occurred since the last measurement. The presence of this strange contrivance on an otherwise flat creosote plain attracted the attention of a kit fox that claimed the territory. Not content with marking the area about the rain gauge with urine and scratchings, it contrived to leap to the top of the device and deposit its droppings through the funnel, which, of course, destroyed the accuracy of the gauge completely.

Hoping to set up a time frame for the fox's arrival, I dropped off more bait at the same time for a few nights. When I judged that a time had been established, I pulled over into the turnoff and sat quietly in the car with my binoculars trained upon the bait station. I did not have long to wait. Before the cooling engine had ceased to snap and crackle, I saw movements materialize at the bait station and, to my delight, saw not the one that I had expected but two of the little desert waifs. They were evidently a pair, for they did not quarrel over the food but shared it amicably. They stayed no longer than necessary to bolt every scrap and then vanished as suddenly as they had appeared.

It seemed that the time had arrived to shed some light on the situation, so, on the following evening, I hung a light with a red filter on the creosote bush above the site. It is said that mammals are not able to see red light, but my experience does not bear this out. This light was connected to the car's system by a long extension cord and its intensity controlled by a rheostat. On this night, the pair seemed to be apprehensive at first under the glow, but they soon got used to it and, on succeeding evenings, paid no more attention to it. At this stage, they began to accept my presence, and I gradually began to spend less time cruising the loop drives and devoted more attention to these fascinating animals.

Now they would come in under full light and eat my offerings leisurely with little evidence of being afraid. I encouraged them to stay longer by feeding small amounts and scattering it about so that they had to search the entire circle under the light. When it was gone, I would go out and replenish the supply. They would retreat beyond the lighted area until I had returned to the car, and then they would rush back to see what goodies I might have left them. Our relationship became a familiar routine of bait and watch with no surprises until, one night, a third fox entered our little circle.

This was, indeed, a surprise! The new arrival was a male, which I judged to be about a year old. The pair would not allow him to share in the bait but would drive him away to a point beyond the light, where he would gaze wistfully while they consumed every scrap of the food. If either of the pair approached him, he would lie down in the submissive attitude, and, while he was in this posture, they would not attack him.

This strange relationship puzzled me for some time until one night, when the pair had eaten their fill, the old male picked up a morsel and carried it over to the stranger. This unwonted act of generosity led me to conclude that this young fox was one of the pair's last year's litter. Evidently, the instinct of providing for the young had not entirely faded in the parent over the passage of time. He did not let this filial emotion get out of hand, however. He continued to share a small scrap or two with the youngster, but only at those times when he had fully satisfied himself first.

I worked with this trio with varying persistence all winter. I say "worked," although, actually, it was a most rewarding experience to be associated with these little animals, and, since I observed them at close quarters through binoculars, I was able to learn much about their physical structure and movements. I had long ago discarded the red filter over the light, and, under the harsh glare of the white rays, every detail stood out.

By December, all three were in full winter pelage. This is buff gray, becoming somewhat darker on the back and lighter underneath. The tail is bushy and terminates with a black tip. The legs are stout and end in quite large feet. The toes are armed with strong claws and bear hairs between them. The ears are very large for such a small animal and stand upright. The insides are lined with long, soft hairs. The eyes are exceptionally large as befits a creature that is as nocturnal as these. On either side of the nose is a dark spot, from which rise a number of long, stiff whiskers.

The life history of these little foxes has been well documented. Males usually mate with a single female but may mate with several, though this is rare. Normally, a den is prepared by both parents. It consists of a burrow dug in soft soil. It may be at the base of a tree or a shrub but sometimes is out in the open. Often, burrows dug by badgers or kangaroo rats are enlarged to accommodate the new family. The young are born in the spring and may number anywhere from four to seven. In a month, they have developed to the point that they emerge and play around the entrance of the den. Now the parents bring them solid food, and, gradually, the youngsters expand their activities and begin to hunt

Figure 4.1
The male of the kit-fox pair at the rodeo grounds.

A: He is in his winter coat, with warm, fluffy fur and bushy tail.

B: During summer's heat, the winter coat is shed, and, thus stripped down, the large ears and eyes become striking, indeed.

on their own. At six months, they are of adult size, the family breaks up, and each individual goes its solitary way until the next breeding season occurs.

During those nights at the bait station, I learned something of kit-fox language. Their voices are high and small, commensurate with their size. They range from a shrill note, almost a whistle, to the low growl with which they warn off a contender. A bark is conversational and is used to call to one another. Any unexplained or unexpected sound a little distance away calls for an alert stance, with ears pricked up, and a warning "wuff" repeated several times. On the few occasions when an interloper has trespassed and attempted to take over, the medley of growls, screams, and yelps that ensues is truly amazing, coming from such tiny antagonists. Perhaps the most remarkable sound they make somewhat resembles a cat's purr. It seemed to me that this was "sweet talk" between the mated pair.

Altogether, my experiences with this trio were so rewarding that I continued to meet with them long after I had obtained all of the photographs I had planned originally and more. Eventually, I weaned myself away by gradually cutting down on the bait supply and missing my evening trysts with them. I doubt that they missed me, but I think of them affectionately whenever I look through the photographs I took so long ago across from the rodeo grounds. I was to encounter several other kit foxes during the time we spent in Ajo, but this first acquaintance remains like a first love, a unique privilege to be cherished forever.

Kangaroo Rats

Moving on, it seemed entirely appropriate that I should choose to work with one of the species associated with these little predators. Probably the most important of these, and certainly the most fascinating, would be the kangaroo rat.

My first field experience with kangaroo rats was gained one moonlit evening on the western edge of the Imperial Valley desert in southern California. My partner, Roy Miller, and I had spent a bitterly cold winter's day searching for a road that was rumored to follow a railroad grade down Carrizo Gorge on the east side of the Coastal Range. It transpired that there never had been such a road down the narrow and precipitous defile. Having established that no road existed, we were mainly concerned to get down into the desert and find shelter from the gale in some small canyon.

As we descended on the highway, we saw ballooning clouds of dust and wind-driven sand looming high above the valley. At the foot of the grade, we turned off the highway into the teeth of the wind and headed cross-country for a low range of mud hills dimly seen through the airborne sand. Turning into the first canyon we came to, we found the relief that we had hoped for. Driving up the wash for a short distance, we located a level place in which to set up camp.

While Roy busied himself building a fire, I arranged our bed. This was before the day of air mattresses and sleeping bags. Our bedding consisted of a few blankets and a thin mattress, which we rolled and tied on top of the car. This gave our outfit a distinctly *Grapes of Wrath* appearance as we rolled down the highway, but it served us very well in the absence of more sophisticated gear. While we were doing this, the sun went down, and, with sunset, as sometimes happens, the wind died completely. The calm that followed, plus a quarter moon high overhead, made a happy conclusion to what had been a very trying day.

After supper, as we sat at the fire enjoying a final cup of coffee, we heard rustlings in the dry leaves under the nearby bushes. Turning a flashlight toward the sounds, we found that they were caused by two of the large kangaroo rats *(Dipodomys deserti)*. Lacking any more suitable food, we tossed them some bread crusts. These they pounced upon and carried away, then returned for more. In no time, they were running around our feet searching for such small offerings as we could spare.

Eventually, we tired of this game and prepared for bed. As we turned in, I told Roy: "I'll bet we have some bedfellows tonight." How true this turned out to be. I had hardly gotten settled when a soft furry object tried to squeeze between my neck and the pillow. Roy was having the same trouble. We agreed that, if we were going to be kept awake, we might as well get some pictures of our tormentors. So, getting up, Roy took out his Speed Graphic and some flashbulbs, and we took a series of pictures. One of the best was a close-up of a kangaroo rat standing on its hind legs in one of my hands while reaching for a tidbit held between the forefinger and thumb of the other. Finally, they, too, tired of the game and went away and left us alone. The memory of that incident whetted my desire to renew acquaintances with these remarkable creatures.

The scientific name of the genus is as apt as the common name—*Dipodomys* (two-footed mouse). As it hops about gathering food or dashes with long leaps toward a burrow, the animal seems, indeed, to have but the two long, muscular hind legs. Closer inspection will reveal that there are two front legs, which are held close to the body at most times but are extremely useful in harvesting the seeds that are the animal's chief diet and in digging the tunnels in the soft soils of the valley floor where they live.

Often this is some of the most barren terrain in the desert. In the Ajo area, it consists of deep alluvial soils, often in conjunction with stabilized sand dunes, supporting scanty covers of shrubs mingled with occasional scatterings of hardy perennial and annual grasses. Amid this desolation, beset by predators of several kinds, the kangaroo rats lead successful, if not entirely pleasant, lives. This is only possible because, over time, they have become so extraordinarily well adapted to survive.

Adaptations

First of the requirements that this small mammal must fulfill is that of existing with a minimum of moisture. The kangaroo rat actually exceeds this demand, for it can exist for long periods without any free water at all. It does this by employing a metabolic process, still not fully understood, whereby it manufactures its necessary moisture from the dry seeds that form its diet. Although this is but a small amount, it conserves this meager supply by living underground through the daylight hours, when the surface humidity is low; by plugging the entrances to its tunnels with earth, so that whatever moisture is within is retained; and by several physiological oddities designed to retain its body moisture.

Behind its tiny nose are several intricate chambers that gather and return some of the moisture that would otherwise be lost through respiration. The kidneys, likewise, recycle the fluids within the body, excreting crystals instead of liquid urine. And finally, these little creatures do

Figure 4.2
Among the adaptations of this remarkable animal, the kangaroo rat, are the large eyes set in both sides of the head, the tiny nasal passages (which conserve moisture), the long whiskers (which help guide its movements in the dark tunnels), and the notches in the ears (which enable them to be folded flat against the head to hold out dust and dirt).

not perspire, another advantage in their ability to survive in a waterless environment.

Another most important requirement for the kangaroo rat is that it be able to maintain its numbers despite predation. This is not easy, given the twofold function of rodents in nature's scheme: to assist in keeping down plant life that, without herbivores, could in some cases get out of control; and to convert this plant food into red meat for the nourishment of carnivores. In this latter role, the kangaroo rats are what is called a "keystone" species—that is, their importance in this game of supply and demand is such that it affects to an important degree the whole ecosystem of the area in which they live. This influence, actually the so-called balance of nature, is reduced to its simplest terms in the desert, where the animal population prospers or diminishes in direct response to the relative abundance or shortage of plant food.

The kangaroo rat, although one of the prime targets of several predators, is well able in most areas to maintain its numbers in spite of their inroads. In its underground labyrinth, it is safe from all but snakes or possibly a roving badger. When it is out gathering food, its large eyes and keen ears warn of approaching danger and its powerful legs carry it in great leaps to the haven of the burrow. Its long tail, acting as a rudder, has a white tip that, bobbing about, distracts the pursuer's attention and probably aids in escape.

There is one hazard they cannot easily survive. That is a long drought that could eliminate the seasonal seed plants that furnish their principal food. Even a limited food supply will result in a diminution of their numbers. These busy little gleaners have been known to so completely harvest the seeds of their annual grasses that hardly any are left to provide plants for the following year. If this occurs, a whole colony can be reduced to but a few survivors.

All of this I knew from reading some of the great amount of research done on these interesting little rodents. I was now in hope of gaining a more intimate knowledge of their way of life. This was not hard to arrange. The wide valley in which Ajo is situated is bisected by a dry (at most times) wash, known locally as Ten Mile Wash. It is bordered by a straggling growth of desert trees: mesquites, blue paloverdes, desert willows, and hackberries. North of the wash, the plain ascends gradually for a distance of perhaps three miles to the base of some low, lava hills known as the Crater Range. At this time, the plain was sparsely covered with bur sage and other low-growing shrubs interspersed with the ever-present creosote bush. The usual small mats of annual grasses were present, but what was most important was a carpet of a *Plantago* species known as Indian wheat. That this is one of their favorite foods was evident from their numerous mounds scattered over the plain.

Traces of an old road led toward the distant hills, but it was evident that the area had lain undisturbed for a long time. This suited my purpose admirably, for I wanted to set up my lights and work under them uninterrupted by curious passersby. My equipment for this project was to consist of an overhead boom light and three strobe units, all powered by 12-volt automobile batteries through an inverter, which stepped the current up to 110 volts AC. This, together with the cameras, tripods, and the ever-necessary three-legged stool, took a considerable amount of time and work to unload and to reload into the car each evening. I was careful, therefore, to select a mound not too far from the road.

Usually, the mounds are not very close together. These animals are not, by any means, gregarious; in fact, they lead solitary lives for most of the time. They are territorial and fiercely defend the area needed to support themselves. This can be quite large, up to an acre in some cases, but in this instance, due to the abundance of food plants, the mounds were not so widely spaced. I was not long in finding one that suited my needs perfectly.

These homes of *D. deserti*, one of the largest kangaroo rats, are spacious in proportion. They are circular in form and range from six feet to as much as ten feet in diameter and up to eighteen inches in height at the center. A number of entrances around the perimeter, and usually several up on the mound, give access to the underground labyrinth within. These entrances are large, up to eight inches in diameter, so that the owner can run in at full speed without having to duck its head. The soil at the mouths of these tunnels becomes worn and deep in dust from the traffic of tiny feet, so that it is easy to tell if a mound is occupied by the tracks and the characteristic marks from the dragging tails of the owner. The mounds are often built under a creosote bush or similar shrub, the network of roots aiding to keep the roof from collapsing.

Since the success of my acceptance into their private lives depended to a large extent on what I had to offer, I gave some thought to what foods they might relish. Fortunately, this has been well researched. Having their moisture needs satisfied from within by metabolic means, these animals ignore the succulent foods loved by most other rodents. Watermelon, lettuce, fruits, and berries do not appeal to them. Peanut butter and cheese, standard baits for other rodents, are also shunned but for another reason: they contain too much oil. On the rat's back, between the shoulder blades, is the opening of an oil gland. The rat uses this oil for dressing its fur. It is used sparingly—just a little too much, and the fur becomes matted. When this occurs, the rat is off to a dust bath, which restores the pelage to its normal silky sheen. These dusting places are to be found among the mounds; whether they are communal, I never could ascertain.

I settled on a wild-bird-seed mixture as a first offering. It went over very well, except for the sunflower seeds in it. This seemed unusual to me, for wood rats prefer them to almost everything else, but the reason must be the same as for peanut butter and cheese: too much oil.

The time finally arrived for my first session with the subterranean dwellers. That night found me at the mound that I had selected. I placed the stool some eight feet from the most-used entrance, put a small handful of seed a foot or so in front of it, adjusted the light to illuminate an area taking in both the stool and the entrance, and sat down and waited. After a couple of hours of inaction, I gave up for that night. Smoothing out the dust at the burrow entrance, I gathered up my equipment and went home by the loop road.

On the following night, the seed was gone, the dust at the burrow entrance was covered with tracks and tail drags, but the net results were the same. On my third trip, I was rewarded by seeing a nebulous figure against the blackness of the inner tunnel, where my quarry crouched watching me. I sat perfectly still, and the image came and went as the rat tried to get enough courage to emerge. This was progress, and I went away encouraged. On the following night, it came to the mouth of the burrow, and, while it still did not come out to the food, I knew that the battle was won in my favor. From then on, it was simply a matter of getting better acquainted.

At first, my slightest movement, or even drawing a breath, was enough to send it into the burrow with lightning speed, kicking a spray of dirt backward as it disappeared. At other times, it might crouch at the entrance and tap at intervals. This is a warning signal to its fellows that danger is present. It is performed by raising a hind leg and striking down on the surface of the ground with that part of the limb between the foot and the knee, what we would term the calf.

Extreme alarm is signaled by a drum roll executed with both legs, usually followed by a dive deep into the recesses of the mound from which the drummer may not emerge for some time. It is quite possible at times during the day to pat the ground gently in front of the burrow entrance and hear an answering tap from deep within. With the super-acute hearing provided by the large auditory bullae of these animals, the tapping method of communication must be quite effective in warning the entire colony.

Once we had arrived at this stage of uneasy familiarity, it was but a case of arranging photographic opportunities. It was not long until this rat was eating out of my hand. Actually, once they lose their initial fear of you, they seem to prefer to be in your hand, picking up seeds with feather-soft movements of their tiny forepaws. It is as though they rely upon the sheer bulk of this huge other creature, whom they have come to trust, to protect them from all danger.

Whether upon the ground or cupped in my hand, the seed disappeared with surprising speed. Kangaroo rats have external cheek pouches of considerable capacity. Lined with short hair, they keep the contents dry until deposited in the storage chambers within the mound. The rat empties them by merely placing a foot behind each and pushing. When a rat carries a load into the burrow, it returns almost at once, eager to carry more away. My little friend showed a fine sense of reasoning. If I put down a small amount of seed that it could carry away in one load, it would take it directly into the underground storage area. If, on the other hand, a larger amount was available, it would carry a load out a little distance away, dig a shallow hole, deposit the seed, cover it hastily, and rush back for more. Apparently, this haste is designed to thwart the possibility of a rival muscling in on the supply.

Our relationship continued very pleasantly on this supply-and-demand basis for some time. Increasingly, I had to take care that I did not step upon my subject as I took pictures and moved about, adjusting my equipment, while it scurried about underfoot investigating anything that might conceivably be edible. This happy state of affairs was interrupted one night with the arrival another kangaroo rat.

This newcomer, a carbon copy of my friend, advanced rather uncertainly toward the seed when "my" rat flew into a rage and charged the interloper. At this show of force, the stranger beat a hasty retreat and was seen no more that night. On the following evening, it was back and, this time, challenged the rightful owner of the food. The encounter that ensued was short and vicious. Like two fighting cocks, they leaped into the air and struck out with their powerful hind legs. The battle was of short duration, and again the visitor left in confusion, but this time it seemed that he would return. By the violence of their struggles, I assumed that they were both males.

They were as alike as two peas in a pod, handsome and full furred, and I was disturbed at the thought that either of them might be scarred during their battles. Accordingly, I prepared two feeding stations, some three feet apart, so that I could sit between them and enforce a truce. This worked out well, and the stranger quickly became as tame as the other.

It was soon evident, too, that he had become the dominant of the two. To test this out, I would occasionally put seed at only one station. At those times, after a token show of resistance, the rightful owner would retreat to the mouth of his burrow and vent his frustration in a series of

Figure 4.3 Kangaroo rats Castor and Pollux were as alike as two peas in a pod. Note their long tails, which they use to guide their flight, and the white brush on the ends, which, it is supposed, distracts a pursuer. The body color of kangaroo rats blends beautifully with the alluvial soils in which they live. Though gentle toward humans, these little animals will fight viciously to establish territories and protect food supplies. I found it necessary to feed them at separate stations to maintain peace.

high, complaining notes. I have not seen any records of kangaroo rats making sounds other than during their fights, so, as far as I am concerned, this was unique.

Castor and Pollux

With the addition of this individual, I found it necessary to name this pair for identification purposes in my notes. I favored something like Damon and Pythias, but, obviously, these names were inappropriate for these two who hated each other so. I settled on Castor and Pollux, fitting enough, I thought, for they were the stars of my project and, like their counterparts in the heavens, were destined to be always separated at arm's length. Their mutual animosity never lessened during the weeks that I spent in their company. I grew to be very fond of them. Despite my efforts to be objective, I could not but be influenced by their trusting ways, and they became my pets in the wild. They, in turn, departed from some of their wild traits in exchange for the foods I lavished upon them. How like humans animals can become. When I would arrive at our accustomed meeting place, they would appear ready to perform whatever I might request, just for a handful of seeds.

One thing that did not change because of this intimacy was their instant reaction to any sudden sound or unexpected movement. The click of a camera shutter and the blinding flash of the strobes would cause them to disappear like magic, only to return before their latent image had cleared from my retinas. The creak of the stool as I shifted position, the noise of a piece of dropped equipment, the rustle of a piece of paper were enough to trigger instant flight, followed by an immediate return, just as if nothing had happened.

Stars and K. Rat Communication

It has been my practice during my years in the desert to occasionally go to some isolated place and spend an hour or two contemplating the stars. It is a practice that I recommend to everyone. It can restore one's perspective to its proper insignificance. For me, it is a spiritual experience, but not one of a religious nature. This is not the vaulted ceiling of the Sistine Chapel overhead with the story of the Creation spelled out in graphic perfection. Far from it! This is three-dimensional space overhead. It stretches out forever, and it yields few answers to the many questions concerning its beginnings; in fact, it continually raises more. Part of its fascination for me is my inability to relate to its vastness. I can understand the span of a yard or the length of a mile, but a light year is a distance beyond my comprehension. Yet, a light year is only an instant in Universe Time when one considers that the light cast by some star may have left its source a hundred or more light years ago. The numbers of stars are likewise beyond belief. Carl Sagan's "billions and billions" of them is beyond understanding.

A night perfect for stargazing came along in December of our first year in Ajo. It was a crisp, cold night in the dark of the moon when I arrived at the kangaroo-rat's mound. I carried my equipment to the site and then sat down in the dark to enjoy the beauty of the night. Not a breath of wind stirred the surrounding creosote bushes, dimly seen in the star-shine. To the north, the Crater Range raised a jagged silhouette against a sky powdered with stars. To the south, the lights of Ajo lay so low against the horizon that they provided no distraction; even the rumble of the ore trains in the open pit was rendered inaudible by distance.

Above me, the Milky Way, paved with stardust, arched across the sky from southwest to northeast. To my right, the Big Dipper hung low over the Crater Range, the end stars of its bowl pointing the way to the North Star. Not particularly brilliant in its own right, the Pole Star marks the extension of the axis around which our Earth revolves. Above the North Star and on a line through it to the Dipper, swung the constellation of Cassiopeia, its five stars forming a luminous letter "W" against the black void.

Following the Milky Way to the southwest, Cygnus, the Swan, was winging its way over the horizon with Deneb, one of the brightest of all stars, marking its tail feathers. Swinging back toward the east, Castor and Pollux, in the constellation of the Twins, blazed high overhead. Behind my right shoulder, the familiar constellation of Orion struck a heroic pose outlined by his three-star belt, his shield, and the sword in his right hand. Rigel at his feet and Betelgeuse at his shoulder have guided navigators since antiquity. Behind Orion and just rising over the horizon, blazed Sirius, the Big Dog, brightest of all the stars. A little farther to the east and higher in the sky swung Procyon, the Little Dog.

Having located these few of my favorite constellations, I settled myself to reflect on the splendor of the evening. My reverie was interrupted by a "tap, tap, tap" emanating from the kangaroo-rat mound immediately in front of me. It was answered by another series of taps a little distance away. Soon, all of the kangaroo rats within hearing were joining in the discourse, if it could be called that. It was evident that they were disturbed because the events on this evening had not followed the routine to which they had become accustomed. Tonight there were no lights, no low murmurs, no moving about as usual. This all seemed very strange; in addition, there was this dark, motionless hulk crouched menacingly in their midst. Was it dangerous? Better sound a warning, tap-tap-tap. What do you think? Tap-tap-tap. I'm not going out there, not I, tap-tap-tap.

I sat for some time, the splendor above me only half-appreciated as my attention was diverted to the coded communications going on all around me. Eventually, I gave up trying to translate them and turned on the light. As I resumed my usual activities, the tapping ceased and all returned to normal. I was to reenact this scenario several times in the weeks that followed, always with the same reactions from the kangaroo-rat colony.

As winter merged into spring, I began to divert my attention from the two loop roads in the valley to an area west of Ajo. Now I visited the kit foxes and the kangaroo rats less frequently. I felt no great compunction in doing this, for the foxes were obviously well able to maintain themselves, and, as far as Castor and Pollux were concerned, I had augmented their underground hoards with large amounts of exotic seeds never encountered by their less fortunate neighbors.

Part V

Down at the Ranch

Listening in the Dark

A road meandered west from Ajo through the territory that I had in mind. It led along the base of some rugged foothills into the area claimed jointly by the Luke Air Force Base and the Cabeza Prieta National Wildlife Refuge and eventually to Charlie Bell Well, a homesite long abandoned. Several arroyos in the hills combined to form a watercourse, usually dry, that crossed the road on its way toward Ten Mile Wash, several miles to the north. Below the road, a basaltic ridge ran along the west side of the arroyo. Along its crest was a low escarpment of the sort known as "rimrock." This seemed to be an ideal terrain to accommodate ringtail cats, and I surveyed it with longing eyes, knowing that there were several obstacles to overcome before I could check on this possibility.

Across the arroyo from this rocky bench was a large level area surrounding an old ranch house and several outbuildings, all in a dilapidated state attesting to many years of neglect. Between the buildings and the arroyo was a large corral built of heavy timbers. Scattered about were various pieces of old farm machinery and mining equipment, most of it rusty and worn beyond any use. The road leading into the ranch was barred by a gate bearing a "No Trespassing" sign. The fence enclosing this ancient homestead likewise bore similar warnings. Under these restrictions, it seemed unlikely that I would ever be privileged to work at the site, so I tried to put any thought of it out of my mind. After all, there were unlimited possibilities to investigate along the main road. In its meandering way along the foothills, it passed through several stands of saguaros, which, at that time, were in heavy bud.

It was also time for the breeding season of the little elf owls, which should be hunting for suitable nesting holes in these massive cactuses. The Gila woodpeckers and the gilded flickers excavate these holes for their nests and, after one season's use, leave them and construct others on the following year. This provides plenty of roomy nesting holes for these tiny owls that are very little larger than an English sparrow. A pair make the selection of a site a cooperative venture with much discussion going on as they move from one cactus to another in their search for just the right home.

At this time, it is relatively easy to locate a pair by homing in on their calls. This can present several hazards, however, as saguaros often grow among thickets of the cholla, known as the "jumping cactus," an extremely unpleasant customer to run up against in the dark. I had devised my own method of locating elf-owl nests by using a parabolic disk, which focused sounds on a microphone above the center and amplified them electronically through earphones. By taking soundings from different points, I could determine the location of a nest quite closely by triangulation. Mounting this apparatus on top of the car, I could sit comfortably below and hear all manner of night sounds in the cactus forest.

Lee and Bonnie Price

I was parked alongside the road on just such a quest one night when a pickup truck came laboring up the grade, the sound of its motor magnified to ear-splitting cacophony in my earphones. Pulling up opposite my car, a man asked if I were in trouble and could he be of help. I assured him that I was alright and, sensing that he must be curious about the apparatus on top of the car, told him what I was doing. He showed further interest, so I invited him over to listen in on the headphones. He came over at once; to my surprise, bringing his wife with him, for I had thought him to be alone. Thus it was that I met Lee and Bonnie Price, who were to aid me in so many important ways during the years to come.

They were on their way home after a long day of doing assessment work on several mining claims that they owned near the border of the Air Force range. I learned that they were "old-timers" in the Ajo community; indeed, Bonnie was the granddaughter of legendary Tom Childs, an early pioneer and one of the original developers of the New Cornelia Mine. Eventually, my conversation veered to the question that I had been aching to ask.

"Do you know who owns the ranch down by the arroyo," I queried.

To my astonishment, Lee said simply, "We do." This was almost too good to be true!

"Would you be willing for me to do some night photography down there?" I asked.

"Sure," he replied. "Maybe it would keep some of the vandals out; they're about to carry the place away." So that was decided as matter of factly as that.

The following morning found me on my way down to the ranch, for I was anxious to find out what photographic opportunities awaited there. The buildings were of little importance in that regard, but the corral was a different matter. Long and wide, it paralleled the arroyo for seventy-five yards, leaving barely enough room for a vehicle to pass between its heavy timbers and the bank. Massive gates divided it into three enclosures, each with its own water trough. The sparkling water within their mossy depths was the magnet that drew the cattle, the wildlife, and even humans to the area, for it was the only water to be found for several miles in every direction. Its source, I was to learn, was in the arroyo whose dry bed lay baking in the sun.

Some time in the ancient past, an outpouring of molten rock had spread out over this landscape, and, during its tortured upheavals, a basin had been formed beneath the area through which the arroyo now ran. Covered by alluvium washed down from the hills, it is that rather unusual formation known as a "perched water table." Surface water collects in it during those few times when storms visit the valley, and, protected from evaporation by the overlay of gravel, it provides a semi-permanent supply of water. The original owners of the ranch had discovered this rare bonanza and, after sinking a well into the sands of the arroyo, had made it the central point of the spread. In an unusual but understandable way, it controlled the entire operation of the ranch, for, being a finite source, it could support only a given number of cattle and fulfill their human needs as well.

Lee operated under no such constraints, for he lived in town and ran only a small herd of cattle on the ranch. Thus, except for those occasions when he was working the herd, the gates of the corral stood open so that the water troughs became accessible not only to the domestic animals but to the wildlife as well. As can be imagined, the latter took such full advantage of the artificial "water hole" in the desert that Lee was obliged to come down and pump the troughs full every couple of days in the dry season of the year.

There were many indications that humans had lived in the area at an earlier and, perhaps, wetter time. Upstream from the well only a short distance, bedrock protruded above the sand, its eroded surface holding shallow pools after every rain. Mortar holes worn deep into the solid rock bore witness that families had lived on the bench above the arroyo and had gathered beans from the mesquites and paloverdes there. Hard heads and basalt and obsidian chips were scattered on the surface of the flat. On the bluff across the arroyo was an overhang, which, from various artifacts scattered about the vicinity, appeared to have been a shelter against inclement weather.

There were bits of shell, too, which had come from the northern beaches of the Gulf of California, a hundred miles to the south. The Hohokam villages along the Salt and Gila Rivers sent parties to the Gulf to bring back shells, which were prized for making jewelry. In the evenings at the overnight camps on the shell routes, these hardy individuals would rough out bracelets and rings from some of these shells, seeking to lighten their burden by even this small amount of discarded material.

The animals that came to the lure of the water were a virtual "Who's Who" of desert wildlife. Absent were only those that frequented the wooded canyons of the mountains or the few that could exist without access to free water. Among the former were raccoons, skunks, and ringtail cats. After all my expectations and despite the favorable habitat along the rimrock surmounting the bluff, I never once saw a ringtail. As for kangaroo rats and pack rats, the area around the corral was so denuded of grass that there was no opportunity for them to exist nearby. Some of the smaller rodents, however, found the corrals, with occasional spillage of grain and heaps of straw in the corners, a suitable habitat. The slow drip from the watering troughs was an added advantage. They shared these quarters with the big hairy desert scorpions, giant centipedes, and sundry and varied beetles and other insects, all of them revolving around in a miniature ecosystem all their own. Sometimes a kit fox might drift in and intrude upon their existence, but, not finding any kangaroo rats in the vicinity, it would move on to more acceptable surroundings.

Several gray foxes and bobcats were nightly visitors, but none of them had the perfection of form and pelage that I desired. I felt sure, however, that eventually the ideal would appear. In all of the four years that I spent at the ranch, I saw not a single coyote. I often heard their evening serenades, but, evidently, their suspicious nature would not allow them to come to the corral so long as the car and my faint light over the water were in the area. In the morning, their tracks gave evidence that they had thoroughly inspected the place after my departure.

Bird Visitors to the Water

The water attracted more daytime visitors to the corral than nighttime ones. By far, the greater number of these were birds. These could be separated into two classes: those that were permanent residents, and those who were termed migrants, some of whom arrived from the north and stayed the winter, while others were only passing through and stayed just long enough to drink and bathe and rearrange their feathers before resuming their journey.

The residents were a sturdy lot, as evidenced by their ability to survive the heat and aridity of the Sonoran summer. Not only did they endure the searing heat, but they raised their broods during its height. The Gila woodpeckers and the gilded flickers had the best of it in this regard, for their young were relatively cool in the nests excavated deep within the trunks of the saguaros. Not so for the cactus wrens and the thrashers, which also built their nests in cactus plants, for these were in chollas, whose spiny branches provided a good bit of shade and presented an impenetrable barrier to predators but were open to every hot breeze that blew.

The doves and the hawks, which our society has come to regard as complete opposites in ideology, are, strangely enough, much alike in their nesting habits. In the desert, the doves usually choose to build their nests in mesquite or paloverde trees. These nests, nothing more than a frail platform of twigs, provide no protection to the nestlings, which come into the world naked and blind. Here, but for the sparse shade of the open canopy, they are exposed to the merciless rays of the midday sun. At this time, the adults take turns standing over the nestlings and shading them with outstretched wings. It is well that the doves mature very quickly and, in the matter of a week, have grown enough feathers to provide for some of their own protection, thus relieving their parents of this onerous task.

The hawks and the great horned owls are forced to build their nests in the most exposed sites of all: in the arms of the saguaros. Even so, they are cunningly placed among the arms of these mighty plants so that a considerable amount of shade falls upon the nest. This is the case so often that it should not be ruled to mere chance. Whether by instinct or reasoning, the birds have arrived at the best solution to a crucial problem. This is an adaptation that is very helpful in surviving the heat from the pitiless sun. Like most of the raptors, young hawks are covered with a fuzzy coat of pure white down as hatchlings. This helps in preventing sunburn and also reflects some heat away from the body. As with the doves, the adult hawks may be seen during the heat of midday standing with outstretched wings over the young. They indulge in another practice that seems to be common to large raptors, that of carrying leafy branches to the nest, apparently using these to provide additional shade to the young. This has been documented a number of times, including accounts of ospreys doing the same thing with seaweed at their nests along the coast.

The most precocious and most vulnerable of the nestlings were the young of the Gambel's quail. As soon as the eggs had hatched and the tiny striped babies had dried, the old birds left the nest with their hatchlings and introduced them to the nomadic life that is the quail's way. Other than taking a siesta in some shady place during the middle of the day, they remain constantly on the move, gathering food and evading predators at the same time. Though they might have done without it, they eagerly took water, and, at least once and sometimes more, the proud parents would bring their young to the small pool that Lee had allowed me to place under a paloverde on the edge of the arroyo. It was easy to identify the various coveys by small mannerisms and traits in the way they came to the water as well as by their numbers. Quail are prolific breeders, as they necessarily must be to maintain their numbers under the predation that they undergo. It was disheartening to have a pair come in with possibly eighteen young and see that number dwindle day by day until, ultimately, only four or five might survive to become adults.

Predation was by no means confined to the young. Occasionally, a covey would come in with only one parent in attendance. It seemed to make little difference if the missing adult were a cock or a hen; the survivor carried on with equal attention to the welfare of its brood. Should both parents be taken away, the chicks would be readily accepted into another covey, such was the devotion of these gregarious birds to the young. Thus, on rare occasions, one adult pair might wind up with as many as thirty chicks, an unusual sight, indeed.

Sonoran Fall

As the summer advanced and the young of the many bird species matured, a subtle change came over the desert. Certain animals began a migration of sorts but not in the general concept of the term. Generally speaking, we are prone to assume that animals migrate to a more favorable climate when the chill of winter forces them to leave their summer habitat. This is only partly true; an even more compelling consideration is that, at the end of their seasonal food supply, they are compelled to seek more favorable conditions elsewhere. So it is in the low Sonoran Desert. By August, the saguaros have bloomed and fruited, and those creatures that have aided in the process and profited from their participation are forced to seek food elsewhere.

The long-nose bats are the first to leave. Having been rewarded with nectar from the flowers and the resultant fruit for their part in pollination, and having reared their young during that time, they set forth along an agave-flowered trail to points in Mexico where magueys and other flowering plants abound. Next to leave are the white-wing doves. Many pairs have reared two broods of young. When the saguaros have ceased to provide a food supply, they go to the feedlots and grainfields for a time, though, as the sun moves southward, they follow it leisurely but purposefully until, by the middle of September, their calls of "who cooks for you" are heard no more in Arizona.

Another associate of the giant cactus leaves early in the fall for a home in Mexico, too. The elf owl is not as closely tied to the saguaro as the previous two. As far as is known, it eats neither nectar nor fruit. However, it has been recorded as catching night-flying insects that come to the saguaro flowers. Actually, although the elf owl is linked with the saguaro forest in most accounts, it finds situations to its liking in desert canyons clear up to the pine belt. It is considered the most abundant owl species in southern Arizona, but, due to its small size and nocturnal habits, little more is known about it than the long-nose bat. It is known to migrate about the first of October; whether it leaves in groups or singly has not been determined.

In marked contrast to the leisurely migration of these denizens of the cactus forest is the spectacular departure of the turkey vultures. Some windless, sunny day in late fall, you might cast an eye skyward and see a large aggregation of these great black birds circling high in the thermals and drifting southward. They float in no structured fashion but are scattered against the blue of the sky like grains of pepper. Their numbers are incredible; where they gather and to what signal is unclear. They winter in Mexico, many of them but a short distance south of the international boundary line. Their return on the following year is heralded as a sure sign of spring by the local people. When they first reappear in the vicinity of San Xavier Mission near Tucson, it has become a historic event paralleling the return of the swallows to San Juan Capistrano Mission in California.

The departure of these and several other species left the way open for other migrants leaving the snows of the northern winter to move in. A great many of these were sparrows and other small seed eaters, gleaning the tiny seeds that had escaped the attention of the doves. The white-crowned sparrows were the most numerous of these. They are neat little gray birds with black and white stripes on their heads, and their sweet, high-pitched songs made a charming chorus as they gathered among the branches of the mesquites lining the banks of the arroyo.

Numerous other species of the sparrow family also made the ranch their winter home. One strikingly different from the rest was the black-throat, or desert, sparrow. Their black throats and heads with white stripes over and below the eyes gave them a somewhat sinister look at complete variance with their nature, for they are gentle, confiding little birds that tame quickly if treated with consideration. I made friends with

Figure 5.1
Sweety, the desert
sparrow, tamed
quickly and by
its boldness
encouraged other
birds to come to me.

one that, at my call, would come to my outstretched hand for the seeds
that were its reward. "Sweety" was my bellwether in a way. I fed the
birds at a weathered, downed tree trunk lying along the arroyo bank.
When I was seated on that log with seeds scattered around my feet and
Sweety perched upon my knee, the rest of the birds took courage from
its audacity, and soon I would have them all around, and even upon, me.

Phainopepla and Mistletoe

One of the more spectacular of the middle-size winter visitors was the
phainopepla, aptly named, for, literally translated, it means "shiny
cloak." This is a slim bird, the males with glossy plumage so blue black
that it reflects sparkles in direct sunlight. A crest of short, stiff feathers
and red eyes are additional features that identify this remarkable bird.
The females are not nearly so flamboyant, being dressed in sober gray.
The species is of the class called "silky flycatchers." It spends the summers
in higher, cooler altitudes in central and northern Arizona. In that environment, it subsists on insects, supplemented with various small fruits
and berries such as the elderberry. Upon the advent of winter, it descends
to the lower desert. There its diet undergoes a dramatic change.

There are few insects available at that time of year, but the mistletoe plants in the mesquite, paloverde, and ironwood trees hang heavy with berries. These mistletoes, for there are several species of them, are a drab sort when contrasted with the large-leafed, white-berried variety that is hung above the doors in the Christmas season and regarded with anticipation or aversion, as the case may be. These desert species are almost leafless and consist of a mass of stems that bear whorls of pink-to-red-colored berries during the winter. They are true parasites that draw their nourishment from the plants unfortunate to have become their hosts. While these infestations seldom kill trees outright, they can weaken them to such an extent that they might succumb to disease or drought.

The method of distribution of this unusual plant is as effective as it is simple. The berries contain a mucilaginous sap that retains its sticky properties when eaten by a bird and, thus, sometimes glues the droppings to the branches below. Many species of birds eat the berries, but the phainopepla is one that chooses a favorite perch and returns to it time and again after feeding. The droppings build up on the branches below each such perch. When proper conditions of moisture and temperature occur, the seeds within such a deposit germinate. The rootlets of these tiny plants seek out and penetrate through any small interstice in the bark, seeking nourishment from the cambium layer of the host plant.

The victim is not entirely defenseless against this attack upon its life system. It builds up a swelling of hard tissue around the point of entrance, which helps limit the loss of its nutrients. In the case of the ironwood, this swelling, or burl, sometimes enlarges to a diameter of up to a foot or more; in rare instances, it may even result in forcing the unwelcome guest from its grip on the branch.

The mistletoe may, in its own right, play host to several bird species. Large specimens may have a diameter of two feet and hang down several feet from the branches to which they are attached. Deep within this tangled mass of interlocking stems, small species such as the gnatcatchers and the kinglets build their nests, finding protection from predators, which they need. Even mockingbirds sometimes nest in the clumps, finding not only shelter but also food, for they, too, love the succulent berries, which persist until late in the spring.

Hawks and War Planes

With the influx of small birds late in the fall, it should follow that their predators arrive with them. One immediately thinks of hawks, and it is true that a number of raptor species do move down into the low desert. However, these are selective in their choice of prey. This is partly because the large buteos, for instance, are too large and slow to catch the smaller birds; on the other hand, the sharpshin and Cooper's hawks do subsist mainly on these species, which they are deadly in their ability to catch. These two are accipters (*Accipter* sp.), which, with their short, rounded wings and relatively long tails, have power and maneuverability superior to that of their prey. They do not swoop upon their victims from great heights, as do the falcons, but prefer to lurk quietly in some tree, hidden by the foliage, and then to dash out after some luckless bird that, by chance, happened to choose the same haven.

On rare occasions, a marsh hawk might visit the area, swooping low with erratic wing beats as it searched the hard-packed earth for the rodents to which it was accustomed in the grassy meadows farther north. At length, being disappointed in the hunt, it would flap away southward toward more appropriate terrain in the agricultural districts of northern Mexico.

One winter we were pleased to be host to a group of Harris hawks. This is not a plentiful species but a distinctive one. It is a large, black, buteo-type hawk with a broad white band across its tail and sometimes, if not worn, a narrower one at the tip. A bright yellow piping of bare flesh about the eyes and at the rear of the beak lends a fierce expression to its face. Formidable it is, for this is one of the few, if not the only, species of raptors that hunts in a group. Lucky, indeed, is the rabbit that can survive the onslaught of a cadre of these savage hunters. In spite of all of its twisting and turning, one or another of its pursuers will succeed in striking it with its talons, and the chase is over.

On only a few occasions, and then only in the wintertime, were we favored with a visit from the king of the raptors. When a golden eagle did come in, it did so only for a drink and a short rest. In comparison with the smaller birds with which we were associated every day, they seemed enormous. Like gliders, they sailed in on broad, flat wings, flapping only at the last moment as they reached for a corral post with outstretched talons. A stare about the area, a rearranging of their feathers, and they were ready for a drink. That accomplished, they took off again with a great flapping of wings until fully airborne and then resumed their journey, soaring away on the wings of the wind to destinations unknown.

No description of our activities at the ranch would be complete without mention of the awesome and sinister war birds that almost daily screamed overhead. Squadrons of fighter and attack bomber aircraft from Phoenix and Tucson airfields practiced their deadly craft on targets located some miles north of the Crater Range. Breaking formation and falling into line, they would swoop like falcons on the target area with guns blazing; then, making a left turn and circling at low altitude, they would cross the ranch, close the pattern, and repeat the attack several times before roaring away to their home fields. It was fascinating to see them as tiny black dots in the distance, enlarging without sound as they approached, until, suddenly, with a screaming whistle of wings and an explosive roar of jets, they hurtled overhead and were gone as quickly as they had arrived.

The wildlife, inured as it had become to many years of this disturbance, paid little attention to the passage of these modern machines, but I, who had done some flying in the days of wood and wire and cloth-covered airplanes, never tired of seeing these latest marvels slicing through the air with unbelievable power and speed.

At night, we were also made aware that we were close to a military installation. I never did learn just why (it is best not to know too much about the activities of the military) flares were set off at high altitude. Local rumor had it that they were reference points for night-flying maneuvers. They were orange in color and suspended from small parachutes. As I recall, they always appeared on nights of the dark of the moon. There was never any sound of aircraft that I could discern, but, suddenly, an orange bloom would blossom against the black sky. It would hang there motionless for several minutes, to be followed by another and perhaps more. Sometimes there might be as many as four at one time hanging there in an eerie silence. After five minutes or so, the first one would go out, to be followed by the others until the sky became totally dark once more, leaving me with an uneasy feeling of having been spied upon by some unseen entity.

As the kaleidoscope of wildlife species constantly revolved about the water according to the seasons, I gradually became more acquainted with the ever-changing relationships that developed between them. Most of these were predictable, involving predator and prey. The roadrunner, that fleet and tireless stalker, grew fat in late summer with a surfeit of grasshoppers; then, when that supply disappeared with the advent of cold weather, it fell back upon short rations of small birds, little rodents, and even carrion, if required. Spring became again a time of plenty, with snakes and lizards coming out of hibernation, and bird's eggs and nestlings available to satisfy that voracious appetite. Early summer filled out the year with coveys of tiny quail moving about, often with a roadrunner lurking around their perimeter, ever alert to snap up a straggler.

Symbiotic relationships, in many cases, are less obvious but are exquisitely well arranged to accommodate both participants. The migrant dove, arriving in the saguaro forest as the cactus flowers are opening, and the yucca moth, which is so closely involved with the yucca that if either would disappear the other would perish, are ultimate examples of the length to which nature binds together two entirely separate life-forms to their mutual advantage. However, in a broader sense, we and all life of the planet are tied together in a mutual effort of survival. As the global inventory of life-forms shrinks, we are all being forced closer to the brink of extinction. Even on the isolated ranch, a decline in the environmental values became apparent in the several years of my presence. There were other unrelated factors that interested me, too, although they affected the general situation to no great extent. Two of these might be identified as dogs and the Night Walkers.

Dogs and Night Walkers

The dogs first attracted my attention one winter's afternoon as I drove down a pair of wheel tracks alongside the arroyo on its way toward the valley to the north. Despite the lateness of the season, the rays of the sun were burning hot as it hung low along the southern horizon. As I proceeded slowly on my way, avoiding the rocks and the chuckholes, a movement across the arroyo caught my eye. As I slowed to a halt, I saw that at some distance away a number of dogs lay in various attitudes of repose under the lacy shade of a blue paloverde tree. I got out my binoculars to scrutinize this company in more detail.

There were twelve or fifteen dogs in the group, all of them large and lean muscled. There were no collars or tags in evidence. They did not seem to mind my inspection in the least; in fact, they viewed me with a studied indifference. After a few minutes of this impasse, I moved on, puzzled at their presence in such numbers and so far from town. I related this occurrence to Lee the next time I saw him.

"Who owns those dogs?" I inquired.

"They come over from the reservation," Lee responded. "Every so often, they make up a pack and move into this area. They usually pick up a few of the town dogs on the way. They work the garbage dump, and catch what they can of the wildlife, and, worst of all, they run the stock and deer."

"Have you lost any of your cattle to them?" I asked.

"Lost them, no," Lee said bitterly. "But a couple of them have lost the brush on their tails, and some have been bitten on the hocks." To my unspoken question, he added: "There isn't much you can do about it. After they've hung around long enough to get hungry, they go home again for a while. They're a vicious bunch, though, and unpredictable—be careful if they're around."

"I will," I promised.

I remembered that, many years before in Avra Valley, west of Tucson, a similar situation had occurred. A sparsely settled community of mobile homes and small ranches had sprung up more or less isolated from the city. Lacking the customary services enjoyed by urban dwellers, the inhabitants created their own or did without. They continued very satisfactorily on that basis until a dog pack became a hazard. This was a miscellaneous group of mongrels of all sizes. They roamed the community, becoming more aggressive as they attacked and killed pets and harassed livestock. It reached a point where the people began to fear for their personal safety. Appeals to the county authorities brought no relief, so, after a town meeting, they decided to take matters into their own hands. Accordingly, a mounted posse was assembled one weekend, and the dog pack was run down and killed. It was drastic action, but, under the circumstances, no outcry was raised. Western people were expected to use whatever means necessary to protect their property and persons.

In spite of Lee's warning, I was unprepared when I did encounter the dogs. One Sunday morning, I went down to the ranch to take some bird pictures. I had prepared a setup on the edge of the arroyo and, using the car as a blind, took the shots by remote control. On this morning, the birds were acting strangely. Although they were familiar with the setup, they kept moving nervously about and looking down into the arroyo. At length, because I was not getting any pictures anyway, I decided to go over to the edge of the arroyo and see what was disturbing them.

Looking down, I discovered that there were two large dogs moving about on the floor of the gully. Shouting at them to "get out of there," I stooped as if to pick up some stones, and they rather deliberately moved up the arroyo, casting baleful glances back over their shoulders as they went. They were no sooner out of sight around the first bend than pandemonium broke loose, and the pack came charging down the wash to gather below me. With barks, growls and snarls, and much baring of teeth, they challenged me to come down to their level, and, if I did, it was clearly their intention to tear me apart. It was now my move, and it seemed not to my advantage. Militarily, I held the high ground, and there was ample ammunition in the form of rocks at my feet. On the other hand, I was vastly outnumbered, and, should they decide to charge me, the bank, though steep, could be surmounted without too much difficulty. I decided not to meet their challenge and, backing off slowly, returned to the car. I got in and rolled up all of the windows. The bedlam ceased as soon as I was out of their sight, and a half-hour later, when it seemed safe to return to the field, there was not a sign to be seen of my erstwhile opponents.

Upon my return home, I got out my .22-caliber rifle, and from then on I carried it in the car on the days that I was in the field. It was fortunate that we did not meet again, for, though I would have been reluctant to kill any of them, I would certainly have done so. Feral dogs have no place in a natural environment. We heard their baying at times, but, as Lee said, they moved in and out of the area as conditions dictated.

I already routinely carried a .38 Special handgun in the car on my night rounds—primarily for the elimination of a rabid animal, should one come to my study area; secondarily against the remote possibility that "Night Walkers" might attempt to make off with the car. That was my term for the illegal aliens who drift into Arizona in search of work. They are not bad people; for the most part, they are simple folk from south of the border looking for work—any sort of work that will improve their lot. They are preyed upon by *coyoteros*, as they are called: riffraff in the border town who promise, for an exorbitant fee, to guide them across the border to jobs in the land of plenty. Too often this consists of merely taking them across the border and turning them loose on their own.

This is ridiculously easy to accomplish. Fences at the border town stop illegal entry at those points, but, a few miles out of town, the border is merely a line drawn between the border monuments. South of Ajo, the border stretches west from Sonoita for a hundred miles consisting of a few strands of barbed wire, which in places are flat on the ground. Mexico Highway 2 parallels the fence most of the way to San Luis on the Colorado River. No one knows how many parties of aliens have been taken out on this road, given a few plastic jugs of water, and pointed north. Their destination is Interstate 8, which also parallels the border but at a distance of some eighty miles. On the irrigated lands along Interstate 8 are fields of cotton and maize, citrus orchards, and stock feeding pens—all potential sources for jobs.

Between the border and this land of plenty, however, lies some of the most inhospitable desert in the world. Much of the trip across this waste trespasses on the Goldwater Air Force Bombing Range, an illegal act in itself. Only a few water holes are to be found on this perilous journey. To miss them would be disastrous; a person could not carry a supply of water sufficient to make the trip without additional amounts provided along the way. To make matters worse, the best chances of finding work are in the summer, when the heat is most intense. Numerous individuals and, at times, whole parties have disappeared attempting this journey of death. The lucky ones are those who have been found by Border Patrol agents and transported back across the border. I quote from an Associated Press release bearing the dateline of Ajo, Arizona, July 7, 1980, in the *Spokesman Review*: "Law enforcement agents using horses and helicopters found the bodies of 11 aliens in the scorching Arizona desert Sunday, bringing to 13 the number of El Salvadorans known to have died after being stranded without water by smugglers. Ground temperatures in the area reach 150 degrees. . . . 'An additional 13 aliens were reported safe, and an undetermined number of men, women, and children may have made their way back to Mexico,' Superintendent Franklin Wallace of the Organ Pipe National Monument said." This incident is unusual because of the numbers involved, but, almost every winter, hunters and Air Force personnel report bodies found in the desert dating from the previous summer.

I never actually saw any Night Walkers, but that they stopped at the water troughs was evident by soapy water and boot tracks seen in the mornings. I have no doubt that they saw the car and had cast longing eyes in its direction. After all, it was still forty weary miles to Interstate 8. I know that I would have been tempted if I were in their situation.

Because of the activities around the corral, I was most often in the vicinity of the ranch, but the surrounding terrain was so varied and supported such a wealth of desert life that I might be absent for several days (or nights) at a time while following new leads. Lee Price was sometimes responsible for these lapses because he knew the area so well and understood what I might use in the way of wildlife pictures.

The Vulture's Nest

It was late in my second spring at the ranch when he came to me one day and asked if I might be interested in photographing a buzzard's nest. *Would I?* What a rare opportunity this would be because vulture nests are seldom found. They are not built in trees or saguaros, as is the case with many of the raptors, but, like the eagle's, they are usually placed in fissures or caves in the most inaccessible places among the cliffs. Lee had come upon this nest entirely by circumstance.

To the west of the corrals were three rocky hills that stood perhaps one thousand feet above the level of the ranch. Each of them was crowned with a capstone with sheer sides perhaps ten feet in height. In checking on the whereabouts of his cattle, Lee was wont to climb one of these hills and sweep the desert below with binoculars. On this particular day, he had climbed the center hill for that purpose. Settling himself upon a suitable rock, he sat with his back to the bottom of the capstone and proceeded to scan the desert below. He had been thus occupied for several minutes when there was a commotion behind him, and, simultaneously, a large black bird hurtled by him, a wing tip brushing his shoulder as it passed. Somewhat shaken by this close encounter, he arose to investigate and found, under an overhang at the base of the wall, a nest of sorts containing two large eggs. He had been sitting directly in front of it!

Climbing the hill the next day and following the directions he had given me, I had no difficulty in finding the site. It was a low overhang no more than three feet in height and some ten feet in width. It extended about eight feet underneath the cliff, the ceiling sloping down to floor level at the back. The floor itself was covered with several inches of debris from an old pack-rat's nest. Sticks, stones, cactus wood, and cactus joints made it difficult to crawl in to the cavity to inspect the nest. Well back in the cave, the two eggs lay in a shallow bowl scooped out of the untidy mess. They were larger than I had anticipated. About the size of turkey's eggs, they were white in color with brownish spots scattered over their surfaces. Although I had not seen the mother leave the nest, the eggs were warm to the touch, proving that the old bird had not been gone long. Perhaps she had seen me from afar with that marvelous telescopic vision and divined my intentions. No doubt she was even then high above me surveying what I was about. Wanting to cause her the least distress possible, I hurriedly crawled in to the cave, picking up a number of cactus spines in the process, took a few flash pictures, and departed.

On my next trip to the nest a few days later, the old bird was there but left while I was still some distance down the hill. No wonder that she heard me, for the weather was hot and the climb steep, and I was puffing from the exertion as well as kicking a few rocks loose as I progressed. This time I was rewarded by seeing a newly hatched chick in the nest. By most standards, newly hatched vulture chicks are not a pretty sight. Their skin is basic sooty black as are their legs, feet, and bills. Excluding these latter body parts, they are covered with dense white down. There was a strong odor of decay hanging in the air, so I judged that even this new arrival was doing its part in keeping the desert clean. The vultures

Figure 5.2
Under an overhanging ledge, on a floor littered with debris, is the vulture nest. Young vultures are covered with white down, as are the young of raptors generally. Vultures cannot be considered beautiful at any stage of life.

feed their young by regurgitation, since their feet, and more particularly their talons, are not adapted to catching or carrying prey. This results in the nest becoming foul smelling in a short time. However, this should not be held against the bird, which has been called "the Flying Garbage Can." There are scavengers associated with most forms of life, and their role is an important one.

My final experience with the vulture's nest was an unhappy one. Situated as it was, with the floor of the overhang level with the outside terrain, the nest left the young vulnerable to any roving predator that came along. The young were fortunate for a while, but, before their pin-feathers had well sprouted, one morning they were gone.

I was bitterly disappointed that I would not have the opportunity to see them mature and take to the air with that marvelous, soaring flight that is unequaled by any other species in the Southwest desert. There was no inkling as to what animal had taken them. It could have been bobcat, coyote, or fox—all were in the area and all were capable of taking them, even over the old bird's resistance had she been there. Although it was a sad blow to me, it should not have been. Looking at it objectively, I had no place in the scenario—I was merely an observer in a drama in which there was no role for me. Would that I could be so objective!

Mountain Lion in the Pepper Tree

Not all of my experiences ended so disastrously, however. Early one morning, I received a call from Bonnie Price.

"There's a mountain lion in a tree near our place," she reported. "Just drive down this way and you'll see a crowd."

Stopping just long enough to grab a camera and some film, I was on my way. About four blocks down Brady Street from home, I saw a crowd of twenty to thirty people gathered around a large pepper tree. The law, represented by a sheriff's patrol car, was there as well.

The tree, a so-called California pepper *(Schinus molle)*, was a large, wide-spreading specimen with a wealth of slender, hanging branchlets crowded with pinnate leaves. The lion, a young female, was lying on a horizontal branch no more than nine feet from the ground. She was partly hidden by the thick foliage except for her long tail, which hung down. Excluding that member, which twitched now and then, she was paying little apparent attention to the crowd, staring ahead with that averted gaze that the large cats in captivity affect when confronted by humans. Obscured as she was by the thick foliage, there was no opportunity to take any pictures, so I circulated among the crowd to pick up what information might be shared.

I found that the Arizona Game and Fish Department in Phoenix had been informed and that officers with a tranquilizer gun were on their way. The crowd settled down to await their arrival. In the meantime, had the sheriff's deputy not been present, someone might have shot her, for, although the mountain lion is protected as a game animal in Arizona, there are always those who would like to see them exterminated. After a wait of another hour, the arrival of the Game and Fish people sent a stir of anticipation through the assemblage.

The preparations were simple enough. A cage in the truck was opened, and all that remained was to tranquilize the center of attraction. A pop from the gun and a flinch from the lion, and, in a very short time, she relinquished her hold on the branch and fell to the ground, her fall cushioned to a large extent by the thick carpet of fallen leaves and twigs that had collected under the tree. All that remained was to slide her in to the cage and wait for her to revive.

Before long, it became apparent that all was not going well. She seemed to slip into a deeper stupor despite her captors' efforts to rouse her. When it became obvious that additional aid would be required, they took off for the company hospital in Ajo, leaving us to wonder what the outcome of the effort would be. The crowd dispersed with the hope that the more sophisticated treatment at the hospital would be successful in reviving her.

We were later informed that she had, indeed, been restored to normalcy and taken to Phoenix. There she was kept for a short time while undergoing tests for rabies and various other ailments. Found to be in good health, she was eventually taken to a remote area far from Ajo and released. I hope that, in this new environment, should she be unlucky enough to come into contact with humans, they might be as charitable as the good people of Ajo. At any rate, she will always bear the distinction of having been treated in a "human" hospital, a unique experience, at least in that part of the desert.

It might seem strange to encounter mountain lions in the low, hot desert, since they seem more suited to the high, cold mountains. However, this is not unusual at all; actually, they are present in some numbers. They are a wide-ranging species, depending on the availability of food. If prey species are scarce, one may roam over a territory of a hundred square miles or more. An old female was known to claim an area just inside the boundary of the Cabeza Prieta National Wildlife Refuge west of Ajo. She periodically produced a litter of kittens and kept that part of the desert supplied with lions for years. Actually, it seems likely that the female captured in Ajo might have been one of her progeny.

In all my years spent in the outdoors, I have seen mountain lions in the wild only twice, both times in improbable places and far separated from each other. One in Everglades National Park in Florida, having emerged soaking wet from a lagoon, crossed the road just ahead of us. The other was on the road between Ajo and the ranch.

It was my habit when going down to the ranch in the morning to drive slowly down a long, sandy grade, where I quite often saw various animals that had not yet retired for the day. The area was sparsely covered with a growth of creosote bushes and bur sage together with numbers of saguaros. On that particular morning, I was coasting quietly along at fifteen to twenty miles per hour when my peripheral vision picked up a movement some little distance to my right. This immediately developed into a long, tawny form racing on a diagonal course to cross the road ahead of me. Along it came, a vision of incredible power and speed, as it bounded across the road with its long tail trailing behind it. I had no time to step on the brakes, even to do anything but marvel at the action going on directly in front of me. Then it was gone. I have no idea whether it was male or female but no matter. The impression of that marvelous exhibition of brute strength, coupled with grace, will remain with me always.

There were other wonders to be encountered on these trips to and from the ranch—wonders in that they involved creatures sometimes far from their accustomed haunts. One morning as I rounded a curve, I surprised a trio of mountain sheep standing broadside in the road. After a startled gaze at the strange contraption bearing down on them, they turned and fled down the road ahead of me. The trio consisted of a ram and two ewes. The ram was a magnificent creature with a massive full curl of horns. Maintaining a speed of ten miles an hour, I followed to see how long they could continue that pace. The ewes did very well, but it was not long until the ram began to tire. His huge head sank lower and lower until, at last, not wanting to drive him to complete exhaustion, I slowed to a halt. They were more than willing to stop as well and stood in the road for a bit looking back at me with flanks heaving. They then left the road, which, of course, would have been their best option in the first place, and were soon lost to sight among the creosote bushes. A strange place to encounter mountain sheep, you might think, since their chosen habitat is high in the rocky cliffs of the mountains. However, they are sometimes seen, as in this case, crossing the open valleys between one mountain range and another.

During my return from the ranch in the late night hours, I would quite often come across various reptiles on the road. To many, the term "reptiles" means snakes, but there are other species besides snakes in this category. Actually, there are more lizards than snakes in the desert. Among these are two species that are so distinctive that they demand some attention. Not surprisingly, they vary as greatly in size as they do in habits. By chance, although that term is erroneous, for nothing in ecology comes about through chance, they happen to be nocturnal: one partly so, the other considered completely so.

Gila Monster

The larger of this ill-assorted pair is the so-called Gila monster *(Heloderma suspectum)*. It is a large lizard, up to twenty-four inches in length, heavy bodied and slow moving. It lives not only in the Gila River drainage of Arizona, but also in adjacent parts of Nevada and Utah, and has been reported as occurring in a small portion of the Colorado Desert of California. It is described as diurnal, but I have encountered it so often at night that I consider it nocturnal as well.

It bears the distinction of being the only poisonous lizard in the United States; the only other venomous species in the world is the allied, but somewhat larger, beaded lizard *(Heloderma horrida)* of northwestern Mexico. The term "beaded lizard" is more appropriate for our species as well, for its rough, pebbled skin is underlain with small, bony granules underneath each surface tubercle. This is what gives rise to the genus term *"Heloderma"* (from the Latin *holotus*, meaning "nail-shaped," and the Greek *derma*, meaning "skin"). The basic color of the skin is yellow to orange, covered with black markings in a random pattern. The feet and the legs are black, as are, usually, the sides of the face. It is a comparatively easy animal to see as it ambles slowly along against the dull green and tan colors of the desert floor.

The poison apparatus of this large lizard is primitive and inefficient to an extreme, but it is not prudent to ignore it. The poison glands are located in the cheeks and the lips of the lower jaw. The venom is pushed into the mouth by muscular action through openings at the bases of several back teeth. The teeth of both jaws are grooved front and back, and it is through these grooves that the venom is designed to flow through capillary action into such wounds as the animal is able to inflict. During a bite, the lizard will clamp its jaws together and, while not relinquishing

Figure 5.3
The Gila monster
is the only
poisonous lizard of
the United States.
It is protected by
law and should not
be molested.

its hold, will, by a chewing motion and through blowing and hissing, attempt to work the poison into the wound. It would seem that the whole mechanism is designed for defensive purposes, and poorly at that.

The food habits of these slow and awkward animals are not well known. It is likely that they are successful at times at eating the young of several species of rodents that live in underground burrows. They are known to take quail eggs, and it is reported that they will climb into bushes and small trees, evidently in search of other birds' eggs. Benjamen Zerby, chief ranger at Saguaro National Monument, reported that he once saw one halfway up a saguaro, evidently hoping to rob a Gila woodpecker's nest.

Any food surplus to its immediate needs is stored in its tail. By checking the relative thickness of its tail, the condition of the animal can be judged. Irene and I were taking numerous trips to the desert in the droughty years of the 1940s. On these jaunts, we frequently came across Gila monsters, which were more numerous in those days. Some would be in poor condition, and, if their situation seemed serious, we would bring them home. After a few weeks on a diet of hens' eggs, they would fill out, and we would release them with tails satisfactorily plumped out.

It was interesting to see their method of eating a hen's egg. Their mouths were not large enough to take one at one gulp, so they would push it around the floor of the cage until they had brought it up against a wall or in a corner. That accomplished, they would gnaw at it with a chewing movement until their teeth had worn a way through the shell. Then they would thrust their long, flat tongue through this opening and work it in and out until, eventually, they had ingested the entire contents. The entire operation, like so many practices of the species, seemed overly primitive but in keeping with the general habits of the creature. Ecologically, we were no doubt in error in capturing these animals, and today it is illegal to keep or molest them in any way.

In 1977, we took a trip from Ajo to Globe, Arizona, a matter of two hundred miles, and on that memorable day we saw four, the lowest at a 1,700-foot altitude and the highest at 4,400 feet. This gives some idea of the numbers and adaptability of this curious and interesting species. Despite being protected by law, however, it is becoming increasingly rare. It would be most unfortunate if this relic of an age long past should be allowed to disappear.

The Gecko

The other nocturnal lizard of which I speak, I encountered frequently on the ranch during the season of early summer showers. In late June, turning over any old board or plank lying on the ground might result in the discovery of one, or sometimes two, little variegated ground geckos *(Coleonyx variegatus)*. These are small lizards; maximum length is about six inches. They might be most appropriately described as being fragile. Their legs are small and weak, their skins soft and semitransparent, and their movements are slow and deliberate in comparison with most species of lizards. The ground color of these little creatures is a dull, light, lemon yellow. This is crossed by several irregular brown bands, and various splotches of the same color are scattered about its body and the back of its head. This results in an indiscriminate pattern somewhat resembling that of the Gila monster, so at times they have been mistaken for the young of that species.

As with many nocturnal animals, the pupils of the eyes are vertical. This allows for more expansion and contraction, depending upon the variability of light, than the conventional round pupils of diurnal species. This response to light becomes troublesome when one attempts

Figure 5.4 Ground geckos are sometimes mistaken for young Gila monsters. These are inoffensive little nocturnal animals. Their food consists mostly of termites and ants.

to photograph this lizard. What happens is that, in order to focus the camera, a fairly strong light is needed. This causes the pupils of the gecko's eyes to contract to narrow slits, making for a rather uninteresting shot. When the focusing light is turned off, the pupils will enlarge again in a few seconds. However, with darkness restored, the lizard is returned to a more familiar setting and moves out of focus at once.

Geckos are unique among American lizards in that they have a voice. This usually consists of no more than a squeak uttered when they are first captured. It is a small voice, granted, but a voice nevertheless. They seem to employ it only as an indication of distress and for no other purpose.

This animal has one more peculiarity, which it shares with several other lizard species: it loses its tail in times of stress. This is supposed to be a defensive tactic wherein, if the animal is about to be captured or is in the grip of some predator, it parts with its tail. This member, now detached from the body of its owner, squirms and contorts about, attracting the attention of the predator, while the erstwhile owner steals away unobserved and lives to not only tell the tale, but to grow a new one. The regenerated tail is not as long as the original, nor does it have quite the same scalation as the first, but, in spite of these small deficiencies, it serves very well.

Given that it is small in size, ground dwelling, and nocturnal, it seems appropriate that this lizard subsists on small insects. It goes its deliberate way, exploring every nook and cranny that might provide a morsel. Occasionally, it strikes a real bonanza in the form of a termite or an ant colony. I recall catching one in the beam of the flashlight one night that was perched several feet above the ground on the furrowed bark of an old mesquite tree. A line of ants was ascending the tree to collect the sweet drops of sap exuding from the young mesquite bean pods. The gecko was contentedly sitting in front of this cafeteria line, snapping up whichever entree it fancied as it went by.

Scorpion

Another nocturnal animal I frequently encountered in many situations was the scorpion. Scorpions were especially plentiful in and around the corral. The litter, which collected in the corners, provided an excellent habitat from which to sally forth at night in search of prey. Foremost among them was the largest species found in the Arizona desert, called the "giant hairy," which measures four inches or more in length. Of a light, semitransparent straw color, they are easily seen under a light at night. Like the spiders, scorpions are arachnids, but, in addition to having eight legs, they have a pair of large claws similar to those of a lobster. This is not too remarkable, for they are distant relatives, albeit terrestrial ones, of lobsters and crayfish. The claws, though they look dangerous, are not powerful enough to harm humans but are used to capture and hold the various small animals upon which they prey.

A scorpion's real danger to humans lies in its stinger, which is located at the tip of its long, many-segmented tail. The tail is carried above the back in a semiarc, curving forward, and can be whipped about with surprising speed and accuracy. The stinger is shaped much like a cat's claw, flattened on the sides and coming to an extremely sharp point. Immedi-

Figure 5.5
The desert hairy scorpion is the largest of the numerous species in the Sonoran Desert. It must be considered mildly poisonous: its sting inflicts intense pain but is not life threatening.

ately behind this point is a bulbous gland containing the poison. A tiny opening on either side of the sting releases venom into the wound when the point is driven beneath the skin of an enemy.

Of the several species of scorpions native to Arizona, only two are considered dangerous, and they to children. However, a scorpion sting is a very painful experience, even if not life threatening, and should be avoided. There is a Scorpion Antivenin Program ongoing at a poisonous-animal research laboratory in Phoenix, Arizona. Thousands of scorpions are processed there, and I have been told that, under the pressure of handling such numbers, some researchers will pick them up by the tail with their bare hands. This can be accomplished without being stung (I was told) by grasping the tip of the tail between the thumb and the forefinger. The stinger is thus held pointing forward between the two fingers and is harmless in that position.

I decided to see if I possessed the courage and the dexterity to accomplish this feat. Suiting the action to the word, I chose one of the large species and placed it on top of an old oil drum, where it posed uncertainly with its tail at the ready. Moving around behind my quarry, I set my teeth, steeled my resolve, slid my hands slowly across the surface of the drum, and, much to my surprise, in a textbook capture, picked up the scorpion by the tail. Once was enough! I have had no urge to test the law of averages against one of these agile creatures again.

Tarantula and Tarantula Hawk

Another arachnid frequently seen on the roads is the tarantula. These gentle giants of the spider clan, although armed with a pair of formidable fangs, pose no danger to humans. They roam the desert in late afternoons and evenings in search of prey or, perhaps, a mate. Hunting them, in turn, are their arch predators, the tarantula hawks (*Pepsis* sp.), large dark-blue-and-orange wasps.

The details of their relationship are well known. Despite a vigorous defense by the tarantula, the wasp is able to sting it, injecting a venom that immobilizes but does not kill. The wasp then drags the spider to a convenient hole, perhaps the home of its hapless victim, lowers it below the surface, and, after laying a single egg upon it, fills the hole with dirt and then departs. In time, the egg hatches, and the larva feeds on the body of the helpless host, eventually emerging as an adult wasp. I have never witnessed the encounter between the wasp and the spider, but I have several times come across the wasp filling the burrow. It does this by circling the hole and loosening the soil with its mandibles, thus causing it to cascade down into the cavity until it is filled. It makes one wonder how the young adult is able to dig its way to freedom.

The adult tarantula hawk is not a carnivorous species, as such. It subsists mainly on nectar from flowers, one of the more favored being the large desert milkweed *(Asclepias erosa)*. This many-stemmed plant, up to five feet tall, grows in clumps in sandy places of the low desert. It is a colorful sight to see a number of these giant wasps flitting about and sipping nectar from the flowers that are borne in umbels at the tips of the stems. They will take other food as well as nectar. We had several Chinese elms in our yard. In the spring, sapsuckers would drill their distinctive patterns of holes in the trunks, seeking the sweet sap that would well out. The wasps would then come to feed on the liquid exuding from these holes.

Although the tarantula is invariably mentioned as the host of these colorful wasps, there are probably other species, not only of spiders but

Figure 5.6
The tarantula hawk leads a rather complex life, not entirely taken up with its pursuit of the tarantula spider. It has a potent sting and, for that reason, should be avoided.

of insects as well, that can serve that purpose. There are also several species of large wasps that prey upon other organisms. The cicada killer of the eastern states comes to mind. It is a large, heavy-bodied wasp quite capable of carrying a cicada for some distance to a place that it has selected for its burial.

I am reminded of an incident that occurred on a hot summer's afternoon at the ranch. I was concealed in a blind, waiting for some birds to visit my sets, when a strange object came flying slowly across my field of vision. It was too small to be a bird, but it obviously had wings of some sort that kept it airborne as it moved erratically along, perhaps six feet above the ground. Directly in front of the blind, it gave a final paroxysm and fell to the ground. Dashing out to the point where it had landed, I found to my astonishment that it was a middle-size grasshopper in the clutches of a large wasp, not one of the tarantula hawks. The wasp straddling the grasshopper was already dragging the supine body of its victim away by the antennae. Disturbed by my arrival on the scene, the wasp left and did not return to its prize. It would have been interesting to see what it might have done with the tranquilized, or perhaps dead, body.

As I tried to reconstruct the scenario, it seemed that the wasp had attacked the grasshopper on the ground and stung it there. The grasshopper evidently had enough vitality to take to the air, and the wasp, keeping a hold on its prey, flew with it until the venom took effect and they fell to the ground together.

The Rain and the Toads

Some day in late July or early August—the date is indeterminate—two events occur almost simultaneously. These are the first heavy rain of the season and the appearance of the spadefoot toads. A change occurs in the seasonal pattern of clouds forming, then piling high in great masses until afternoon. Anvils form, and, preceded by a hot wind, a few drops of rain, muddied by the dust picked up on the way down, pelt the thirsty soil.

This time is different. You can't put your finger on it, perhaps the air is a little more humid, the clouds more swollen with the burden they carry. The folks downtown notice it with anticipation.

"Think we might be goin' to get a rain?"

"Shore hope so; we need it bad."

Down on the ranch, the wildlife, with sharpened instinct, know that this is it! The nocturnal species are ready for a night of activity after the rain is over. The clouds build higher and higher, a dead calm settles over the desert, everything is in readiness for the show to begin!

Suddenly, a stab of lightning shatters the stillness. The townspeople run for their cars and roll up the windows; others secure belongings that might blow away and carry indoors those things subject to water damage. A continuous rumble of thunder grows closer, while the lowering clouds shut out the rays of the sun. Then, with a great swoop, the downdraft ahead of the storm descends upon the town.

Driven by the wind, empty garbage cans bounce and crash down the streets, while the air is filled with papers and refuse that have collected along the gutters. The alleys contribute to this aggregation with debris that may have lain there since the last such storm. Out in the valley, a pall of dust a thousand feet high is driven before the rain. The desert is caught in the grip of the storm. Fine gravel stings the face, and dust cuts visibility to only a short distance. Great saguaros sway before the blast, and trees and bushes thrash wildly under its grip. Wildlife, forewarned by the thunder, have taken to cover, there to remain until the storm has subsided.

Hard on the heels of the wind comes the rain. At first, a few drops seemingly as large as marbles clatter on the tin roofs and splatter the ground. Their numbers increase quickly, the staccato on the roofs develops into a roar as it seems the heavens have opened up, and the deluge overwhelms all before it. Lightning flashes and thunder roars, while the cloudburst continues unabated for half an hour.

The streets become rivers from curb to curb. Hastily filled sandbags fail to keep the flood from entering the business houses. Out on the desert, the washes and the arroyos overflow with torrents of muddy water seeking its own level on the lower ground. Eventually, the storm has spent its force. The rush of rain slackens to a pattering of final drops, the thunderclaps fade to a low rumbling in the distance, and a silence, all the more profound because of the recent pandemonium, settles on the desert.

In town, the residents get into their cars and take to the streets. This is a custom of the little towns in the southwestern deserts. When the storm has spent its force, their citizens get out to assess the damage. This neighbor's patio cover has blown away, that yard has two uprooted trees across the driveway, the bakery and two stores are flooded and are being swept out as quickly as possible. It's all a rare happening that must be appreciated to the utmost.

On the open desert, all is clean and sparkling in the afternoon sun. The birds come out of their hiding places, oil their feathers, and arrange them anew. Deep in their burrows, the desert tortoises have learned through some sixth sense of the storm and emerge to plunge their heads deep into the nearest puddle. Here they drink deeply to replenish their water supply, which, at this late date, has been running dangerously low. They have specially adapted glands above their shoulder blades in which they store water. The snakes, too, come out in force in late afternoon to revel in the coolness and the humidity of their usually hot and dry habitat.

At nightfall, a strange sound not hitherto heard arises from the vicinity of the puddles brimming in the lower areas. Singly at first, then swelling as more voices add to the chorus, the toads sing praises to the rain that has brought them out of their long imprisonment underground. Actually, these loud croaks are a part of the breeding cycle whereby the males endeavor to entice the females to their sides. There is an urgency

Figure 5.7
One of the smallest but also the loudest of the toad species in the desert is the Sonoran spadefoot. A small scale of black hornlike material on the bottom of each hind foot forms the "spade" with which they dig into the moist ground.

to all of this, for these sources of water are even now beginning to seep into the ground, and, in the days to come, evaporation will take a further toll.

The toad most responsible for the clamor is the Sonoran spadefoot, *Scaphiopus couchii*. Never was a scientific name more apt: from the Latin *scapium*, a digging tool, and *pus*, a foot. There are several toad species in the Sonoran Desert; this is one of the smallest and is considered the most common. In the vicinity of the ranch, it was scarce because the bajada was well drained, with the exception of some pools in the bed of the arroyo, of which more later.

Amphibians are rare in the desert. Obviously, conditions in this parched land are not favorable for them. The term "amphibian" means double life and refers to such animals as live in water in the larval stage and on land in the adult form. The spadefoot would seem to lead a double life in the adult form as well, for it spends as much time underground as it does on the surface, if not more. It must do this to survive the long dry periods common to its environment.

The life history of the spadefoot may as well begin with the gathering of their numbers at a large puddle left by one of the infrequent big rainstorms during the monsoon season. Though it now seems an ideal breeding place, in a month it will be dry—baked hard as the surrounding plain by the desert sun. On this evening, however, it is several inches deep and an ideal place to deposit eggs. The female lays several hundred of them in long, ropy strings, while, at the same time, a male fertilizes them. By the next morning, a change in the embryos is already noticeable, and, from then on, their development is unbelievably rapid. In only a few days, the puddle is swarming with tiny tadpoles. Their hind legs appear first, followed on the next day by the front ones, while, at the same time, the tail is being resorbed. In ten days from the time the eggs were laid, the tadpole, now a miniature toad, is ready to start life out of the water.

Though we saw or heard no spadefoots in the vicinity of the corrals, they were around, for one of the bedrock pools up the arroyo was teeming with tadpoles. I was privileged to watch their development from day to day. They had no visible source of food, but it had to consist of almost microscopic plants and possibly primitive forms of animal life. Fairy shrimp are found in many of the pools among the rocks, the eggs surviving long periods of drought.

The toll on the hundreds of baby toads when they leave the water is heavy. Birds, lizards, and even scorpions take large numbers of them. This is just as well; were all these thousands of toads allowed to mature, a plague of biblical proportions would result.

The mature toads, meanwhile, having fulfilled their purpose, have been living on the fat of the land as represented by the burgeoning numbers of insects that appear during the rainy season. With the end of the monsoons, they are ready to enter the next phase of their life cycle. This should be accomplished before the soil has dried out too much.

Now the spades for which the species is named come into play. These are tiny, single plates of a hornlike material attached to the bottom of each hind foot. Selecting a place to its liking, the toad begins oscillating its hind legs and the rear of its body back and forth. As a hole begins to form, the animal literally backs into the cavity. Before long, its back is level with the surface of the soil. From that point on, the soil it displaces works up over its back until soon the toad is at the bottom of a shaft, the upper end of which is plugged with loose material from below. When the shaft has reached a depth of from one to two feet, the toad ceases its labor and, sheltered from heat and cold by the insulating properties of the soil, sinks into a deep torpor.

Respiration and heartbeat slow to the absolute minimum required to sustain life. Now it sleeps the days away until another monsoon on the following year brings it out of hibernation/estivation again. For the young of the year, it must be a grim battle to attain the size to accomplish this retreat from the aridity of their habitat. Surely, many of them must perish.

As I have mentioned, one of my first concerns at the ranch was to provide a small pool for the convenience of the birds, especially the ground dwellers such as the quail. Placed underneath a low-branching palo-verde tree on the edge of the arroyo, it offered shelter as well as water. It was immediately utilized by the local birds and soon became a place known to migrants as a rest stop on their journeys. It became equally popular with the nocturnal creatures, large and small. When I worked the corrals at night, it became my habit to sweep the area at intervals with the flashlight to check on what visitors might be about. Sometimes I would surprise a fox or a bobcat taking a drink at the pool.

Colorado River Toad

One evening, as I passed the flashlight's beam over the pool, I received an answering flash of yellow fire from the center of the basin. Going over to check on the owner of this brilliant eye, I discovered a Colorado River toad contentedly sitting in the four inches of water. His pulsating sides were setting up a miniature ground swell in the tiny pool, for *Bufo alvarius* is a massive creature. Largest of our Sonoran Desert toads, a large specimen will attain a length of eight inches and is wide and heavy in proportion. Its flaccid sides expand and contract as it hops about, the effect being, as a friend of mine once stated, "a hot-water bottle on the move." It is a voracious feeder, taking insects too large for the smaller species to subdue. Crickets, grasshoppers, moths, and the large black cockroaches native to the Southwest all fall prey to this corpulent amphibian. For this reason, it is welcomed to some yards; however, other characteristics render it unwelcome in others. A gland on either side of the head secretes a milky fluid that is extremely poisonous to dogs, and many a cherished pet has succumbed to it.

Figure 5.8
The Colorado River toad is by far the largest toad in the Sonoran Desert. It acts as a very efficient control on animals up to half its size.

It has one other trait that has pretty much gone unrecognized. One year in Tucson, as the monsoon season came on, our Scout troop built an educational exhibit featuring the four species of toads common to the area. These were confined in an open-topped, glass-sided enclosure mounted on a table. Here they were conveniently situated for close-up viewing, and the visitor could even reach in and touch them, although this was discouraged. The toads were fed a diet of mealworms, which was deemed sufficient for the short time they were to be on display.

All went well until, one day, the smallest of the four seemed to be missing. A diligent search failed to locate it among the rocks and plants in the display, and we concluded that some child must have picked it up and taken it home. This was a small matter; it was easily replaced by another. In no time, it, too, had disappeared. Then the truth dawned upon us! An inspection revealed that our obese friend was even fatter than usual.

The toad at the ranch seemed to be a solitary individual. Perhaps it had eaten up all the competition. Where it spent its days, I did not discover; it may have dug itself into the damp earth beneath the watering troughs, but every night it could be found in the pool under the palo-verde tree. I was fascinated by its eyes and took a number of close-ups, but no picture could duplicate the flash of yellow fire reflected from the flashlight's beam. An ancient folktale had it that the toad had a precious stone in its head. In William Shakespeare's *As You Like It*, act 2, scene 1, line 12, Duke Senior says:

Sweet are the uses of adversity
Which like the toad ugly and venomous
wears yet a precious jewel in its head.

My friend of the birdbath went that one better with a brilliant topaz on each side of his massive head.

"Rat"

About two miles west of the corrals, on the way to the Cabeza Prieta National Wildlife Refuge and only a few feet off the road, stood an organ-pipe cactus. There is a notion that the organ pipe, a plentiful species in Mexico, comes north of the border only in Organ Pipe Cactus National Monument and that the population within the United States is contained wholly within the monument boundaries. As a matter of fact, there are many colonies of this cactus north and east of the monument. One is located in the Ajo Range south of Ajo, and the lone plant of which I speak was even several miles farther to the north.

It was a beautiful specimen with ten or twelve stems rising symmetrically to a height of eight feet with never a mar nor frostbitten tip. Much as I admired it, this plant was no more exceptional than many that I had seen in the monument and in Mexico. What really drew my attention was the untidy mass of debris enclosed within the base of its encircling arms. Ever since I had taken the photographs of the wood rat (*Neotoma* sp.) in Saguaro National Monument, I had hoped to work with another. Here was my hope fulfilled, and I set about making the acquaintance of this one at my earliest convenience.

That time arrived at the end of the rainy season, when drier and cooler weather found me knocking at the door of his ramshackle dwelling. Figuratively, of course, I had learned to respect the spiny defenses that *Neotoma* sets up to repel strangers.

This one was a white-throated wood rat *(Neotoma albigula)*. Its genus name (from the Greek *neos*, meaning "new," and *temnein*, meaning "to cut") reflects its habit of cutting new growth of shrubs with its sharp incisors, and its species name combines the Latin words *alba*, meaning "white," and *gula*, meaning "throat." It is a species that has attracted a growing interest in the scientific community in recent years. It is a highly adaptable creature that makes its home not only on the open desert, as in this case, but also up in the rocky clefts of the mountains. Under some particularly advantageous overhang, countless generations of wood rats may have used the same quarters.

These animals are cleanly creatures, and somewhere in their homes will be an area set aside for toilet purposes. For want of a better term, these are called "middens." In the course of time, deposits of urine, which crystallize as they evaporate, build up into a time capsule containing entries of leaves, other plant fragments, pollen, bones, and sticks—a veritable checklist of everything in the vicinity. By dissolving these middens, analyzing their contents, and dating them through several means, one can compile a natural history of the area reaching back hundreds of years. Obviously, wood-rat nests in the open, where they are exposed to the weather, cannot yield such data, but the day-to-day habits of the animal are so unique in many respects that they merit some mention.

First of all, *Neotoma* is not a rat in the sense of *Rattus*, comprising several species of European rats. Ours is a clean little animal, and, although it has a musky odor, it is not one born of filth. Though a creature of the desert, the white-throat is prodigal in its use of moisture. It survives this anomaly by eating cactus and other succulent plants in drought times. This seems a logical answer to a shortage of water, but the fact is that cactuses contain chemicals that make them unsuited for long-term consumption by most animals. The saguaro cactus, for instance, contains a high percentage of oxalates, compounds that are poisonous to rodents in general. The wood rat, however, is one that can ingest this juicy flesh with impunity. Laboratory animals have survived quite adequately for extended periods on a diet of saguaro-cactus flesh alone. In the field, it is not unusual to find a saguaro that, from the base, has a tunnel winding upward for some distance around the trunk, having been eaten out by one of these rodents. Seedling saguaros are taken whenever available.

The wood-rat house, if it can be called that, fills a dual purpose. It serves the owner as a protective barrier against enemies and, to some extent, provides insulation from heat and cold. Underneath the untidy pile of whatever has come handy are several passageways leading to the various service areas. Some are set aside for storage, one at least for a toilet, and the best for a nest. The nest is constructed of the finest and softest materials available. Even in an area that seems composed of nothing but sticks, and stones, and thorns, there are fibers, and soft bark, and downy seeds to be gathered by this inveterate collector.

Wood rats have a legion of enemies, but, protected by their fortress home, they survive the attacks of snakes, owls, and other carnivores quite well. In the past, though, they also had reason to fear humans. Their house, a barrier to all other predators, rendered them particularly vulnerable to the arch predator. Indians set their nests on fire. If the occupant fled the burning mound, it fell victim to stones and clubs; if it remained, it wound up as roast rat—whether rare or well done made little difference. To later arrivals in the desert, wood rat was quite acceptable as an entree. Its flesh was esteemed in times of sickness. Major Edgar Alexander Mearns, a United States Army surgeon, in *Mammals of the Mexican Boundary of the United States* (Washington, D.C.: Smithsonian Institution, 1907), says: "Captain Martinez of the Army Engineer Corps of Mexico informed me that physicians of northern Mexico commonly ordered broth made from the wood rat for the Indians and peasants whom they are called upon to treat, just as our physicians prescribe chicken broth and beef tea."

When the wood rat remains in populated areas and takes up residence in homes, it becomes known as the "pack rat." Lacking its mundane booty of cactus and sticks, it turns to such other articles as strike its fancy. These are usually bright or colorful objects—the very things that the human occupants of the house might least prefer to lose. In the wild, this tendency renders these rats susceptible to persons, such as myself, who photograph them carrying away all manner of things that ordinarily would not be found near their nests.

My offerings to my "Rat," for I had no other name for him, were in two forms: those that I gave him free and clear, and some for which I was an Indian giver, letting him have them for an evening and then taking them back when the session was over. Among the former, he had favorites. He would scatter tinfoil, can lids, and brightly colored plastics over the top of his house and periodically rearrange them as fussily as any housewife with her furniture. Among my "Indian-giver" offerings were

Figure 5.9 The white-throated wood rat, also known as the pack rat, shows no fear of the vicious spines of the teddy-bear cactus. Rat finds that there is always rearranging to do around the house.

my watch and car keys, which I tethered with black cord so that they could be picked up but not carried away.

As our relationship continued, Rat became less inhibited by my presence. I, for my part, relaxed and enjoyed watching the normal activities that he resumed through this familiarity. *Neotoma* is a busy little creature. Unlike the kangaroo rat, which had several periods of activity each night, this white-throated wood rat was continually on the move doing a variety of chores around his house. There were trails to clear of obstructions (placed by me), favorite objects to rearrange on his roof, cactus joints to de-spine, and, of course, the seeds and crusts that I brought had to be carried and stored away for future use. He accepted sunflower seeds from my hand without hesitation—until one night when he took an investigative nip at the fleshy pad between the second and third joints of the fourth finger of my left hand. It was only a pinch to satisfy his curiosity, and, at my startled yelp, he backed off, but at that point I had no desire to further test the keenness of his long, sharp incisors.

I spent a lot of time with Rat, a poor choice of names perhaps, but, when one maintains a steady monologue with a friend, it seems only proper to call him by some name. I learned a lot about him, and at the same time I discovered a few basics long ignored about myself. We spent nights together when the moon was high and all the world was silver and sheen. We spent nights when the wind thrashed the creosote bushes and keened through the spines of the organ pipe. And, on some nights, we met in the same world draped in black velvet and bereft of light and sound. These last were the times when I felt most akin to Rat, as, together, we faced the nameless terrors of the night. His instincts warned him against the very real dangers posed by snake and coyote, and mine, carried down from the distant past, admonished me that man serves no good purpose in being abroad in the dark and that danger lurks there.

Your Visit with Rat

Perhaps you, my reader, might care to share such an evening with Rat? If so, I suggest that you join my little friend for a few hours of complete isolation from others of your gregarious kind. Several hours of absolute aloneness except for the presence of that little animal. I predict that he will assume a new importance in your sense of values. Are you willing to have your long-dormant instincts surface for just a little while? Possibly you don't grasp what I'm asking? Then, suppose that you learn by doing.

You know the place; you have visited it with me in these preceding pages. An organ-pipe cactus marks the spot, several miles west of Ajo on the lonely road leading to Charlie Bell Well in the Cabeza Prieta National Wildlife Refuge. I've picked a night for your visit. It's in the dark of the moon with cloud cover promising a black night without even starshine.

Take my car—it knows the way. It's been there often enough. You'll find extension cord, a light, and the three-legged stool; that's all you'll need. And, oh yes, a bag of sunflower seeds and some crusts for Rat.

You set off in the deepening dusk with anticipation. The old car, survivor of a hundred desert trips, rattles and squeaks, but the motor sounds good as you coast down the long grade leading to the ranch and beyond. It's already dark when the organ pipe looms up ghostly white in the glare of the headlights. There you turn the car around and park against the berm of the narrow road. No need to put out warning reflectors; no one ever comes along on this road after dark.

With flashlight under your arm, you unroll the coil of extension cord thirty feet from the car to the organ pipe and hang the viewing light low on one of the arms directly over Rat's nest. Next you scatter a handful of sunflower seeds there, working them well into the debris, and, with that accomplished, you sit down on the three-legged stool and wait. You have not long to wait. Rat has seen these preparations many times, and, before you are well settled, he is out combing through the trash, seeking out the seeds that he dearly loves.

The silence, which was shattered by your noisy arrival, now settles in again. With its return, you, for the first time, become aware of the inky blackness of the night. The car, though only thirty feet away, is barely visible against the darkness that enfolds your world. Except for the dim circle at your feet, there is no glimmer of light to be seen in the hundred square miles of desert that surrounds you. Sound is equally nonexistent. Save for the blood throbbing in your ears and the faint baying of the pack of renegade dogs coursing a deer on far-off Child's Mountain, it is quiet as the tomb. In a little while, even their horrid clamor fades away, and you are alone in a world that has no bounds of height, or width, or depth—only a tiny circle of light and a little wood rat.

You wonder about the dogs. They were miles away, that's true, but could there be another pack, a splinter group such as was willing to attack in broad daylight at the ranch? The thought makes you uncomfortable. You sweep the area with your flashlight's beam. Nothing there. Of course not, you tell yourself and settle down once more on your stool. But . . . could there possibly be something lurking behind you . . . watching . . . waiting? You find your ears straining to hear any sound, the hair on the back of your neck prickles, and your back muscles cringe at the thought. You try to focus your attention on Rat. He's not apprehensive. You attempt to copy his attitude. Not to fear.

Suddenly, there is a sharp snap behind you! Rat bolts for the entrance to his nest. Your heart leaps into your throat; your back flinches from you-know-not-what. You fumble desperately for the switch on your flashlight, finally you manage to turn it on. Shakily, you sweep the area once more with its beam. Again nothing—the gooseflesh on your back slowly settles down again. You feel silly, sheepish! You're not really frightened, you tell yourself. You've just let your imagination get to you. You wish, though, that Rat would return. You reflect that his company is better than none, that his presence might serve to banish this foolish anxiety that you, yourself, have created.

In time he does return, quite as though nothing had happened. You force yourself to become engrossed in placing teddy-bear joints in his runways and watching him push them around with no respect for their wicked spines. He willingly carries away whatever you have to offer, whether it be a bit of tinfoil or a plastic fork. You are reassured by his presence. He will sense when danger threatens. Come to think of it, though, he was really frightened. There must have been something out there a while ago. Your uneasiness returns, and you are relieved when it is time to go.

On the way back, you attempt to analyze your reactions. Reason tells you that there was nothing to fear. Then why the gooseflesh down your neck and between your shoulder blades? Why the surge of adrenaline at the snap, which was probably no more than a rock contracting as it cooled under the evening's chill? Was it because, deep in your genes, the instincts of early humans still remain? How many generations are you removed from those of the cave who would not venture out at night because of the dangers that lurked out there, waiting, watching.

When you drive into the yard, I come out on the porch. "How did it go?" I ask.

"Fine, just fine," you reply.

We spend a few minutes in desultory chitchat, avoiding anything pertinent to the evening's happenings. You get into your car and go on your way. I know pretty well what you experienced, and you know that I do. Aloneness in the desert night is not for everyone.

Foxy

There came the day when I had gathered a surfeit of wood-rat pictures. With Rat's cooperation, I now had poses ranging from serious to ridiculous. During this time, I had, to a certain extent, neglected the ranch, and it was with a renewed interest in the possibilities awaiting there that I resumed my evening visits. I continued my practice of checking the soft soil around the water troughs for tracks every evening, and, to my delight, I found tracks indicating that a large bobcat was making daily visits to the corral for a drink. When I arrived just after nightfall, the tracks were always fresh, a sign that he made his visits during the hours of late afternoon or dusk. This seemed to present a good opportunity to get some pictures, but first I wanted to see the animal. A bobcat is a rugged, aggressive creature, and, like an alley cat, an old tom wearing the scars and blemishes of years of combat is not a pretty sight. Therefore, before I wasted time planning for a setup, I determined to get a good look at him.

To that end, late afternoon found me at the corral one day. The corral fence, as I have explained, paralleled the arroyo with barely enough room for a one-lane road between them. The segment of fence along the arroyo was some two hundred feet long. It was a sturdy affair. The posts, old railroad ties, were set two feet into the ground and about eight feet apart. The rails of heavy lumber were far enough apart for a small animal to get through but narrow enough to hold a steer. The top rails, about a foot below the tops of the posts, were two-by-sixes. The whole structure was checked and warped from years of exposure to the weather. I give you these boring details in order to explain what happened later.

On the day in question, I arrived at the corral just at sundown. I drove the car up to the corner of the corral and as close as possible to the side of the fence. There I had a good view down the entire length of the enclosure. I had barely time to focus my binoculars when I detected a movement in the low brush along the arroyo bank, and out came a gray fox about halfway down the length of the corral. He crossed the road and, effortlessly as a butterfly, floated up to the top of a post. He sniffed all over the crown of it, and then I realized what he was after. As an inducement to attract Gila woodpeckers and flickers to the area, I had baited the tops of some of the posts with pieces of doughnuts stuffed deep into the cracks of the wood. With their long beaks, the birds had undoubtedly removed all of the bait, but the fox, with his keen sense of smell, knew that there had been food there and was hopeful of salvaging a few crumbs.

Figure 5.10 Foxy would come to my whistle day or night if he was within hearing. I always made it a point to reward him with some small bit of food.

After a thorough search, during which time he found nothing, he proceeded to the next post in my direction, walking the two-inch width of the top rail as sure footedly as a gymnast on the balance beam. I sat spellbound watching this performance as he proceeded, post by post, ever nearer to me. Finally, when he reached the last post next to me, I was leaning forward over the steering wheel in order to look up through the windshield at the top rail. As he advanced down this last segment of rail just above me, he suddenly became aware of my presence. He stopped as our eyes met, and time stood still for possibly five seconds as we looked deep into each other's eyes.

Some kind of communication passed between us; I know not how to explain it, but a bond was forged that existed from then on. After this brief interval had passed, he continued on to the corner of the fence, and, in the rearview mirror, I saw him jump to the ground. Reaching into the bait box on the floor beside me, I broke out a doughnut and slowly opened the door and stepped out. He was only about twenty feet away.

"Don't be afraid," I called out and threw him a piece of doughnut, which he located at once. I threw him another and then held one in my hand and said: "Here it is, Foxy, come and get it." He came up to me without hesitation, as somehow I knew he would, and, from then on, our friendship was based on a mutual trust and respect for each other. Our relationship continued as equals. I gave him food, not as a reward for what he did for me but as a gift. He was happy to do the poses that I asked him for, not for food but because he liked me.

I made it a point never to intrude on his private life. I never laid a hand on him, feeling that taking such a liberty was beyond the limits of our understanding. His den was somewhere in the vicinity, I knew, but I never tried to locate it. I knew it was close by because I could whistle for him at any time during the day, and, in a minute or two, he would come to me, slipping like a gray shadow through the bushes. I kept his existence a closely guarded secret, knowing full well what interest the news of a tame fox would spark in town. Irene was the only one with whom I shared our secret, and even she came to the ranch only occasionally to witness some new tactic that Foxy had learned. As our association continued, he more and more anticipated what I might concoct and divined what part he might play in this new endeavor.

Bounded by a few trees, the little flat on the edge of the arroyo became a set wherein I would arrange the simple props that would show Foxy off to the best advantage. While I would move these things about for the next picture, he would sit on his haunches, head cocked at an angle, with his ears at the alert, while his eyes followed my movements with lively interest. When we had finished a session, I would feed him a few pieces of doughnut and tell him: "That's all, Foxy, see you tomorrow," and he would take off.

Foxy was by far the most photogenic of my wildlife subjects. I judged him to be a two-year-old, just fully adult, and, like most young males at their height of virility, his juices were flowing. He was a handsome creature, and it was evident by his bearing that well he knew it. His coat was without a blemish, and his tail, the most striking feature of a fox, was fully furred. We took pictures in every setting we could think of, and, at length, when I ran out of ideas, he would come and watch me take bird pictures on the long, summer afternoons.

As the heat waned and the crisper nights of fall arrived, a circumstance developed that filled me with foreboding. Rumor had it that a trapper from New Mexico had arrived and was working the general area. There was nothing unusual about this. The Arizona Game and Fish Department issues trapping licenses, and, as long as the trapper operates in the designated areas and within the guidelines, it is illegal to harass him or to molest his traps in any way. There would be no trapping on ranch property, but it ended along the roadway at the upper end, and across that road was public domain.

I debated whether to contact this trapper and appeal to his better nature, but, as a matter of fact, I felt that it would be to no avail, and I never had the opportunity to meet him anyway. There really seemed to be nothing to do but hope that he would not work in the vicinity of the ranch. As the days passed and I heard no more about him, I began to hope that he had left the area.

Then, one afternoon, no Foxy appeared to my whistle. I went up and down the arroyo calling, but he was not in the area or he would have come to me. Sick with anxiety, I searched for a long time, but it was hopeless. I never saw my trusting little friend again.

I have often wondered what I might have done, under the circumstances. I cannot even be certain that Foxy came to his end in a trap. There are many everyday hazards awaiting wildlife. Nevertheless, the picture that haunts me is of my friend anguishing in a cruel steel trap, while I, whom he trusted even with his life, did nothing to help him.

After Foxy's disappearance, the ranch held such painful memories for me that I gradually discontinued my visits there. I had taken most of the pictures that I needed anyway, so I turned my attention to the Cabeza Prieta National Wildlife Refuge and the Pinacate Desert in northern Mexico. The latter is a wild, uninhabited region of lava flows and sand dunes lying between the head of the Gulf of California and our border with Mexico. Either area holds enough of interest to keep one occupied for several lifetimes. Time has no regard for the aging of bodies, however, and, after five years of living in Ajo, it seemed advisable to seek a second retirement in a larger town. So we reluctantly moved to Phoenix.

Our thoughts often turn to our former abode, however, and occasionally we drive down for a day and renew acquaintances with old friends. On our most recent trip, we packed a picnic lunch and drove down to the ranch. The wheel tracks into the place were not as well worn as in the days when I was making daily trips there, but they indicated that Lee was still doing his weekly rounds of inspection and watering the stock. We parked alongside the arroyo underneath a paloverde tree and set out a card table and chairs in its sparse shade.

The place had changed little except that, like us, it had grown older and more decrepit. The cattle troughs were full of clear, sweet water, and the moist earth around them was patterned with animal tracks, but the basin that I had built against the edge of the arroyo was dry and full of dead leaves and twigs. The corral timbers were more checked and bleached a silvery gray by the sun. The old mining machinery was scattered about the area as before but was a little more rusty. Vandals had savaged the house and the outbuildings and carried away the doors and windows. Their empty frames stared like sightless eyes out across the flat. The place seemed dead and forlorn compared to the days when I had seen it crowded with birds and all of the other small creatures that came to my baits.

While we ate there in the shade, I reminisced with Irene about some of the events that had taken place all around where we were sitting. Some of them were so vivid in my memory that it was like reliving them. When it was time to leave and we had packed up our gear, I walked over to the place where I had once set up my cameras and whistled one last time for Foxy, as though that might bring him back to me. The cliffs across the arroyo mockingly echoed my unanswered summons. That was all.

Addendum

In retrospect, as I look back to that summer on Miller Peak, I cannot but reflect on how much I have been favored. In the many years since that time, my contacts with people have ranged from simple country folk to some in high government office; however, equally important to me are my memories of Tubby, and Buck, and Foxy, and a whole host of lesser creatures. How fortunate it is to have one's work and personal interest coincide as mine have.

In writing about these experiences with our animal friends, I have studiously avoided any use of anthropomorphism. In simple terms, the word means "animals acting like humans." This is unfortunate because, actually, animals react in some situations just as humans would. It would seem quite appropriate if there were an opposing term meaning humans acting in animal fashion. After all, the genus *Homo* contains the most highly evolved mammals in the animal kingdom. Unfortunately, we humans have developed to such an extent, and in such ways, that we no longer fit into any useful niche in the natural world. At the same time, neither have we risen to the heights to which our intelligence entitles us. Our chief importance as an animal has become a negative one: we are the only creatures with the ability, and now, it seems, the destiny, to destroy the environment of the world as we know it.

Konrad Lorenz said it well when he wrote: "I believe I have found the missing link between animals and civilized man. It is us." I would go one step further and describe us as higher mammals who have picked up an amazing number of bad habits along the evolutionary trail.

The deterioration of our environment has developed slowly but inexorably. It has come about through a matter of simple logistics: the world has only finite resources with which to supply an ever-increasing population. There are other matters that enter into this, such as pollution, but these are incidental to the main problem. Efforts at conservation of resources and recycling of waste materials, admirable as they are, can only delay the inevitable.

A friend, whose opinions I value highly, explains it this way: "Draw a graph with a line representing our natural resources descending at an angle from the upper left-hand corner. Then draw another representing our increase in population arising from the lower left-hand corner. After these two lines cross each other, it ain't going to be pretty." In fact, we have already passed that point; we have used up much of our renewable resources and are drawing down our reserves at an alarming rate.

Our situation reminds me of a wastrel who has come into a substantial inheritance, tax free, of course. At first, he lives very comfortably on the income provided through investments. As his tastes become more sophisticated, however, he finds that these do not provide enough funds, so he begins to draw on the principal. This, in turn, reduces his income from the investments, and, eventually, he winds up broke.

We, too, are drawing upon principal. Forests are being destroyed everywhere, topsoil is being carried away, mining and grazing are taking their toll. Even the sea, once thought to be an inexhaustible source of food, is now found to be vulnerable to the exploitation taking place. Habitats of wildlife, and humans as well, are shrinking as "development" takes them over. National parks and wilderness areas are being loved to death as our population yearns for even a brief time to get away from it all. These are not recreation areas in the sense of being amusement parks; they are literally re-creation areas for the recharging of the soul— some of the few places where we human animals can return to the natural world from which we sprang.

Pressures are mounting to open up even these areas for exploitation. The catchphrase "multiple use" is advanced as the way to get maximum benefit from them for the most people to justify such intrusion. Do not be misled by this phrase. Multiple use leads only to multiple abuse. Natural areas cannot withstand such treatment. Most of America has been subjected to multiple use. These parks and wilderness areas are all that are left of an America that was.

In zoos, an animal that continually walks back and forth behind the bars of its cage is known as a "pacer." Such creatures are not desirable as exhibits. They spend their lives in utter frustration at being kept away from their natural environment.

Guard our natural areas at all costs and keep them inviolate. Do not condemn future generations to be captives in a zoo of our own making.

About the Author

George Olin was born in Luverne, Minnesota, in 1907. He has spent most of his life in the outdoors, from the lakes and forests of Minnesota to the mountains and mesas of the Sonoran Desert of Arizona.

George graduated from high school in 1925 and attended North Dakota State College for two years. At that time, he encountered financial problems and left for a nomadic life on the road.

He followed the harvest from Kansas to Saskatchewan, lumberjacked in the high Rockies, and worked on construction jobs. Of a trip from Salt Lake City to Los Angeles, he says: "I saw the desert for the first time, and I fell in love with it." He eventually took a steady job in Los Angeles and there met and married Irene. She shared his interests, and every spare moment found them in the nearby desert with camera and notebook.

In 1947 they left the crowded city and for two years trailered over the Southwest in search of the perfect home. They found it in Tucson and made it their base of operations. Except for eight years spent in the eastern United States, they continued to explore the environment of the desert, especially at night.

George's writings include three books and many articles on the desert Southwest; his photographs have appeared in these and other publications.

Library of Congress Cataloging-in-Publication Data

Olin, George.

Up close : a lifetime observing and photographing desert animals / George Olin.

p. cm.

ISBN 0-8165-2003-8 (cloth : alk. paper) — ISBN 0-8165-2004-6 (paper : alk. paper)

1. Desert animals—Sonoran Desert—Anecdotes. 2. Photography of animals—Sonoran Desert—Anecdotes. 3. Olin, George. I. Title.

QL116.O44 2000

591.754'09791'7—dc21   99-050880